Embracing IMPERFECT

365 DEVOTIONS FOR LIVING AUTHENTICALLY

LINDSAY FRANKLIN

ZONDERVAN

ZONDERVAN

Embracing Imperfect
Copyright © 2024 by Zondervan

Published in Grand Rapids, Michigan, by Zondervan. Zondervan is a registered trademark of HarperCollins Christian Publishing, Inc.

Requests for information should be addressed to customercare@harpercollins.com.

Zondervan titles may be purchased in bulk for educational, business, fundraising, or sales promotional use. For information, please email SpecialMarkets@Zondervan.com.

ISBN 978-0-310-15541-6 (audio)

Library of Congress Cataloging-in-Publication Data

Names: Franklin, Lindsay A., author.
Title: Embracing imperfect : 365 devotions for living authentically / Lindsey A. Franklin.
Description: Grand Rapids, Michigan : Zondervan, [2024] | Audience: Ages 13-18 | Summary: "Everyone wants to have a perfect life, and as Christians, we're called to follow Jesus's perfect example. But when we inevitably fall short, it's easy to spiral into anxiety and self-doubt, fearing we'll never be good enough. This 365-day devotional delivers a powerful reminder that God doesn't expect us to be perfect or handle everything ourselves. Each Scripture-based affirmation in Embracing Imperfect explores what it means to see yourself as God does, allowing you to let go of crippling perfectionism and embrace his amazing promises and plans"—Provided by publisher.
Identifiers: LCCN 2024005611 (print) | LCCN 2024005612 (ebook) | ISBN 9780310155553 (hardcover) | ISBN 9780310155386 (ebook)
Subjects: LCSH: Christian teenagers—Prayers and devotions. | Youth—Prayers and devotions. | Devotional calendars. | BISAC: YOUNG ADULT NONFICTION / Religious / Christian / Devotional & Prayer | YOUNG ADULT NONFICTION / Social Topics / Self-Esteem & Self-Reliance
Classification: LCC BV4850 .F725 2024 (print) | LCC BV4850 (ebook) | DDC 242/.63—dc23/eng/20240315
LC record available at https://lccn.loc.gov/2024005611
LC ebook record available at https://lccn.loc.gov/2024005612

Scripture quotations are taken from The Holy Bible, New International Version®, NIV®. Copyright © 1973, 1978, 1984, 2011 by Biblica, Inc.® Used by permission of Zondervan. All rights reserved worldwide. www.Zondervan.com. The "NIV" and "New International Version" are trademarks registered in the United States Patent and Trademark Office by Biblica, Inc.®

Published in association with Books & Such Literary Management.

Cover design: Cindy Davis and Patti Evans
Interior design: Denise Froehlich

Printed in the United States of America

24 25 26 27 28 LBC 5 4 3 2 1

IMPERFECT

I see you. I see the never-ending cycle of striving, straining, achieving. The gut punch of realization when success doesn't bring the fulfillment you thought it would. The inevitable burnout, the dips into depression, the wondering what's the point of it all, anyway. Why try so hard when it's never enough?

Worse, I see the moments those lofty goals aren't met. The crushing truth that, try as you might, you can't always win. Not every grade is going to be an A+. Not every dream can be realized, no matter how hard you focus. And, if that's true, why bother working so diligently, stressing so expertly, cradling your anxiety like a beloved pet, using it to drive your Very Good Work?

Not only do I see all of that, I feel it. I see you because I am like you, intimately familiar with this vicious cycle. If most or all of the above sounds relatable—if you understand the highs and lows I've described, the hamster wheel of performance and unmet standards—you, my friend, may be a perfectionist.

Our achievement-based culture sometimes talks about perfectionism like it's a good thing. A synonym for "diligence" or "excellent effort" or "attention to detail." But the reality of true perfectionism is darker, more insidious, and has far-reaching implications for our mental health, our relationships with others, and our spiritual walks. And something I'm sure of: the Lord wants to free you from the prison of perfectionism.

Over the next 365 days, we're going to look at the truth behind perfectionism, how to identify the unhealthy patterns in our lives, what the Bible says about our identity and purpose, and so much more. My hope is you will walk away from this devotional feeling the freedom Christ offers to us, secure in your identity as a child of God, so you can move into recovery from perfectionism.

Let's get started.

THE DRIVE TO BE PERFECT

●●●●●●●●●

"Come to me, all you who are weary and
burdened, and I will give you rest."

MATTHEW 11:28

To start at the beginning, we should first define perfectionism, this insidious beast we're going to combat over the next 365 days. After all, we have to name the dragon before we can properly battle it.

Perfectionism is the drive to appear, to feel, to *be* perfect. It sounds so simple when phrased that way, but let it sink in for a moment. Perfectionism is the desire for flawlessness in the way others perceive us, the way we feel inside, and the way we actually *are*. That's an insanely tall order. That's an *impossible* order.

And what's the result of this burning drive we will never satisfy? "Weary and burdened" is putting it lightly. But don't lose hope, friend. Jesus's words in this verse tell us he's here for those who feel overloaded, overwhelmed, burned-out. That's you. That's all of us. There's hope and there's rest on the horizon!

REFLECTION Do you sense an overwhelming drive for perfection in your life? How do you feel when you think about it? Take a few moments to journal your thoughts. This is your starting point, and you'll want to refer back to it in the coming weeks, months, and years to see how far you've come.

ALL-OR-NOTHING THINKING

Sow your seed in the morning, and at evening let your hands not be idle, for you do not know which will succeed, whether this or that, or whether both will do equally well.

ECCLESIASTES 11:6

It's important to distinguish *perfectionism* from *high-achieving*, which is working hard in order to be more successful at something. While perfectionists often do achieve at a high level, there are important differences in the way each group thinks, and we're going to spend some time looking at that.

Perfectionists have a thinking pattern called "all-or-nothing thinking." Psychologists classify this as a "cognitive distortion" because it causes perfectionists to view their world in a way that isn't necessarily accurate, let alone healthy. For a perfectionist, unless their (lofty) goal of everything going just right is completely met, they view their effort as a failure. There is no such thing as "good enough." There is all, or there is nothing. Succeed or fail.

It's easy to see why this is a harmful way to think. It's easy to see why we become overwhelmed and despairing. Most people fall victim to all-or-nothing thinking at some point, but when it becomes habitual, it's a difficult pattern to break.

REFLECTION Where are you suffering from all-or-nothing thinking? Is it your schoolwork? A sport or hobby? Your relationships? Write out some specifics you can refer to later as we unravel this negative thought pattern.

A GOOD JOB IS GOOD ENOUGH

●●●●●●●●●

From the fruit of their lips people are filled with good
things, and the work of their hands brings them reward.
PROVERBS 12:14

Similar to perfectionists, high achievers shoot for the stars.
They set lofty goals for themselves. They push past their comfort zones and really go for it. They aren't afraid to imagine
winning first place, getting a 4.0 GPA, or nabbing a starring role
in the school play.

But high achievers don't consider themselves failures if they
fall short of their goals. Second place is a worthy achievement.
A 3.7 GPA is excellent. A supporting role is a win. For a high
achiever with a healthy mindset, effort matters. A good job is
good enough. *Did I try my best? Then I already won, no matter the
outcome*, the healthy high achiever thinks.

Does this mindset sound relatable or completely foreign? If
it's relatable, you may be well on your way to rejecting perfectionism and embracing a high-achiever mindset instead. If it's
foreign to you, stay tuned. There's hope for all of us!

REFLECTION Can you remember a time where you fell short of meeting
a huge goal? How did you feel afterward? Did the disappointment fade
quickly, or does it still sting to think about it?

HIGHLY CRITICAL

But test them all; hold on to what is good.
1 THESSALONIANS 5:21

Paul was talking about testing prophecies in this verse, but the idea of testing anything and everything comes pretty naturally to a perfectionist. That's because perfectionists have laser vision, ready to identify and fixate on every fault and error.

Holding on to what's good? That's harder for us. Our highly critical nature means we pick out faults in everything around us, which can be helpful when something is broken and needs to be repaired. But some of us even pick out faults that don't actually exist. Yikes. This laser vision becomes harmful, hurtful, and unhelpful when it's focused on the humans around us—and our own already-bruised hearts.

REFLECTION Do you struggle with a highly critical nature? What is one past situation where this has helped you (like fixing something before it gets worse) and one where it has hurt you (like in your relationships with others)?

SUPPORTING ACCOMPLISHMENT

I also told them about the gracious hand of my God on me and what the king had said to me. They replied, "Let us start rebuilding." So they began this good work.
NEHEMIAH 2:18

High achievers may also be gifted with a positive version of their critical nature. We call that "attention to detail," and it's a great asset. But high achievers also focus on supporting accomplishments—both their own and the accomplishments of others.

The Bible tells us not to be prideful, but saying, "I used God's gifts to give this my best effort, and I'm proud of the result" is not the kind of pride the Bible warns us against. It's okay to like what you produce. And it's even better to lift up those around you, taking pleasure in their hard work and joy. This kind of positivity nurtures your relationships and feeds your soul in the process!

REFLECTION What recent accomplishment do you feel proud of? How about someone else's win that brings you joy? Maybe your best friend, sibling, or parent recently hit a big goal. After writing down these wins, take a moment to celebrate with that person!

PUSHED BY FEAR

There is no fear in love.

1 JOHN 4:18

Imagine swimming through a deep lake, far from shore, with frigid water enveloping you and the current pulling at your limbs as you try to paddle for land. Now throw in some piranhas nipping your heels, and you've got some strong imagery for what it feels like to be a perfectionist pursuing their goals.

We perfectionists are pushed by fear, always attempting to outrun the feeling we might fail, the worry we won't measure up. Slipping under the surface always feels like it's a breath away, and we battle against that powerful current as if our lives depend on it.

We'll dive much deeper into this idea—and what the Bible has to say about this type of fear—but for now, hear the apostle John's words today: there is no fear in love, friend, and God is love (1 John 4:16). Reject the fear that's chasing you!

REFLECTION Do you ever feel like fear is the "motor" driving you toward your goals? Take a moment to imagine yourself reaching the shore of the lake described above—stepping onto the sand and safely climbing into the arms of your Savior. How do you feel now?

PULLED TOWARD GOALS

For it is God who works in you to will and to
act in order to fulfill his good purpose.
PHILIPPIANS 2:13

High achievers have big goals. They work hard to reach them.
But instead of being pushed by fear, trying to outrun the sense
they might fail, they are pulled toward their big goals. They're
ignited by an inner drive, a fire burning within, and they move
with purpose toward the finish line.

It's easy to see that a high-achiever mindset sounds healthier and more appealing than a perfectionist mindset. But here's
something else to consider: Does being pushed by fear sound
like what the Bible describes when it talks about the work we do
for God? Or does being pulled toward our goals seem more in
line with the peace and purpose Scripture describes for followers of Jesus?

If you feel like you've been "pushed by fear" in the past,
don't worry! The Lord gives us the opportunity and gift to grow
through him, and recognizing something we'd like to change to
be more like Jesus is an excellent first step.

REFLECTION Do you resonate more with the idea of being pushed by fear
or being pulled toward your goals? What's your biggest goal right now?
Take a few minutes to think about what's motivating your work toward that
goal.

UNREASONABLE GOALS

●●●●●●●●●●

I have received full payment and have more
than enough. I am amply supplied.

PHILIPPIANS 4:18

Big goals are a good thing. Shooting for the stars is great. But what happens when a perfectionist sets a goal that's nearly impossible to reach? As people prone to all-or-nothing thinking, anything short of reaching the big goal can be interpreted as a total failure. Even when we know logically this isn't true, sometimes our emotions still crash around us as though it were fact.

Even worse, sometimes a near-unattainable goal *is* met, and the perfectionist still rejects their success. "Yes, I won first place, but the judges were probably biased. The competition must not have been very good this year. Maybe it was a mistake." Or perhaps, "Yes, I got all As this semester, but my percentages could have been higher. I got a B on my math final. Did I really deserve an A in that class?" Some will simply move on to the next impossible task on their list. Others get caught in a loop of rejecting and doubting their past successes.

Does any of that feel familiar? If so, you may have unattainable goals and a problem with rejecting your own success.

REFLECTION Think about one of your biggest wins in life. Have you ever doubted its legitimacy? Reject those doubts right now and reframe, telling yourself, "The Lord gifted me with the ability to achieve this goal, and I'm so grateful!" How do you feel about the accomplishment now?

THE FUN OF STRETCHING

Now may the God of peace . . . equip you with
everything good for doing his will.
HEBREWS 13:20–21

For a high achiever, shooting for the stars isn't emotionally risky. Because if they "fail" and instead land in the stratosphere, they think, *Wow, I'm in the stratosphere, and that's amazing!*

For the high achiever, stretching is fun. Pushing the boundaries of what could be possible is an adventure, and if the high goal is met, great! Let's stretch even further to redefine our limits!

Does that kind of positivity about your work seem like a distant, far-off mindset? If so, that's okay. For now, rest in the knowledge that the God who equips the faithful high achiever to have peace, positivity, and gratitude about their successes wants to equip you in the same way.

REFLECTION Can you think of a time when you fell just short of your big goal? Maybe you didn't win the top prize, but you were a finalist. Take a few minutes to think about landing in the stratosphere—and how awesome that is.

FOCUSED ON RESULTS

What we have received is not the spirit of the world,
but the Spirit who is from God, so that we may
understand what God has freely given us.

1 CORINTHIANS 2:12

Perfectionists focus only on results, and honestly, who can blame them? The world focuses on results too. In a business context, sometimes the only thing that matters is "the bottom line" (whether or not something is financially profitable—and exactly how much money it rakes in). The biggest rewards are reserved for those who get the best results.

But we don't have to embrace this mindset, friend. A life of following Jesus isn't about a single outcome or a one-time event. It's a lifelong journey with many seasons, phases, and eras along the way, and there's lots of growth to be had in each. Let go of a results-only mindset and embrace the journey!

REFLECTION Think for a few moments about the major milestone of graduating high school. That end result (a diploma) is pretty cool, but what about the journey getting there? Write down some important things you have learned (or expect to learn) along the way.

ENJOYING THE PROCESS

He who began a good work in you will carry it on
to completion until the day of Christ Jesus.

PHILIPPIANS 1:6

Maybe you've already guessed that high achievers aren't focused only on their results. They also care about the process of getting there. The process is the part with laughter, learning, and all those glorious side quests. The process is the part where we build relationships, grow our skills, and mature into followers of Christ who look ever more like him.

Not only should we notice the process, we are even allowed to *enjoy* it. I know, crazy! But think about it. It's great to have an end result like a flawless performance in the fall play. That's awesome. But consider the value—the *fun*—of the weeks of rehearsals leading up to it. The friends made along the way. The backstage silliness, the inside jokes, the progression from how the show looked at the first rehearsal to how it looked by the end. Even if the final result wasn't flawless, the journey to get there was still worthwhile.

REFLECTION Do you find yourself fixated on results? Think about your last completed project. No matter the end result—positive or negative—write down at least three valuable things you took away from the process of working on that project.

CRUSHED BY UNMET GOALS

Even youths grow tired and weary, and
young men stumble and fall.

ISAIAH 40:30

"Youths grow tired and weary." Does that sound relatable? Think about the last time you didn't meet your goal, the last time you felt like you failed. Were you absolutely crushed by it? Flattened? Disappointed beyond description?

It's a common feeling for perfectionists, and it's no wonder. When everything short of perfection is perceived as a failure, how is it possible not to be crushed at every stumble, weary before you've even begun? Even healthy high achievers can get burned out when they take on too much at once or experience big disappointments. They can begin to feel beat up by their circumstances.

Friend, this is such a heavy burden to bear. And, truly, you don't have to. In the coming months, we're going to look at many biblically based reasons why you don't have to carry such a heavy load—and practical tips for training ourselves to think in a better, healthier way.

REFLECTION Take a minute to visualize the heavy weight you've been carrying on your shoulders. Now picture Jesus telling you you're free of it. Set it down at his feet and describe how much lighter and freer you are.

BOUNCING BACK

●●●●●●●●●

Day **13**

But those who hope in the LORD will renew their strength.
They will soar on wings like eagles; they will run and
not grow weary, they will walk and not be faint.
ISAIAH 40:31

Just to be clear, you can be a recovering perfectionist and still hope in the Lord. In fact, if you're reading this book, I suspect that's exactly who you are—someone who struggles with perfectionism, loves Jesus, and wants to learn a better way.

One part of this "better way" we're hoping to learn is a skill high achievers have: bouncing back after failure. They feel disappointed too, of course. That's a normal human response when we're let down in some way. But high achievers quickly put that failure and disappointment into its proper place, refuse to let it define their self-worth, and move on to the next project or goal.

If that sounds like a distant, unachievable ideal, I have good news! Keeping your hope in the Lord central—relying on his strength, believing in his love for you, recognizing who you are as a child of God—will help you put disappointments in their proper place.

REFLECTION Consider your last big disappointment. Can you describe your emotions afterward? Were they heavy, crushing, dark, smothering? Looking back, do you think your emotions were outsized compared to the event?

FEAR OF FAILURE

"Meaningless! Meaningless!" says the Teacher.
"Utterly meaningless! Everything is meaningless."
ECCLESIASTES 1:2

Perfectionists have a very serious conundrum. Like all humans (except Jesus when he was on earth), they are imperfect. Yet they're constantly striving toward perfection, berating themselves when they fall short of that impossible standard. It's not too hard to see how this mental loop—the drive to be perfect, the inability to achieve it, the perception of total failure—leads to all kinds of heartache for those of us who struggle with perfectionism.

We might even begin to feel like everything we do is meaningless, every effort futile. That no work is worth doing, no goal is worth pursuing, no dream is worth chasing. We might become so afraid of making a mistake that we do nothing.

Friend, if you're in that place, allow me a moment to hug you through the pages. Then hear this truth: You are loved, created on purpose, and your future is filled with good works to pursue. Don't give up, and don't allow fear to freeze you!

REFLECTION Can you think of something you wanted to do recently but didn't because you were afraid to fail? If that opportunity is still open to you, prayerfully consider pursuing it now. If not, what's another leap you might take instead?

HEALTHY RISK

"Meaningless! Meaningless!" says the Teacher.
"Utterly meaningless! Everything is meaningless."
ECCLESIASTES 12:8

Did you notice how this verse in Ecclesiastes says the exact same thing as the verse in the previous devotion? That's because today we're going to think about the idea that "everything is meaningless" in a slightly different, more positive way, similar to how a high achiever might.

When we recognize our tasks, projects, and goals are usually not life-or-death situations, that they shouldn't make or break our existence or completely shatter our sense of self, it gives us the freedom to take healthy risks in life. It gives us the space to say, "Hey, why not?" when faced with an exciting challenge.

The only thing that truly matters in an eternal, life-or-death sense is our relationship with God. And God's love for you is already secure. When our reverence for him is the center of our lives, we have the freedom to explore this world he's made and take some (healthy) risks—win or lose, succeed or fail. The outcome is, in one very real sense, meaningless. So, why not?

REFLECTION Take a few moments to write how you feel about this new way of looking at your goals—and the future risks you might take. Is it exciting? Strange?

PROCRASTINATION

Be very careful, then, how you live—not as unwise but
as wise, making the most of every opportunity.
EPHESIANS 5:15–16

Some people might assume perfectionists are people who tick
all the boxes on their to-do lists as quickly as possible, burning through their assignments in an effort to snag that deeply
desired 100 percent, that perfect score, that A+.

But it's actually very common for perfectionists to struggle
with procrastination. Often it's fear of failure that holds us back,
making us too worried about our performance to even begin.
Other times, impostor syndrome crashes down on us, convinc-
ing us we aren't really up to the tasks set before us, no matter
how well we may have performed in the past.

Some of us even hide our procrastinating tendencies because
others perceive us as high achievers who have it all together, and
we don't want to shatter the illusion we have everything under
control, even when we're desperately behind.

REFLECTION Are you a procrastinator? If so, think about some of the
difficulties procrastination has caused in the past, like extra stress, missed
deadlines, or work that was rushed or sloppy.

DIVING IN

No discipline seems pleasant at the time, but painful.
Later on, however, it produces a harvest of righteousness
and peace for those who have been trained by it.
HEBREWS 12:11

If the previous devotion left you feeling a little down about your procrastination habits, don't worry. There's good news today. High achievers tend to dive right in to their work, and we can learn to do that too.

When we take some pressure off the ultimate outcome, that can make it easier to leap into our tasks with all our hearts—and reframe the procrastination-inducing ideas that hold us back. Rather than thinking, *If I don't do this perfectly, it's a complete waste of time*, try, *This is an opportunity to practice the discipline of "just starting."*

Instead of looking twenty steps down the road toward the finished product and panicking about that result, we are instead choosing to focus on the first, most important step— just starting.

REFLECTION How do you feel about the idea of "just starting"? Write out some positive statements about taking the first step on a big project (for example, "Completing step one is all I need to focus on today"; "Getting started is a big win").

DEFENSIVENESS

●●●●●●●○○○

Do not be quickly provoked in your spirit,
for anger resides in the lap of fools.

ECCLESIASTES 7:9

It's probably clear by now that people who struggle with perfectionism have a lot of internal angst, doubts about their self-worth, and maybe even questions about how God could possibly love them. It would be easy to think perfectionists are curled-up balls of self-consciousness, too timid to snap back at anyone for any reason.

While that can be true for some of us, it's actually common for perfectionists to feel and act defensively when confronted with their mistakes. While there may be a lot of turmoil churning on the inside, perfectionists feel pressure to maintain a facade of flawlessness, and that makes it difficult for us to admit mistakes to others—and sometimes, even to ourselves. We become highly sensitive to criticism, often responding in less-than-godly ways.

There's a lot of biblical wisdom to lean on when it comes to controlling our anger (or defensiveness) and being honest about mistakes, and we will look at many specific ways to do this in the coming months. But today's verse is a great place to start!

REFLECTION The last time someone confronted you with a mistake or you were presented with evidence of a less-than-stellar performance, how did you react? If it wasn't great, how could you have responded better?

THE VALUE OF CRITICISM

●●●●●●●●●

Day **19**

**Wounds from a friend can be trusted,
but an enemy multiplies kisses.**
PROVERBS 27:6

Let's be honest: no one loves to be criticized. Criticism can be hard to hear, especially for people who are used to performing well, whether they're high achievers or perfectionists.

But high achievers are often able to quickly place criticism where it belongs. This "proper place" will vary, depending on the circumstances of the critique, but when it's coming from a close friend, a trusted mentor, or a beloved parent, we can be pretty sure those words were meant to help, not harm.

Since it's such a big, difficult concept, there's a whole section on how to handle criticism well later in this book. For now, let this wisdom from Proverbs sink in: hard truth from a friend can be trusted, but empty flattery can hurt you in the long run.

REFLECTION Can you think of a time when a trusted person gave you some criticism that was really hard to take? How did you respond? Would you do anything differently now, if it were to happen again?

LOW SELF-ESTEEM

●●●○○○○○○○

For he chose us in him before the creation of the world to be holy and blameless in his sight.

EPHESIANS 1:4

The idea of self-esteem can be tricky for followers of Christ. We're not supposed to regard ourselves the same way the world does, and avoid becoming prideful, selfish, or arrogant. We're not supposed to put ourselves above God or put our own desires before the needs of others. So why is it bad to have low self-esteem?

When I use the term *low self-esteem* in this book, I'm referring to the deep fear people (perfectionists especially) have about their value as human beings. They fixate on their failings and shortcomings and struggle to believe they were loved by God before the creation of the world, chosen to be holy and blameless in his sight.

Embracing the truth that God loves you—that he created you on purpose and chose you, specifically—is healthy self-esteem. It's esteeming God's stated truths about you above the dark struggles that want to convince you of the opposite.

REFLECTION Consider for a moment the depth of love for you described in Ephesians 1:4. What is your initial emotional response? Does it fill you with awe? Joy? Or does it make you squirm a little?

HIGH SELF-WORTH

In him we have redemption through his blood, the forgiveness of sins, in accordance with the riches of God's grace.
EPHESIANS 1:7

Godly self-worth acknowledges that we are precious to the Lord. Full stop. It's not about our achievements; it doesn't take into account our successes or failures. It does not depend upon our abilities or even our personalities. We have inherent value because God says we do. Jesus died on the cross to prove how much we matter to him.

Spiritually healthy self-esteem says, "I am a child of God. I live for him. My life matters—God says so." Perfectionists, who are naturally performance-focused, may struggle to really understand and embrace this. We might say it with our mouths but wonder inside how it can be.

Truly, it is a puzzle. It's amazing that God would die for *anyone*, let alone a lot of sinful humans. But that's the beauty and mystery of grace, the unmerited favor we didn't earn but is lavishly poured out on us anyway.

REFLECTION When was the last time you contemplated God's grace toward you? Think about it for a few moments, then journal about your emotional response to those meditations.

WHAT DRIVES YOUR DRIVE?

I live in disgrace all day long, and my
face is covered with shame.

PSALM 44:15

As we've outlined some characteristics of perfectionism, has it felt like looking into a mirror? If so, you might be wondering where your perfectionism came from. There are many possible answers to that question, and we're going to work through a few.

Perfectionists are driven to perform well . . . but have you ever asked yourself what drives your drive? If the underlying emotions prompting you to succeed are fear, shame, low self-esteem, or guilt, you're probably living in a perfectionist prison. These negative emotions may net good results sometimes, but they're definitely harmful to a person's heart and to their relationship with Jesus.

The Lord wants us to live in freedom, not in the shackles of disgrace and distress (Gal. 5:1). No matter what prompted these negative drivers to appear in your life, let's prayerfully work on breaking those chains.

REFLECTION Take a few moments to journal through the emotions beneath your drive to succeed. For each negative emotion, write out at least one biblical truth to combat it. Example: shame—There is now no condemnation for those who are in Christ Jesus (Romans 8:1).

HIGH-EXPECTATIONS ENVIRONMENTS

●●●●●●●●●●

Start children off on the way they should go, and
even when they are old they will not turn from it.
PROVERBS 22:6

For some of us, the desire to be perfect is an inborn personality
trait, perhaps worsened by some unhelpful thought patterns
we've accidentally nurtured over the years. For others, something external prompted this drive within us.

Growing up in a high-expectations environment can be one
of these outside factors. Some perfectionists struggle with their
parents' or caregivers' heavy expectations. Others might have
been in a very competitive learning environment, part of an
elite sports group, or immersed in a world where talent is closely
judged. Sometimes in these you-vs.-them groups, performance
is prized, rather than growth, effort, or participation.

An environment that tells us "mistakes will not be tol-
erated" can be difficult to withstand. If you've felt the heavy
blanket of a high-expectation environment wrapped around
your shoulders, you can start removing that weight today. It'll
take some time to leave it completely behind, but remember
Jesus offers us acceptance just as we are.

REFLECTION Has a high-expectation environment factored into your
inner drive? If so, take some time to imagine shedding that weight—but
also take a few minutes to find grace for those who may have inadvertently
stirred up these thought patterns for you.

EXPECTATIONS FROM WITHIN

●●●●●●●●●

We all stumble in many ways. Anyone who is never at fault in what they say is perfect, able to keep their whole body in check.
JAMES 3:2

Not all perfectionists have external factors shaping them. Many of us grew up in homes where mistakes were okay and our performance was repeatedly encouraged, our efforts supported, our failures and shortcomings forgiven.

Still, the drive to appear perfect, to *be* perfect, exists inside us. Why? That's a difficult question to answer, except to say each person is created with their particular personality, and every personality type has a predisposition toward certain struggles. Someone who is carefree and outgoing might struggle with impulse control. Those who are careful and meticulous are likelier to be perfectionists.

If you relate to the idea of perfectionism being mostly inborn, just remember this: God created your personality on purpose. You can hold on to the good, wonderful traits and gifts he gave you while rejecting those unhealthy elements that seek to push you farther from his love for you.

REFLECTION Write out the top ten things you like about yourself, but focus on your personality and your heart, not your performance (so "I have a mathematical brain" rather than "I get good grades in math," or "I care deeply for other people," not "I do a lot of community service").

SHAMING EXPERIENCES

The LORD God made garments of skin for
Adam and his wife and clothed them.
GENESIS 3:21

Sometimes our personalities are such that we're vulnerable to the struggle of perfectionism, but we don't fully embrace it until a triggering event occurs.

Experiences where we felt shame—whether because someone humiliated us or we felt embarrassed all on our own—can definitely contribute to perfectionism. Shame is an intense emotion, and a deeply negative one. It's not the same as godly conviction when we've done something wrong and we're moved to repent. It's more like the sudden feeling of nakedness Adam experienced in the garden after he'd sinned for the first time.

Keep in mind what God did for Adam and Eve. Their shame was caused by something they *had* done wrong, but God still clothed them and covered up their nakedness. Even in our dark moments, we are worthy of care and love.

REFLECTION If you've had a lot of shaming experiences in the past, don't worry, you don't have to list them! But take some time to think through them and write about your feelings. If you're still struggling with the hurt, ask God to meet you there.

CHASING PRAISE

Those who flatter their neighbors are
spreading nets for their feet.

PROVERBS 29:5

It makes sense that someone who lives under constant scrutiny, crushed under the weight of high expectations, might slowly become a perfectionist. It's a bit strange to imagine the opposite is also true—but it is! For some people, receiving excessive flattery and puffed-up praise can inadvertently train them to be perfectionists.

When we receive outsized accolades for our accomplishments, especially when we're very young, it sometimes trains our young brains to focus on those rewards. We crave that validation, revel in that praise, and we want to repeat that experience over and over. And when we hear those kind words, we subconsciously think, *They love me because I do well. I must always do well to hold on to their love.*

Loving encouragement, especially from parents, is a wonderful gift, but like all good things, our sinful nature can sometimes twist it into something that hurts us.

REFLECTION Have you experienced very supportive parents, teachers, or mentors—now or in the past? If so, you're blessed! Take a moment to write out your gratitude for those who have encouraged you, and think about whether you've ever gotten caught up in chasing praise.

ACHIEVEMENT-BASED WORTH

●●●●●○○○○○

Day 27

You, dear children, are from God and have
overcome them, because the one who is in you
is greater than the one who is in the world.

1 JOHN 4:4

Once the early perfectionist roots have taken hold, new root systems sometimes sprout to further support our rotten "trees" (or thought patterns). After years of living with unhealthy ideas and beliefs like the ones we've been talking about, we often base our self-worth on what we are able to achieve or accomplish. We think, *I am a worthy person if I perform at a high level. My life matters because of what I am able to achieve. If I don't achieve, I matter less.* This root grows deep and long, and it can be difficult to dig out.

Later in this book, we're going to explore in depth God's love for us, godly self-worth, our identities in Christ, and so much more. For now, think about whether this particular type of thinking is something that's taken hold in your heart. If so, you can commit to uprooting it using biblical truths!

REFLECTION Write out some statements you've believed about yourself and your achievements like those above. Take a hard look: Are those statements true or false? If they're false (the ones above definitely are!), write out a biblical truth that combats the false belief.

DISTORTED THINKING

*The heart is deceitful above all things and
beyond cure. Who can understand it?*
JEREMIAH 17:9

All-or-nothing thinking is going to come up a lot during our time together, and that's because it's a big problem for perfectionists. And not just perfectionists—we all have a succeed/fail, good/bad, worthy/unworthy mentality at times.

But while some things are black or white, night or day, many things exist in a gray area. This gray area can seem contradictory for an all-or-nothing thinker. A piano recital that wasn't perfect was still a success? A test with some incorrect answers was still a win? A person who makes mistakes is still lovable?

Yes, to all of the above, friend!

REFLECTION Do you have a problem with black-and-white thinking, especially when it comes to your accomplishments or self-worth? Write down some words associated with absolutes: *all, always, never, every, must.* See if you can go a day (or even a week!) without using them.

THE NEED FOR CONTROL

*In his hand is the life of every creature
and the breath of all mankind.*
JOB 12:10

One root of perfectionism that tends to run deep and spread wide—into many areas of our lives—is the need to feel in control. In control over our situations, over our lives, over the way people perceive us or how much they care for us. Sometimes this even extends to wanting to control others' actions.

I probably don't need to state the obvious—this need for control is toxic to our mental and spiritual health. It's often toxic to those around us. The only One who is truly in control of anything is God. Most of us know this already, but it's one thing to know something in your head. It's another thing to embrace it with your whole heart and live like it's true. But when we do, it's freeing! The whole world doesn't rest on your shoulders, friend! God hasn't asked us to do his job.

REFLECTION Do you struggle with needing to be in control? Ask yourself where this need might have come from. Have you been through some trauma or chaos? Or maybe it's just a learned habit? Dig deep so you can start to uproot it!

THE PRESSURE TO LOOK PERFECT

Your beauty should not come from outward adornment. . . . Rather, it should be that of your inner self, the unfading beauty of a gentle and quiet spirit.
1 PETER 3:3–4

Our culture is unkind to perfectionists. When someone is struggling with the desire to look, act, and be perfect, the world responds with intense pressure, telling us perfection is, indeed, the goal. And those who fall short are worth less than those who seem to hit the mark.

Look no further than social media for proof, with its highly curated and slickly edited images and videos. Countless people have been touched up by cosmetic procedures or use complex makeup tricks to alter their looks. The overriding message? The way you look isn't good enough. You must buy our products, follow our accounts, and do as we do to reach the standard. The pressure to look perfect on the outside can be overwhelming.

Want some great news? This message is in direct opposition to what Scripture tells us. The Bible says we are to care more about our character than our looks—and that God looks at our hearts, not our outward appearance.

REFLECTION Do you feel pressure to look perfect on the outside? If so, spend some time today thinking about a "beauty routine" for your soul—praying for others, studying your favorite book of the Bible, spending time doing a beloved hobby.

THE PRESSURE TO BE RICH

For the love of money is a root of all kinds of evil.
Some people, eager for money, have wandered from
the faith and pierced themselves with many griefs.
1 TIMOTHY 6:10

Not only does our culture tell us it's important to be physically beautiful, it also stresses the idea that wealth is to be chased. Sure, we say things like, "Money doesn't buy happiness!" But we also use the signals of wealth—nice homes, fancy cars, expensive gadgets, pricey designer clothes, fine jewelry—as status symbols that determine one's social worth.

Perhaps a simple reading of this verse from 1 Timothy gives you a good idea how God feels about this. Instead of encouraging us to chase wealth, Scripture warns about the dangers of wealth. There's nothing wrong with being materially blessed or appreciating your house, car, clothes, or anything else you have. But the Bible warns us repeatedly that money can become a snare, and it's something we should be careful about!

REFLECTION How often have you felt pressure to be wealthy? Have you ever bought into the idea that having enough status symbols would make you happy? Memorize some verses about chasing wealth so the next time that pressure pops up, you can combat it with biblical truth.

31

THE PRESSURE TO BE SUCCESSFUL

Commit to the LORD whatever you do, and
he will establish your plans.

PROVERBS 16:3

Our culture tells us it's important to be wealthy, but it also tells us it's important to be successful. These two are not always synonymous. You can inherit vast wealth, having done nothing to earn it, or you can be wildly successful in a field that doesn't pay well. The world tells us the very best thing is to have both money and success.

But have you ever wondered if maybe God has something different in store for your life? The way we have success in God's eyes is by first committing to him whatever we decide to do, then allowing him to direct our steps. That type of successful life may or may not involve a career the world values. But God always values that kind of humility, trust, and obedience.

REFLECTION Have you given much thought to your future goals? (If you're a perfectionist, you probably have.) What if God asked you to wipe that entire vision board clear and start over with his plans instead? Take time to consider how closely your future plans align with his.

THE PRESSURE TO BE HOLY

●●●●●●●●●●

Day **33**

> "Be careful not to practice your righteousness in front of others to be seen by them. If you do, you will have no reward from your Father in heaven."
>
> **MATTHEW 6:1**

Here's where it gets a little tricky. It's easy to contrast the pressure we feel from the world with what God says in Scripture—the world's lies versus God's truth. But what about the pressure to be perfect that we sometimes feel from within the church?

Holiness is a good thing. A wonderful thing, in fact. God is holy, and, as followers of Christ, we should be seeking to grow in holiness in our lives. But a problem arises when churches expect perfection from sinful humans, preaching condemnation for mistakes we've already repented of. Or, perhaps even more common, when churches become very focused on the *appearance* of holiness, whether or not true holiness exists beneath it.

We're all messy works in progress, and having to pretend otherwise is exhausting . . . and eventually harmful. Putting on that type of performance leaves us unable to be our authentic selves.

REFLECTION When do you feel like you're able to be your truest self? Are you able to let down your walls and be authentic, or do you feel like you need to wear a mask with your church family?

THE PRESSURE TO BE WORTHY

Day **34**

> We are not trying to please people but
> God, who tests our hearts.
>
> **1 THESSALONIANS 2:4**

There's immense pressure from the world to meet its markers of perfection. Sometimes there's pressure from the church to present a perfect, holy image. But oftentimes the most intense pressure of all comes from within us: the pressure to feel worthy.

If I'm a world changer, then I'm worthy of the space I take up on this planet. If I affect others' lives, then I'm truly successful. If I just meet one more milestone, hit one more goal, I will no longer doubt my value.

I hope none of that sounds familiar to you, but if it does, you're not alone. The desire to feel worthy, to feel as though our life matters, is a very human emotion, and it's common for perfectionists. We're going to dive into how this mindset negatively affects us and, most importantly, what God has to say about it!

REFLECTION Write out the words, "My life matters." What emotions does it trigger? Can you do it without cringing? Does it bring you a sense of peace and joy? Do you truly believe the words you just wrote?

THE HAMSTER WHEEL OF EARNING LOVE

Am I now trying to win the approval of human beings, or of God? Or am I trying to please people? If I were still trying to please people, I would not be a servant of Christ.
GALATIANS 1:10

Oof. If only it were so easy to reject the need to please humans! It's hard for most (if not all) of us, especially when we're constantly feeling internal pressure to be worthy—in our own eyes, in the eyes of others, and maybe even in God's eyes.

This mindset plops us squarely onto an emotional hamster wheel. Picture a frantic little rodent, scrambling with all his tiny heart, turning the wheel over and over but never actually getting anywhere. That's what it's like when we try to earn love, whether it's self-love, the love of others, or God's love. When we believe love is based on our performance, we scramble and sprint, only to wind up in the exact place we began, exhausted and bedraggled.

Here's a not-so-secret truth: God's love doesn't work this way. Jump out of the hamster wheel and find out why.

REFLECTION Do you relate to the image of the tiny hamster darting toward nothingness? If so, I want you to picture yourself allowing the wheel to slow, then stop. Pause, and imagine what the stillness would feel like after running on the wheel for a long time.

But God demonstrates his own love for us in this:
While we were still sinners, Christ died for us.

ROMANS 5:8

Take a moment to reread that verse, even if it's already familiar to you. God demonstrates his love for us in this crystal-clear way: Christ died for us while we were sinners. Every human still sins, of course, even after they believe in Jesus. We're not perfect. So what Paul meant here when he said "still sinners" is that we were dead in our transgressions. Spiritually asleep. Not yet fully embraced as a child of God the way we would be once we understood Jesus's sacrifice for us.

And still, Christ died for us. When we were like *that*. He loved us enough to die for us. Does this sound like something you have to earn? Does it sound like an exhausting hamster wheel? A condition based on your performance or your perfection?

No, this is God's free gift to everyone. The very nature of his love.

REFLECTION Set a timer for ten minutes and do nothing else but meditate on this verse and what it means for your life. If you go past ten minutes, all the better. Then write down what thoughts come to mind.

HEALTHY CONVICTION

●●●●●●●●●

"When he comes, he will prove the world to be in the wrong about sin and righteousness and judgment."
JOHN 16:8

The "he" Jesus was referring to here is the Holy Spirit. He was explaining what the Holy Spirit would do when it was poured out on the world after Christ's death and resurrection.

Many other translations use the word *convict* instead of *prove*, and feeling conviction is something Christians talk about a lot. But what does it mean?

While the message of God's love—his acceptance of us, even though we fail—is extremely important, it's also important to understand this function of the Holy Spirit: he will nudge us (or sometimes smack us over the head) when we're engaging in sinful behaviors that should be removed from our lives. It's very important to learn to discern the difference between Holy Spirit–conviction and perfectionistic shame. One is from God; the other is not!

REFLECTION Can you think of a time in the past when you were convicted by the Holy Spirit about something you knew wasn't honoring God? How did that feel compared to shame-based, perfectionist guilt?

HEALTHY GROWTH

But grow in the grace and knowledge of our Lord and Savior
Jesus Christ. To him be glory both now and forever! Amen.
2 PETER 3:18

Another truth that's very important to keep in mind when we
talk about God's abundant love of us is the fact we should spend
our entire lives growing. It's healthy! Thinking back to Romans
5:8, consider how God loved us *so* much when we were spiritually dead that he physically died so we would not have to stay
spiritually dead. The point wasn't to leave us stuck where we
started. Instead he rescued us, and now our job is to grow in our
walk with Jesus.

Thankfully, this truth doesn't conflict with any of the good
things we've been learning about shunning unhealthy perfectionist thinking. Notice I said *grow in*, not *arrive at a destination*.
The point isn't that we must be perfect in our reflection of
Jesus. That's impossible! Instead, we should continue to shape
ourselves and our lives in a way that honors God—a process
that won't be fully complete in this lifetime.

REFLECTION For a moment, sit with the idea of the never-complete process of growing in Christlikeness. Does it feel uncomfortable, or liberating?
Write out the words, "I am a work in progress—and that's okay."

"BE PERFECT . . ."

Day 39

"Be perfect, therefore, as your heavenly Father is perfect."
MATTHEW 5:48

Wait, what? Haven't we just spent over a month saying we *can't* be perfect and that perfection isn't the goal anyway? What do these words from Jesus mean, then?

The Sermon on the Mount, found in Matthew 5, contains some of Jesus's most challenging teachings. In today's verse, he'd just outlined several ways in which the law of Moses didn't go far enough in its demands. Jesus said God cares not just about the outward actions but *also* the inward heart. He was speaking to an audience whose religious leaders kept the letter of the law but not the spirit, and Jesus was challenging his listeners to expand their idea of the holiness requirements for salvation.

Importantly, Jesus was saying, "This is the standard," but elsewhere he said, "You are not capable of meeting it on your own, which is why I've come to help" (John 3:16–18, paraphrase).

REFLECTION As you move through your day, pay extra attention to your inward heart—your thoughts and feelings. How well do they align with Jesus's example? Are there areas you'd like to work on? Pray for God's help and guidance in doing so.

"IF YOU WANT TO BE PERFECT..."

●●●●●●●●●●

> Jesus answered, "If you want to be perfect, go, sell
> your possessions and give to the poor, and you will
> have treasure in heaven. Then come, follow me."
>
> **MATTHEW 19:21**

Another verse where Jesus told us how to be perfect? Well . . .
sort of. Again, he was not telling us we must be perfect to earn
God's love. Instead, he was answering a question from a rich
young ruler who'd asked what he must do to get into heaven.
This young man, with a startling lack of self-awareness, had just
insisted he completely kept a list of commands Jesus outlined,
including "love your neighbor as yourself." Jesus's response—
and the man's unwillingness to do what he asked—exposed the
man's insincerity. He wanted his spot in heaven, but he didn't
want to *really* follow Jesus.

Jesus's words also highlight the fact God's definition of *perfection* is never going to be the same as the world's. The man
had wealth and status. Maybe even influence. Perhaps he even
had good morals. But Jesus said to be *perfect*, he had to go even
further—radically loving others and refusing to rely on his
material wealth. A tall order in any century!

REFLECTION Read Matthew 19:16–22. Do you think the young man in
this story was a first-century perfectionist? What about his thinking suggests he might have been?

. . . .

. . . .

. . . .

. . . .

FINDING PEACE

The Spirit you received does not make you slaves, so that you live in fear again; rather, the Spirit you received brought about your adoption to sonship. And by him we cry, "*Abba*, Father."
ROMANS 8:15

As we meditate on the desire to be perfect, I want to leave you with one crucial idea: being a follower of Jesus offers the love, peace, and adoption as children of God that will free us from our perfectionist prisons.

Practical tools to help change our thinking in this area can come from many different sources. But the heart of our peace comes from the knowledge that our place in God's family is secure. We matter because he says we do. We aren't "worthy" in the sense that we can earn salvation on our own. But we *are* worthy in the sense that our salvation matters enough that God chose to die for it.

Hear the freedom in those truths. Embrace the love in those words. And find peace for a mind and heart that's probably very weary from striving toward an impossible goal.

REFLECTION Take some time today to sit with Jesus. Quietly—in a place that's comfortable and cozy for you. If it feels elusive, ask God to fill you with the peace described above.

MYTH: PERFECTIONISM DRIVES SUCCESS

●●●●●●●●●●

Yet when I surveyed all that my hands had done and what
I had toiled to achieve, everything was meaningless, a
chasing after the wind; nothing was gained under the sun.

ECCLESIASTES 2:11

Sometimes we know a behavior or mindset is unhealthy for us,
but we still have a hard time letting it go. Often this is because
we're holding on to false beliefs about the unhealthy mindset,
erroneously thinking it's helping us in some way. We're going
to bust some of those perfectionist myths right now, as well as
over the next few days.

Myth: "My perfectionism drives my success." It's easy to
see why we believe this. *Yes*, we think, *I know I'm anxious and
depressed, but my drive to be perfect is what makes me so successful.*

Truth: You are successful despite your perfectionism, not
because of it. Even without your perfectionistic fear propelling you forward, you would still have the same skill, talent,
and aptitude. In fact, your ability to succeed would probably
increase without the added pressure that comes with being a
perfectionist. You can shed unhealthy driving forces and retain
your talent.

REFLECTION Is there a piece of you that's reluctant to let go of perfectionism? If so, why do you think that is? What might happen if you let go
of this myth?

....

....

....

....

MYTH: PERFECTIONISTS GET THINGS DONE (AND WELL)

Day 43

> Let us not become weary in doing good, for at the proper time we will reap a harvest if we do not give up.
> **GALATIANS 6:9**

Myth: "I am able to get more things done because I'm a perfectionist." Not gonna lie, I feel this one! It's very easy for me to tell myself that if I release all my perfectionistic tendencies, I will not be able to accomplish as much as I usually do.

But remember how perfectionists are often procrastinators? How they can become frozen and overwhelmed with starting because they're already worried about the end result being good enough? Yeah, I feel that too.

Truth: Letting go of perfectionism allows us to hit deadlines more easily. We can manage our time better—and without debilitating fear and anxiety—when we focus on making progress. Letting go of all-or-nothing thinking helps us focus on keeping our commitments and giving each project our best, rather than being so wrapped up nitpicking our efforts that we fail to do what we're truly capable of.

REFLECTION Is there a big project you're currently procrastinating on? Clear your mind of any associated fear or anxiety (prayer is a great way to do this), and ask yourself, "What is the first small step I can take to begin this project?"

MYTH: PERFECTIONISTS ARE
DETERMINED AND RESILIENT

Day 44

I do not run like someone running aimlessly; I do not fight
like a boxer beating the air. . . . so that after I have preached
to others, I myself will not be disqualified for the prize.

1 CORINTHIANS 9:26–27

Myth: "Perfectionists don't let obstacles stand in their way, and
they *will* find a way to succeed because they are determined and
resilient." *Anxiety is the gasoline that runs my motor*, we may think.
It helps me to keep driving toward all the goals I want to reach in life.

If this is you, I want to hug you through the pages right now.

Truth: Your perfectionism actually makes you hypersensi-
tive to criticism. Perfectionists are more prone to social anxiety,
performance anxiety, depression, and writer's block.[1] All of
these are roadblocks to success, not the gasoline that makes
your engine run. You are talented, capable, and intelligent, and
that is what helps you shoot for your goals, no unhealthy thinking patterns required.

REFLECTION Would you describe yourself as determined and resilient?
Think about times you've shown both these positive traits in the past. Was
your perfectionism a help or a hindrance in those situations? (Try really
hard to untangle this!)

MYTH: "THIS IS JUST HOW I AM"

Therefore we do not lose heart. . . . Inwardly we are being renewed day by day.

2 CORINTHIANS 4:16

Myth: "This is the way I am, and I cannot change it." To be fair, this is a common belief with *many* different struggles, not just perfectionism. People often feel like those things they battle against—whether perfectionism, a particular sin, a negative attitude, or thousands of other issues—are simply part of who they are, never to be improved or addressed.

Truth: You don't have to live this way. If you're reading this book, my hope is that you have the desire to change. And you can! We may not change perfectly (see what I did there?). We may not be able to fully eradicate all of these thought patterns from our minds, but we can grow in our understanding of them. We can learn to recognize the harm they do and how to spot them. We can add tools and techniques to our arsenal to combat them when they try to take over. We can be healthier and more peaceful followers of Jesus.

REFLECTION Spend a few minutes in prayer today, asking the Holy Spirit to help you change. When our goals align with God's will, the Holy Spirit is always there to help, encourage, and support us.

MYTH: "PERFECTIONISM IS WHY PEOPLE LIKE ME"

●●●●●●●●●

One who has unreliable friends soon comes to ruin, but
there is a friend who sticks closer than a brother.

PROVERBS 18:24

Myth: "My friendships are based on my performance. If I don't
perform well, people won't like me as much, and my perfectionism helps me perform."

Oof. This one. You've likely never thought about it in quite
these words, but have you ever felt your friends wouldn't be your
friends if you were less successful? Or have you wondered how
much your relationships are based on your ability to do well? To
be the overachiever? The star of the show?

Truth: I want you to hear this with all the love in the world.
Our friends like us regardless of our perfectionism, not because
of it. We're going to explore the many ways perfectionism can
damage relationships, but trust me on this: The people who love
you aren't sticking around because you're a perfectionist. They're
there because they love *you*.

REFLECTION Make a list of some of the people you're closest with,
whether they're friends, family, or mentors. When you think about your
relationships with those people, do you find any evidence that suggests
their love for you is performance-based?

DANGERS OF PERFECTIONISM: ANXIETY

Day 47

Do not be anxious about anything, but in every situation, by prayer and petition, with thanksgiving, present your requests to God. And the peace of God, which transcends all understanding, will guard your hearts and your minds in Christ Jesus.
PHILIPPIANS 4:6–7

This sounds like a straightforward directive—do not be anxious—and yet it's a complicated matter for someone who struggles with anxiety. We *want* to obey. We *want* to banish anxiety from our minds and hearts, but for some it can be a lifelong challenge to do so.

Anxiety is not something only perfectionists experience. Anyone can be anxious, but perfectionists are likelier to struggle with it than most people. It makes sense. If you're always worried about your performance, fear of failure nipping at your heels, that's bound to significantly eat away at your peace of mind.

But there's hope for those struggling to manage their anxious thoughts. We can combat our anxiety while also addressing what may be the underlying cause for many reading this book—toxic perfectionism that's working overtime to steal your peace.

REFLECTION Is anxiety a problem for you? The next time an anxious thought arises, visualize grabbing hold of that thought and handing it over to Jesus. This is a strong reminder that you're not alone in trying to shoulder your fears.

GOD'S GOT YOU

"Take my yoke upon you and learn from me, for I am gentle
and humble in heart, and you will find rest for your souls."
MATTHEW 11:29

Everyone experiences anxiety sometimes, when our fears
and worries get blown out of proportion to the event at hand.
Anxiety robs us of our joy and makes us feel powerless—which
is a doubly terrifying thought for a perfectionist who feels like
they need to be in control.

Whether we are perfectionists, high achievers, or deal with
anxious tendencies, the Lord wants to give each of us rest. He
desires peace for his children—a break from worry, fear, striving, and stressing. Our Savior said, "You will find rest for your
souls" (Matthew 11:29). Jesus has us safely tucked under his
wing. He knows every situation we face, every worry burden-
ing our hearts. He knows all about our desire to live up to an
impossible standard. And still, he offers us rest.

How can we tap into that sense of rest when anxiety threat-
ens to overwhelm us? Let's start by reminding ourselves that
God is in control, so we don't have to be. Let him take on the
burdens that are weighing you down. God's got you, friend.

REFLECTION Think of some ways you can quickly remind yourself of the
rest Jesus offers you. You can memorize Scriptures like the one above. You
can write reminders here, or on index cards that you tape up in your room
or tuck into your binder.

PEACE IN THE BODY

Let the peace of Christ rule in your hearts, since as members of one body you were called to peace. And be thankful.
COLOSSIANS 3:15

When it comes to the truth, our feelings aren't always a good judge. Sometimes they are big helpers, like when our intuition correctly tells us to be wary of a situation before we have a reason to feel that way. But sometimes, when we're dealing with big, negative emotions like shame or anxiety, our feelings whisper lies to us. If you're a perfectionist, you're probably no stranger to overwhelmingly strong feelings trying to whisper harmful lies in your ear.

Anxiety tries to tell us awful things—that the world is a terrifying place, that we're all alone in it. That we can never feel safe or secure. But these feelings don't reflect our reality as children of God. The Lord is always with us, and even more concretely, he has given us a place where we can find community, strength, and safety: a body of trusted fellow believers. We can access the peace God wants for us when we surround ourselves with people who remind us of the truth—that we are valued and loved!

REFLECTION Has anxiety ever caused you to feel isolated? If you've struggled with anxiety, what are some other feelings it has caused for you? Write down some truths to help you combat feelings that don't reflect reality.

NO CONDEMNATION

●●●●●●●●●

When anxiety was great within me, your
consolation brought me joy.

PSALM 94:19

Mental health can be difficult to discuss in faith communities.
For many Christians, their experiences while trying to get the
help they need have not been positive. Sometimes verses like
today's have been used to shame those suffering with anxiety
and even cast doubt upon their faith and love for Jesus.

If this has been your experience, I'm sorry. Recently, there
have been positive shifts toward removing the stigma around
mental health struggles, and we can pray this continues. Verses
that encourage us to trust God, let go of anxiety, and seek peace
should be read as comfort. They remind us we're not alone—
God sees us and cares for us. And he supports us as we learn to
embrace new thought patterns and biblical truths.

Experiencing anxiety or struggling with perfectionist
thought patterns does not mean you're irrevocably broken. It
means, just like every single Christian, you're an imperfect work
in progress, being lovingly shaped and looked after by our ever-
present Lord.

REFLECTION Is it easy to be open about your mental health struggles?
Or have you dealt with shame because of them? If so, take a few moments
to release that shame during prayer. *Everything* can be brought before the
Lord. Approach his throne with confidence!

GOD KNOWS OUR STRUGGLES

I sought the LORD, and he answered me; he
delivered me from all my fears.

PSALM 34:4

Miraculous healing can happen for all kinds of illnesses, including mental health concerns. Some people have been instantly cured of their anxiety. But for others—including Christians who are just as faithful, loving, and genuine—anxiety is a lifelong battle. Maybe it's the thorn in their side—the thing they pray about, like the apostle Paul did with his, and one God chooses not to remove (2 Corinthians 12:7–10).

But here's a truth every one of us can rest in: God knows about our anxiety. He's aware of our perfectionism and all that comes with it. He *sees* our struggle, and he cares about it. No one likes to experience affliction, whether in our bodies or our minds. But we can feel assured that we have a God who sees and comforts us through the pain of those afflictions.

REFLECTION Is there something in your life that you've asked God to take away and he's chosen not to? That can be tough to endure. But think about the ways God has continued being faithful to you, even in the midst of that affliction.

DANGERS OF PERFECTIONISM: DEPRESSION

The Lord is close to the brokenhearted and
saves those who are crushed in spirit.

PSALM 34:18

I have good news and not-so-excellent news. The less-than-stellar news is that a perfectionist mindset puts a person at greater risk for depression. This is also not surprising, given the constant feelings of unworthiness and failure circling like sharks around the struggling perfectionist.

The good news: as with anxiety, if you struggle with perfectionism, you are not powerless against this struggle. We're going to talk about some biblically based mindfulness practices you can adopt to help, but if this is a bigger battle for you, please remember it's okay to seek outside help. Mental health professionals, trusted mentors or pastors, your parents, and your friends can all be part of that support system. There's no reason to battle dragons by yourself when you can have a whole supportive crew fighting by your side.

REFLECTION If depression is something you struggle with, have you ever felt like you need to hide this part of yourself from God? You don't. He is there with us in our joy and brokenheartedness. Take a moment to invite God into the process of combatting these feelings.

GROWING IN GRATITUDE

Every good and perfect gift is from above, coming down from the Father of the heavenly lights, who does not change like shifting shadows.

JAMES 1:17

When dark emotions feel like they're blanketing us, it's easy to believe we're surrounded on all sides by negativity and heartache. And when we get into that mindset, we tend to overlook the many blessings we do have.

Being thankful for our blessings doesn't negate the hard things we're facing. Ignoring heartache or grief isn't healthy, and we don't have to tell ourselves not to feel those things because we have [fill-in-the-blank] blessings. But we can make a choice to focus on our blessings instead of our struggles. And it is always appropriate to overflow with gratitude when something good happens, even when we're facing otherwise hard circumstances.

Try spending a whole week intentionally choosing gratitude when you feel yourself fixating on the darkness. Take note of all your blessings, large and small. You might be surprised at how many wonderful things God has placed in your life that you never even noticed before.

REFLECTION Use a gratitude journal to try the above experiment. Jot down anything and everything that comes to mind. How many of these things are those you routinely notice and thank God for? How many were new discoveries?

●●●●●●●●●

I know that there is nothing better for people than to
be happy and to do good while they live. That each
of them may eat and drink, and find satisfaction
in all their toil—this is the gift of God.

ECCLESIASTES 3:12–13

Have you ever been struck by a sudden feeling of *Wow, I really love this*? Sometimes that feeling strikes when we're doing something we enjoy. Other times it can hit during the most mundane tasks—like taking the dog for a walk or organizing your school supplies (just me?). It's a huge blessing that we're able to feel happiness as we work, play, rest, learn, grow, and move in the world God has made.

Taking pleasure in the small joys of life can be part of a godly practice of gratitude. Especially for perfectionists, who tend to focus on achievement, taking the time to notice small joys is an excellent habit to build.

It seems obvious to thank God for the big answers to prayer. Perhaps it's less obvious to thank him for the little things—ice-cold refreshment on a hot day, a perfect afternoon with friends, a beautiful pack of new pens. Give it a try—you might find the little things can have a big impact!

REFLECTION Set a timer for five minutes. Without thinking too hard, write down as many things that bring you joy as you can, no matter how big or small. See how many you can come up with!

GOD IS WORKING HIS PLAN

And we know that in all things God works for the good of those who love him, who have been called according to his purpose.
ROMANS 8:28

We serve a very big God. Holy, gracious, just, omniscient, omnipresent, omnipotent, loving, faithful. The list of his awe-inspiring attributes goes on and on, to the point we will never completely wrap our human brains around God's full character.

Yet, when we understand who God is—as much as we're able—when we have some inkling of what his character is all about, only then can we truly appreciate verses like this. God has a plan for the world, his people, and each of our lives. Scriptures like this assure us those plans will be used for our ultimate good. And that's because our all-knowing, ever-present, perfectly good, and eternal God is always operating within his character.

God works *all things* for the good of those who love him—including you. That's a promise. It doesn't mean we won't sometimes face legitimately difficult circumstances. But we can rest assured God is with us, always working for our good.

REFLECTION Have you ever been through something that was very difficult at the time, but looking back you can now see how God worked that situation for your good? Can you sometimes see those big-pictures goods, even in the difficult moments?

BEING A POSITIVE PRESENCE

Day **56**

> May the God of hope fill you with all joy and peace
> as you trust in him, so that you may overflow
> with hope by the power of the Holy Spirit.
>
> **ROMANS 15:13**

When we're feeling depressed, it's easy to become really focused on ourselves and our own problems. This can set off a descending spiral of negative emotions, propelling us farther into that pit of hopelessness.

Want to know something that can help? Looking outward to those around you, seeing where you might be able to help *them*. Your friend going through grief may need a listening ear. Your sibling struggling with anxiety might love to get a hug from you.

Bringing positivity into someone else's life does not mean blasting sunshine into their faces while they struggle. Most people prefer a gentler approach when they're hurting. Instead, we can focus on being what this verse describes—a person so filled with joy and peace that we can't help but exude hope. The best part is that we're not expected to do this on our own, because the source of our joy, peace, and hope is the Holy Spirit.

REFLECTION Is there someone you know who could use some extra support right now? How might you bring them peace and comfort in a gentle way?

WORKS IN PROGRESS

●●●●●○○○○○

You were washed, you were sanctified, you were justified in the name of the Lord Jesus Christ and by the Spirit of our God.
1 CORINTHIANS 6:11

Salvation is something most followers of Jesus are deeply grateful for. We understand that the Son of God became a man and died for our sins—and we recognize how huge that is. How it brought us from death to life, separation from God to reconciliation with him.

But sometimes believers overlook a related blessing—our sanctification. After we've crossed over from spiritual death into spiritual life, God doesn't leave us in that brand-new, baby Christian state. Right away, he begins to rework us into his image so we can look more like Jesus in the way we act, think, and feel. The Holy Spirit lives inside us, facilitating this process. He guides us, pointing out the areas of our lives that don't honor God. And then he helps us change those things.

Friend, this is a beautiful truth, especially for our recovering perfectionist hearts. We are all works in progress. We're not perfect. We're not yet complete. But we are *growing* to be like him day by day.

REFLECTION Have you been a believer as long as you can remember, or do you recall what it was like before you knew Jesus personally? Do you remember what it was like when you were a less mature Christian? How has God been shaping you over the last few months?

DANGERS OF PERFECTIONISM: LONELY AND WORTHLESS

Turn to me and be gracious to me, for I am lonely and afflicted.

PSALM 25:16

If you've guessed by now that perfectionism is the icky little gift that keeps on giving, you're right. Not only does it put us at greater risk for anxiety and depression, it often leaves us feeling lonely, worthless, and insecure.

These feelings are deeply human, spanning across the millennia of recorded history. How do we know? Lines like this in Scripture tell us that ancient people struggled with these sorts of feelings. Even King David, the author of this psalm, whom God called a "man after my own heart" (Acts 13:22), felt this way sometimes.

But no matter how common they may be, those dark feelings are not true. And certainly God doesn't want us to embrace lies about ourselves. In the coming days, we're going to take an in-depth look at our insecurities—what they are and how to overcome them. But let's start by reiterating that you are loved, valued, and never alone.

REFLECTION How often do you feel lonely? Do you struggle to make friends, or are you surrounded by people and still feel like no one understands you? Can you think of any reassurances from Scripture to help you with your feelings of loneliness?

DEFINING INSECURITY

Be alert and of sober mind. Your enemy the devil prowls
around like a roaring lion looking for someone to devour.
1 PETER 5:8

Everyone wants to measure up. Sure, our ideas of "measuring
up" vary quite a lot. We're all trying to meet different standards,
depending on our values, our cultures, our personalities. But
most people can admit, "Yes, I would like to meet the standard
for success."

Everyone feels like they've fallen short at times, but for a
perfectionist, this universal human experience has harsh consequences. Falling short plants seeds of inadequacy in our hearts,
and those seeds sprout into anxiety in our minds. Eventually,
that anxiety grows into a full-sized tree of insecurity. That can
make us feel unsure, unconfident, and unsafe.

Insecurity is not unique to perfectionists, but it does affect
us in some specific ways we're going to look at. As followers of
Jesus, we have the most powerful tools available to uproot those
diseased trees and plant instead healthy saplings rooted in the
truth of God's Word. Ones that help us see we do measure up.

REFLECTION What are some of the standards of success you hope to
meet in your life? Jot down the first few that come to mind. Consider some
that are spiritual or character-based (for example: I would like to be a person firmly rooted in God's Word).

PERFECTIONISM AND INSECURITIES

The LORD makes firm the steps of the one who
delights in him; though he may stumble, he will not
fall, for the LORD upholds him with his hand.

PSALM 37:23–24

Why are insecurities such a big deal for perfectionists? You may have already guessed at some of the reasons. When we feel inadequate and unsure, it's like putting a magnifying glass over our fear of failure. Amplifying it. Burning it into our already-anxious thoughts.

When we've also set impossible standards for ourselves with an all-or-nothing mentality, it's easy to see how this becomes a vicious cycle that feeds our insecurities. We will look at specific examples of insecurities—and most importantly, how to work through them, banishing them in favor of God's truth—but for now, reread the verses above. Though we may stumble, we will not fall, for the Lord upholds us with his hand. Whatever insecurities you're struggling with today, God is there, holding your hand. He won't let you fall!

REFLECTION Do you feel like insecurities are hindering you? If you're ready, write down your biggest insecurity. Are there some biblical truths that challenge this insecurity? Write them down too.

NEVER ENOUGH

> But you, LORD, are a shield around me, my
> glory, the One who lifts my head high.
> **PSALM 3:3**

Sometimes, the nefarious little creature living beneath all our insecurities is the lying voice that says, *Nothing I do is good enough. I will never be enough.*

Please banish that thought right now. While it's true Scripture says we can't do enough to earn our own salvation (Ephesians 2:8–9), that's not the same message this lying voice is trying to get you to swallow. Jesus is the only one who could keep the law perfectly and therefore is the only one who can save us. But that does *not* mean you are worthless. That does not mean you're not "good enough" in God's eyes.

In fact, God decided we are so worth it, he came to Earth himself to save us. Does that sound like something he'd do for a bunch of "never enough" humans who don't matter to him? We can't earn this gift, but we are beloved and precious in his sight, and he is the one who lifts our heads.

REFLECTION Have you heard the whispering voice lately, telling you you're not enough? Replace that voice with this truth: God loves you, radically and wildly, and you are precious to him. How does that make you feel?

JEALOUSY IN RELATIONSHIPS

Anger is cruel and fury overwhelming, but
who can stand before jealousy?

PROVERBS 27:4

Insecurities can show up in many different areas of our lives, and one of the most common is jealousy in relationships. When we don't feel sure of ourselves, when we doubt whether we're acceptable or worthy, it sometimes causes jealousy to arise in our relationships.

Maybe we're convinced our parents love a sibling more than us. Maybe we become irrationally angry whenever we see two of our friends spending time together, feeling left out or even hurt by the mere fact they're in each other's company.

Sometimes the unfairness is real, and sometimes the hurt is legitimate, but it's never wise to give the unwieldy beast of jealousy space to hang around in our hearts. It tends to cloud our judgment and disintegrate our relationships.

REFLECTION Has jealousy crept into any of your friendships lately? What about family relationships? If so, think about the root of that jealousy—is it something you need to address with someone, or is it coming from insecurities about yourself?

SOCIAL WORRY

The words of the reckless pierce like swords,
but the tongue of the wise brings healing.
PROVERBS 12:18

For an insecure person, social situations can be terrifying. Being unsure of yourself and lacking confidence can lead to the kind of self-consciousness that makes you feel like everyone is watching you. Not only watching you—dissecting and judging and deciding you don't measure up.

If that sounds familiar, I'm so sorry! It's not fun to feel like you're living under a judgy microscope. The good news is, once we've identified our own insecurity as the root of our problem, it's a lot easier to dismantle this wonky worldview that leads us to think everyone is watching us.

Truthfully, most people aren't paying as close attention to us as we pay to ourselves. When we become more secure in who we are—more confident in our identity as God's children—that helps us shed this unhealthy cloak of self-consciousness. Ditching that cloak allows us to be more authentic and open, drawing people to us rather than pushing them away.

REFLECTION Do you experience social worry? Sometimes social situations are an issue for us if we haven't found "our people" yet—those with shared interests and passions. What are some ways you could reach out to others who share some of your interests?

BODY IMAGE

Day **64**

> "The LORD does not look at the things people
> look at. People look at the outward appearance,
> but the LORD looks at the heart."
>
> **1 SAMUEL 16:7**

When I say "insecurity," what's the first thing that comes to mind? If you thought about anything related to physical appearance, you're not alone. Often when people talk about insecurities, they mention the immense pressure to live up to our cultural standard of beauty. This applies to both men and women, though typically there's extra pressure placed on girls and women to look a certain way.

It's pretty wild how much cultural beauty standards have changed over the centuries, and even how much they vary from culture to culture. Yet over the years and across the world, people have felt the same pressure to measure up—and the same discomfort if they've been judged as falling short.

The best news: These standards are completely irrelevant to God. He is not at all concerned about what we look like on the outside and is instead solely focused on the part that matters—our hearts.

REFLECTION When you wrote the top ten things you like about yourself on day 24, the focus was on personality. This time, I want you to write down ten things you appreciate about the body God carefully crafted just for you.

BASIC NEEDS

●●●●●●○○○○

"So do not worry, saying, 'What shall we eat?' or
'What shall we drink?' or 'What shall we wear?'"
MATTHEW 6:31

Oof. This verse is hard if you've ever dealt with the insecurity of not having your basic needs met. Sometimes it's called "food insecurity" or "housing insecurity," as it typically involves those two things. *Many* people all across the world experience these types of insecurities daily.

More than the other types we've talked about so far, this type of insecurity stems from feeling unsafe, often because you *have* been unsafe in this way in the past. In other words, it's not an irrational fear. Though in the verse we're looking at today, Jesus told us not to worry about such things. Why?

Giving in to worry is never good for our hearts, whether the fear is founded or not. That doesn't mean we're not supposed to think about our basic needs, of course. In fact, we are encouraged to calmly trust God, plan well and be wise with our resources, and share generously with others, especially if we've been blessed with abundance. God provides for all his children in the end.

REFLECTION Whether you've experienced insecurity over basic needs being met or not—but especially if you haven't—brainstorm a list of ways you can help those in your community dealing with this problem right now. Is there any way you can take action this week?

PERFORMANCE

I will instruct you and teach you in the way you should
go; I will counsel you with my loving eye on you.

PSALM 32:8

Perhaps the insecurity nearest and dearest to the perfectionist's
heart is the one that's tied to our performance in school and later
our jobs. School and work environments tend to give us objective measures of performance that perfectionists both crave and
dread. Those lofty goals we set for ourselves—when reached—
give us the validation we desire. "Yes, you are good enough," they
tell us, assuming we're able to receive that message.

But when we don't reach those goals, the opposite message
is etched into our minds over and over again. Insecurity takes
hold. We don't feel sure of our abilities or confident of our skills.
Even if we've had many successes in the past, that insecurity
begins to dominate our thinking.

How about some good news? Our school and job performances don't *actually* measure who we are or what value we hold.
Yes, we should work hard and perform all tasks to the best of
our ability. But God's love and our worth are not based on our
performance—in school, at work, or anywhere else.

REFLECTION How strongly are your feelings of self-worth tied to your
grades or achievements? Write out some affirming statements of truth about
this: "God loves me, no matter what score I get on my tests." "I matter, even
if I don't have straight As."

SIGNS OF INSECURITY: FEELINGS OF INADEQUACY

Not that we are competent in ourselves to claim anything for ourselves, but our competence comes from God.
2 CORINTHIANS 3:5

We've looked at some areas where insecurities commonly pop up, but you might still be wondering if this applies to you. *Am I insecure? If so, how is it affecting my life?*

One of the big telltale signs you're dealing with some insecurity is persistent feelings of inadequacy. These can show up as a vague sense of never feeling quite good enough at anything you do, or it can feel like a big, scary thundercloud constantly booming your shortcomings loud enough to rattle your brain.

There's a whole section in this book devoted to insecurity because it's such a common feeling. It's almost baked into our existence as humans. But that doesn't mean we must learn to live with it. We can work on overcoming these feelings of inadequacy rather than letting them be influential voices in our lives.

REFLECTION Memorize the above verse from 2 Corinthians. Our competence comes from God. Full stop. Next time feelings of inadequacy try to overwhelm you, write about how it would feel to rely on God's competence instead.

SIGNS OF INSECURITY: LOW SELF-ESTEEM

Therefore, if anyone is in Christ, the new creation
has come: The old has gone, the new is here!
2 CORINTHIANS 5:17

Remember those feelings of worthlessness we talked about
before? Our insecurities love to whisper into our ears, telling
us we don't matter. When we start to believe that lie—or even
when we regularly *wonder* if it might be true—it chips away at
our self-esteem.

Low self-worth, low confidence, low self-esteem—these are
all signs you might be struggling with insecurity. If that resonates for you today, here's some good news: we are supposed
to be works in progress. God has not asked us to be perfected,
completed projects. And when that does eventually happen, it's
going to be *his* work, not ours. We were never asked to meet a
standard he knew we couldn't reach.

So those mistakes, slip-ups, and blunders? They say nothing
about how much you matter to God. God esteemed you enough
to create you, to love you, to die for you. Use that truth to combat insecurities that are trying to lie to you!

REFLECTION Sometimes we're very unkind when we look inward at ourselves. But what do you think your closest friends would say if I asked
them why they love you? Write down five to ten ideas. Or, if you're feeling
adventurous, ask them!

SIGNS OF INSECURITY: CAN'T COPE

Day **69**

Anxiety weighs down the heart, but a kind word cheers it up.
PROVERBS 12:25

Here's an insecurity red flag that might be less obvious: people who are insecure often struggle to cope with stress.

Anxiety, coupled with a lack of resilience, makes stress feel absolutely overwhelming, impossible to overcome, and completely flattening. For you, this could look like shutting down during stressful times in life. It could manifest as major irritability. Or the symptoms could even be physical—insomnia, a racing heart, and body tension can all be signs you're not coping with stress very well.

Let's take a suggestion from this verse in Proverbs. To help deal with your stress today, focus on the positives in your life right now. It doesn't mean you pretend you're not stressed. It just means you are making a choice about where to shift your focus to help get out from under the stress that wants to flatten you.

REFLECTION Quick—write down the first five things you think of that always make you smile. If more than five things come to mind, write them down too!

SIGNS OF INSECURITY: ANXIOUS ABOUT RELATIONSHIPS

A friend loves at all times, and a brother
is born for a time of adversity.

PROVERBS 17:17

Everyone probably feels a little twinge now and then worrying they might have upset or offended a close friend. It's normal to have speed bumps in relationships of all kinds, and it's normal for friends to fade in and out of our lives during different seasons (you probably don't have the *exact* same list of best friends you had in elementary school).

But if you find these thoughts to be very consuming— frequently questioning the status of your friendships, wondering if your loved ones still love you, or lying awake at night replaying conversations over and over—these are signs you might be struggling with insecurity.

While not every single relationship we have will be a forever friendship, remember what this verse says: a friend loves at all times. That's a two-way street, and your friends have *chosen* to be in your life. If you're committed to openness and authenticity in your friendships, there's no reason to worry about your friends abandoning you! You can trust that they love you as much as you love them.

REFLECTION Does this fear sound relatable to you? Jot down the names of your closest friends, then take a moment to pray for each of them. What's one thing you can do to let them know they're loved?

SIGNS OF INSECURITY: POOR DECISION-MAKING

●●●●●●●●●

"Everyone who hears these words of mine and
does not put them into practice is like a foolish
man who built his house on sand."

MATTHEW 7:26

When we hear "poor decision-making ability," we might think
of someone being very reckless and making bad choices, which
is one way to interpret that phrase. But for someone struggling
with insecurity, it means something quite different.

People who are insecure feel unsafe and unsure, so when
they are faced with big decisions—or even small decisions—
they often freeze. They ruminate, contemplate, worry, and
wonder. Instead of taking a leap, they stand on the precipice,
worried about doing the wrong thing, and so they ultimately do
nothing. Which can be a big problem when quick thinking and
fast decisions are required.

When we learn to release control to God, when we learn
to feel safer and more secure in ourselves, it starts to feel less
like the weight of the world rests on each and every decision. It
becomes easier to make a choice without the crushing fear that
accompanies insecurity.

REFLECTION Are you able to make wise decisions when you don't have
much time to deliberate? If not, think about what's at the root of that. Is it
because you just need more time to think, or is insecurity the real problem?

SIGNS OF INSECURITY: OVERLY CRITICAL

●●●●●●●●●

My guilt has overwhelmed me like a burden too heavy to bear.

PSALM 38:4

When a person is insecure—unsure of their value, ability, or worth—they can become hypercritical of both themselves and others. Those are two sides to the same coin, which often flips back and forth. We feel afraid we don't measure up, so we nit-pick everything about our performance. And because we feel so worried about our own worth, sometimes we project that unforgiving laser vision onto others, nitpicking *them*, whether out of habit or because it makes us feel better about ourselves. Which can then further feed our insecurity when we play back our reaction or see how others treat us in response.

Ouch. It's almost painful to read it spelled out like that. When put in those terms, it's also very clear that, if we are experiencing this sign of insecurity, we definitely need to focus on banishing it from our lives, for our sake and the well-being of those around us!

REFLECTION Do you feel the impulse to nitpick other people? What about yourself? Take a few moments to dig down into where that's coming from. What can you do to keep that impulse in check?

SIGNS OF INSECURITY: MASKING WITH CONFIDENCE

Day 73

He answered, "I heard you in the garden, and I
was afraid because I was naked; so I hid."

GENESIS 3:10

Have you ever felt the need to shout about your own accomplishments? Do you dismiss others' input without consideration of their ideas? Ignore your shortcomings when they are pointed out?

These can be signs of someone who is arrogant, of course. But oftentimes, people who do these things—especially if those people are perfectionists—are not suffering from too much confidence but rather a *lack* of confidence. True confidence and self-assuredness don't need to convince everyone else how good they are. They don't need to overstate their abilities and ignore their shortcomings. If you notice some of these behaviors in yourself, and you know your real feelings don't match what you're outwardly projecting, you may be showing signs of insecurity. Like Adam in the garden, we tend to hide when we're ashamed, and false confidence is one way to hide. And similar to Adam, we have a God who is ultimately there for us, even when we are in a fragile place.

REFLECTION If you've been masking with confidence, imagine removing that false mask now. What's underneath? Dare to look your true self in the mirror and say, "God loves the real me, flaws and all."

73

SIGNS OF INSECURITY: SOCIAL AVOIDANCE

●●●●●●●●●●

He heals the brokenhearted and binds up their wounds.

PSALM 147:3

Some insecure people hide behind masks. Others literally hide. When engaging in a community feels risky, some of us will opt out altogether. "What if they don't like me?" we ask. "What if they reject me? What if I fall short?" These questions can plague us to the point we decide not to engage at all.

Remember when we said perfectionism can lead to loneliness? This is one of the underlying reasons. When we're afraid of being judged as less than perfect, it seems better to just keep to ourselves.

But the Lord created human beings for community. We're not meant to be isolated islands; we need each other, and we need God. There are many Bible verses devoted to the value of friendship and how communities of believers should interact with each other—in harmony, with grace, and always in love.

REFLECTION Have you ever opted out of a social gathering because you felt insecure? What about an entire community, like a group at school or church? Write out some benefits you might get from joining such a group.

SIGNS OF INSECURITY: MISTRUST OF OTHERS

> "The thief comes only to steal and kill and destroy; I have come that they may have life, and have it to the full."
> **JOHN 10:10**

Jesus's words here are absolutely true. The thief—Satan—does come to kill and destroy. This is his only objective, and we'd do well to remember that, giving him no space in our minds or hearts. But have you ever found yourself looking at other people as though *they* are here to kill and destroy?

Okay, maybe that's a little dramatic. But when we build up our defensive walls, skeptically viewing others from atop them and wondering why they're really hanging around us, a similar thought might enter our minds. When we're unsure of ourselves, it can make us unsure of everyone else.

Sometimes we have good reason not to trust others. It's important to be discerning and remember you don't need to allow everyone access to your most vulnerable self. At the same time, having life to the full means being spiritually alive in Christ and developing fruitful, open, loving relationships with others. Boundaries are important (more on this later). But those boundaries must be balanced with a willingness to connect with others and shelf our insecurity-based mistrust of their motives.

REFLECTION Do you struggle to trust others? Think about the last new person you opened up to. How long ago was this? Is there anyone you'd like to be closer to, but have been holding back because of fear or mistrust?

SIGNS OF INSECURITY: POOR COMMUNICATION PATTERNS

The tongue has the power of life and death,
and those who love it will eat its fruit.

PROVERBS 18:21

Communication is hard, but it's also important. As a result, a lot of time, money, and energy is spent teaching communication—between married couples, friends, parents and kids . . . the list goes on. Nobody is born knowing exactly what to say or how to say it well. It requires skill, patience, and practice for anyone to become a good communicator.

For an insecure, perfection-prone person, this practice can be difficult. *Really* difficult. And as "mistakes" are made, it can cause you to draw into yourself, until you have a hard time communicating your needs or telling people how you feel. Especially when others' not-perfect communication styles make us think we're safer keeping things to ourselves.

Does it often seem unsafe to speak up? Are you afraid of rejection if you say what you mean or express what you're going through? If so, insecurity is winning the battle. But overcoming insecurity is possible by recognizing our fears, remembering good communication takes practice, and, importantly, reminding ourselves it's okay to say how we feel in a loving, tactful way.

REFLECTION Was there a time recently when you stayed silent instead of speaking up about your needs? Think through whether this choice was made in wisdom (sometimes it is!) or in fear.

SIGNS OF INSECURITY: PERFECTIONISM

He says, "Be still, and know that I am God; I will be exalted among the nations, I will be exalted in the earth."
PSALM 46:10

Which came first, the perfectionism or the insecurity? Truly, these two traits are so intertwined, it's impossible to say which is causing the other. And it doesn't really matter.

What does matter is recognizing that insecure perfectionists are simply looking for a way to control their worlds—the external one as well as their emotional, inner world. If you often feel unsafe and unsure, you might find yourself flailing about for something to hold on to in order to feel more secure—achievement, accolades, rigid structures flawlessly executed. In short, perfection.

If that feels relatable, I want you to take a deep breath right now, all the way into your lungs, drawing all those unhealthy thoughts into one ball. Now exhale them out. Friend, God is the one in control. He's the only one who can give you the security you crave. Release yourself from a burden that isn't yours to carry.

REFLECTION If you recognize insecurity (or a need for control) at the root of your perfectionism, I want you to take a few more breaths like the one described above. Now write out how you feel about releasing control to God instead of trying to carry it all yourself.

FREEDOM FROM INSECURITY: RECOGNIZE IT

●●●●●●●●●●

Watch your life and doctrine closely.

1 TIMOTHY 4:16

Maybe you're now convinced insecurity is something that can harm a person's life (let's be honest, I probably didn't need to convince you of that). Perhaps you're saying, "Yes, that's me. I have some issues with insecurity." But maybe you're also wondering, *Now what?*

Don't worry. We can be free of our insecurity, we can untangle negative thought patterns, *and* we can learn new ways to live. The first step in dealing with our insecurity is simply to recognize that we have it and identify where it lives in our lives. We must take off our masks, shun all our wonky coping mechanisms, and be raw and honest with ourselves.

This can be uncomfortable, especially if you're used to holding yourself to a high, make-or-break standard. It's awkward to look in the mirror and say, "I'm insecure." But it's so important to start here, as it will allow us to learn new patterns.

REFLECTION If you feel ready, journal about your insecurities. If you need to, write them on a separate sheet of paper you can rip up and throw away when you're done. What are the top three insecurities you'd like to work on?

. . . .

. . . .

. . . .

. . . .

. . . .

. . . .

FREEDOM FROM INSECURITY: MANAGE YOUR FEELINGS

Be merciful to those who doubt.
JUDE V. 22

Knowledge is power. Maybe you hadn't fully realized how insecurity affects your life, but now that we've put the topic under the microscope, you see it. The moment you see something clearly for the first time and decide you don't like the view can be scary. But it's also empowering.

Because if you just discovered some of the feelings you've been struggling with—the fears, the doubts, the unsureness—are insecurities, now you are prepared. For example, when jealousy flares in one of your friendships, you can ask yourself, "Am I feeling this way because I'm insecure?" If the answer is yes, you can see those feelings clearly and manage them appropriately, combatting them with the truth.

Managing our feelings is hard work. Taking responsibility isn't easy. But it's so worth it!

REFLECTION Have you recently been in a situation or conflict that you now recognize was a result of underlying insecurity? Was anyone else affected by that situation? If so, think about how you might clear the air with that person.

FREEDOM FROM INSECURITY: DEPEND ON GOD

Day 80

Immediately the boy's father exclaimed, "I do believe; help me overcome my unbelief!"

MARK 9:24

This exclamation from the boy's father is so relatable. In one breath, he said he *does* believe but also asked Jesus to help him believe more. He had faith, but he also doubted, and, importantly, he recognized he needed Jesus's help to overcome his doubts. He needed Jesus to show up.

It's okay for us to cry out to God this way too. We have faith, but when insecurity, doubt, and fear are big struggles for us, we need his help to overcome them. It's not only okay to rely on God's help with these things, it's necessary. If we rely on our own strength to overcome all our issues, we are setting ourselves up for failure and frustration.

Don't be afraid to call out to God the way this boy's father did. We believe—help us overcome our unbelief!

REFLECTION Is there anything you've been muscling through, trying to rely on your own strength to manage? Take a few moments to pray about it, asking God to help you release control to him.

FREEDOM FROM INSECURITY: YOU WERE FORMED BY GOD

Day 81

●●●●●●●●●●

For you created my inmost being; you knit
me together in my mother's womb.

PSALM 139:13

When you look in the mirror, what do you see? If you deal with insecurities about yourself, whether on the outside or the inside, this is a loaded question. The answer might be painful or difficult, maybe even unbearable.

I want you to listen to me very carefully: you were formed by God, on purpose and for a purpose. No matter how insignificant we feel sometimes, no matter how much we question whether we measure up, the truth is God crafted us. We're unique, but we were all made in his image.

When we really own this truth, it becomes clearer that all the things we worry about and struggle with when it comes to our worth and our sense of identity are . . . peripheral. Less consequential than we worry they are. The God of the universe *formed us*. Let that sink in!

REFLECTION Most of us spend a lot of time critiquing ourselves, but how often do we stop to thank God for his wonderful handiwork in crafting us? Write out a prayer of thanksgiving for the specific *you* God created.

FREEDOM FROM INSECURITY: STAND IN GRACE

●●●●●●●●●

Since we have been justified through faith, we have peace with God through our Lord Jesus Christ, through whom we have gained access by faith into this grace in which we now stand.

ROMANS 5:1-2

When we get caught up in the performance trap (thinking how well we do is the measure of our self-worth), and when we are riddled with insecurities (constantly feeling unsure and unsafe), it's easy to lose sight of some really fundamental truths.

As followers of Jesus, we stand in grace. This is the very foundation of our faith as Christians—that because of Jesus, we have access to God's grace without having to do anything to earn it, and we can live confidently in this fact. As long as we have faith, we are judged by no other measure. Not our performance, not some external idea of what "good enough" looks like. Simply our belief in Jesus and *his* goodness.

And even if we've heard this before, it's so easy to lose sight of. To know it in our heads but forget it in our hearts as we move through our busy, stressful, day-to-day lives. When we remember grace is real and bring that truth to the forefront again and again, unraveling our insecurities becomes easier and easier.

REFLECTION Have you taken time lately to ponder your salvation, the free gift of God's grace you've received through faith in Jesus? Write out some thoughts or prayers about it right now.

. . . .

. . . .

. . . .

. . . .

FREEDOM FROM INSECURITY: NOT CONDEMNED

●●●●●●●●●

Therefore, there is now no condemnation
for those who are in Christ Jesus.
ROMANS 8:1

Sometimes it can feel like we have a little well of criticism and condemnation stored up somewhere deep inside. It may be directed outward at times, onto those around us, but often we are the unhappy recipients of our own bitter well water. There is no shortage when it comes to criticism we're willing to heap upon ourselves.

Friend, it's time to stop that well from filling. Right now. If the only words you have for yourself are criticism and condemnation, you are holding yourself to standards God never wants you to have. Your sins? Forgiven. Your shortcomings? Overlooked. Mistakes, foibles, failures? Removed from you as far as the east is from the west. There is *no* condemnation for those who are in Christ Jesus.

We are to pursue holiness in our lives and repent when we do wrong, of course. God cares about how we live. But even though we fail in so many ways, he still doesn't condemn us. Why are we condemning ourselves?

REFLECTION When was the last time you felt truly free and comfortable in God's presence? Maybe it was a long time ago, before insecurities took over. Take a moment to meditate on the fact there is *no* condemnation for you in God's sight.

FREEDOM FROM INSECURITY: NO FEAR

Day **84**

Perfect love drives out fear, because fear has to do with punishment.
1 JOHN 4:18

We've already established that fear is a big motivator for most perfectionists. The precise doom we fear may vary, depending on our goals, values, and the root causes of our perfectionism, but at the end of the day, most of us are afraid of something. We seek to control our environments so we can prevent our worst fears from happening. When we can't maintain this control or meet our own standards, we begin to feel anxious and insecure.

Does this sound familiar? When it's laid out so plainly, it's pretty obvious this is not the way God wants us to live. It doesn't sound at all like the peace available to us as followers of Christ. It doesn't sound at all like the assuredness of love God gives us.

And yet those things are ours to claim. We can have peace, and we already have God's love!

REFLECTION Take a few moments to visualize the fear inside you. Now imagine God's perfect love shoving it away. Maybe for you it looks like a knot of darkness, blasted away by a light so powerful, the darkness doesn't stand a chance.

HIS POWER IN OUR WEAKNESS

For when I am weak, then I am strong.
2 CORINTHIANS 12:10

Insecurities can leave us feeling vulnerable, small, and weak. Nobody likes to feel that way. We'd love to believe we're strong, capable, and able to handle everything life throws our way.

But the truth? The truth is that we *are* weak and small all the time, at least when we compare ourselves to God. And you know what? That's okay. Not only is it okay, it's good. When we acknowledge how weak we are—that we aren't able to handle everything; that our lives, our futures, and our souls don't actually rest on our shoulders—then we are *free*. We are free to turn to the Source, the One who truly does carry the weight of the world on his back.

The best news of all? Unlike us, he is equipped to handle the job—perfectly.

REFLECTION Have you ever thought of your weakness and vulnerability as an asset? If you're used to being strong and powering through life's difficulties, this might be a new concept! Take a few moments to feel the freedom of being strong in your weakness.

DANGERS OF PERFECTIONISM: RELATIONSHIP POISON

What causes fights and quarrels among you? Don't they come from your desires that battle within you?

JAMES 4:1

One of the greatest dangers of perfectionism? It can become absolute poison in your relationships. Why does this matter so much? Because humans are built for community, and fellowship with other believers is extra important for followers of Jesus. We *need* each other, and when our negative thought patterns are harming our relationships, this can become a major problem.

But don't lose heart. We are going to look at several perfectionistic poisons and immediately counter them with biblical antidotes. After a couple of weeks, you're going to have a full toolkit to help grow and nurture healthy relationships in your life.

REFLECTION Up to this point, have you considered whether perfectionism has affected your relationships? Write down some goals for the most important relationships in your life. How would you like to see those relationships grow over the next year?

....
....
....
....
....
....
....
....
....
....

POISON: LACK OF OPENNESS

Better is open rebuke than hidden love.
PROVERBS 27:5

Crushing fear of failure isn't exactly conducive to open communication or transparency in relationships. What do I mean by transparency? Letting someone see the real you. Not being afraid they will reject or judge you. Choosing honesty and authenticity.

Even for someone who isn't a perfectionist, this can be really scary. No one likes to be judged or rejected. No one likes to have a person look at the real you and say, "No, thanks." But the fear is often magnified for someone whose ultimate standard is always *perfection*.

Yet in order to truly build deep and lasting friendships, openness is required. Otherwise, those around us are merely connected to a mask—a front we put up to protect ourselves from being hurt. When you let them see the real you, you have the chance to form a relationship that leaves you feeling known and loved, even in your toughest moments.

REFLECTION On a scale of 1 to 10, how open are you with others? Is it a sliding scale, depending on the situation? If so, that's okay. Appropriate, even. But take some time to think through how authentic you are in general.

ANTIDOTE: ACCEPTANCE

We love because he first loved us.

1 JOHN 4:19

Openness is a challenge for a lot of people, especially if we've been burned in the past. But there's a really helpful antidote to counter the poison of being fearfully closed off: acceptance.

The first step is accepting ourselves as we are—God's unique and treasured children, wonderfully created in his image. If we can really own that identity, it's powerful! Others' opinions fade into the background. The voices critiquing or rejecting us are muted. We have God's seal of approval, and what else could we need? We are already accepted.

The second step is accepting others. Returning their openness with kindness. Seeing them for who they are and saying, "Thank you for sharing your authentic self with me!" You don't have to say those words out loud—that's probably weird. But we can show our loved ones we feel it in hundreds of ways, big and small.

REFLECTION Brainstorm ways to show your loved ones you accept them. If you have a friend who struggles with insecurity, can you compliment her on something you admire? Is your brother a fellow perfectionist? Tell him something you love about him that isn't performance-based.

POISON: BEING OVERLY CRITICAL

If you bite and devour each other, watch out
or you will be destroyed by each other.
GALATIANS 5:15

We've mentioned this before—that laser focus we so often direct at our own fragile hearts sometimes gets turned outward. The ugly truth is that it can—and does—sear those around us. If you've ever been judged by a highly critical person, you know how this feels: as though nothing you do is correct, and no matter how hard you try, it'll never be good enough.

Ouch. We've spent a lot of time examining why it's harmful to do this to ourselves. It's not any better when we direct it toward others. Most perfectionists don't act this way maliciously (so if you're telling yourself you're a terrible person, you can let that go right now). It's just that the perfection standard tends to apply to *everything* in our lives, and that often includes those around us.

REFLECTION Have you accidentally seared someone with your critical laser beam recently? What about in the past? Write out some thoughts about the situation, and pray about whether this warrants an apology to the other person.

ANTIDOTE: SHOWING GRACE

Accept one another, then, just as Christ accepted
you, in order to bring praise to God.

ROMANS 15:7

If we could only talk about *one* antidote in this entire book—to
give to yourself and others—it would be grace. Grace, grace,
and more grace. An entire mountain of it, please and thank you.
Luckily, we're able to add lots of tools and antidotes to our arse-
nals, so we don't have to limit ourselves to just one approach.
But ultimately, they all come down to a single thing at their
core: grace.

When someone makes a mistake? Grace. When your high
standard isn't quite met? Grace. When someone fails spectacularly? Grace. This doesn't mean we should accept abuse (never)
or that we shouldn't have boundaries with people (more on that
later). It doesn't mean we stop trying to do better and encouraging those around us in their quests to do better too.

But when the temptation arises to pull out the laser beam of
judgment and direct it toward your loved ones in a searing blast,
block that beam with a shield of pure grace.

REFLECTION Is there someone in your life who needs your grace right
now? What are a few ways you can show them you still value and love
them, even if they messed up?

POISON: CHOOSING ISOLATION

An unfriendly person pursues selfish ends and against all sound judgment starts quarrels.

PROVERBS 18:1

Being in community can be scary. It can bring up a slew of questions about ourselves: *Am I accepted here? Am I valued? Where do I fit in? Would they even notice if I left? What if I have nothing to bring to the table?*

These questions can plague anyone, but they hit perfectionists especially hard. Because if we even *suspect* the answer to one of those questions might be negative, our instinct can be to pull back. Withdraw. Remove ourselves from the possible devastation that might occur if we put ourselves out there and get rejected.

But this isolation isn't healthy, even for the most introverted among us. We all need people. Some of us may need only a person or two, but no one is better off in complete isolation. Especially when the questions we ask ourselves are often answered in the positive, not the negatives we fear, when we join in real community.

REFLECTION Has there been a community or group you wanted to join but didn't, afraid you might not be accepted? Or an activity you wanted to join at school, but you opted out because you were afraid your performance would be judged? How would you handle the situation if you faced it today?

ANTIDOTE: CHOOSING COMMUNITY

Two are better than one, because they
have a good return for their labor.

ECCLESIASTES 4:9

If you thought the antidote to the poison of choosing isolation
might be choosing community, you guessed correctly! For some
of us, this must be an active, intentional process. We have to
make a habit of telling ourselves over and over, "Connection is
worth the risk. People are worth the risk." For others, this may
feel more natural. The longing for community may have been
simmering just beneath the surface, and now you're giving it
permission to bubble over.

Wherever you fall on that scale, hear this truth: People
truly are worth it. *You* are worth it. It's okay to be choosy about
the people you want to invest in. But investing somewhere is
key, especially when you can bring openness, authenticity, and
acceptance into those treasured communities. Building healthy
relationships requires some risk, but the reward is great!

REFLECTION Think back to the reflection from yesterday. Is the opportunity to join that group still open to you? If not, is there a similar group you
could join? Or do you have a completely new idea for a community you'd
like to connect with?

POISON: CONTROLLING OTHERS

There is only one Lawgiver and Judge, the one who is able to save and destroy. But you—who are you to judge your neighbor?
JAMES 4:12

Some perfectionists really do keep their perfectionism turned inward. But for others of us, the desire for perfection extends beyond the borders of our bodies, minds, and performances. We wish to achieve perfection in *everything* associated with us, which means those around us need to be perfect too—and we try to "help" by asserting our will over theirs in an effort to get them to our idea of perfection.

Eek. Put that way, it's very obvious why this is poison to our relationships. When we expect everyone around us to be perfect, it not only makes us prone to nitpicking, we might even *demand* they adjust their behavior, nudging them ever closer toward our idea of "good enough."

It's a wonderful thing when friends push each other to be better. But this must be done from a healthy place—one of love and encouragement, not one that desires unattainable standards and applies pressure to try to make that impossible perfection happen.

REFLECTION Do you think your perfectionistic tendencies are only directed inward? Or have you accidentally projected them onto others at times?

ANTIDOTE: SEEKING PEACE

 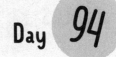

Carry each other's burdens, and in this way
you will fulfill the law of Christ.
GALATIANS 6:2

You may think the antidote to projecting our perfectionism
onto others is to have no standards or expectations of our loved
ones. But that's not the case. It's good to push Christians toward
greater holiness, for example. It's reasonable to expect support
from friends (and it's important we support to them too). It's
good to maintain loving boundaries.

The real antidote to controlling others is to seek peace, both
within ourselves and our relationships. Did a friend hurt your
feelings? Rather than hold them to an unforgiving standard of
perfection, find peace within yourself by sifting through your
feelings first. Were you extra sensitive today? Was the intent
behind their comment actually malicious?

Once you've sifted through your feelings, it becomes clearer
when those conflicts require discussion with the other party.
And when we confront others in situations like this, we can do
so with reconciliation on our minds, rather than impossible
standards and a spirit of unforgiveness.

REFLECTION Are there any relationships in your life that have suffered
because of too-high standards? Think about whether you need to talk
something through with them, and pray for wisdom moving forward in all
your treasured relationships.

POISON: OVERANALYZING

"How can you say to your brother, 'Let me take the speck out of your eye,' when all the time there is a plank in your own eye?"
MATTHEW 7:4

If you've ever lain in bed at night, running through all the things you should have done differently that day, you might have a problem with overanalyzing.

Small mistakes often bother perfectionists excessively. And when it comes to relationships, wanting to perfect everything is harmful, even toxic, especially when we constantly point to others' errors or can't let go of things. In a way, we're trying to focus on a tiny issue we see in others to distract us from the big plank of perfectionism that drives our behavior.

The same goes for when we overanalyze ourselves. Not only does it further stress our relationships by making the people we care about feel they need to reassure us we're fine, we can become so focused on picking apart conversations, mistakes we made, and other people's possible motives that we drive ourselves further and further into a spiral of monitoring everything in and around us, trying to avoid future stress by never letting a tiny thing slip.

If this sounds anything like you, know there's relief in sight.

REFLECTION On a scale of 1 to 10, how often do you overanalyze people, whether yourself or others? Do you think this has harmed your relationships in the past?

ANTIDOTE: MOVING ON

And we urge you, brothers and sisters, warn those who
are idle and disruptive, encourage the disheartened,
help the weak, be patient with everyone.

1 THESSALONIANS 5:14

If overanalyzing, nitpicking, and replaying are problems for you,
can I give you the secret to a freer life? Ready?

Practice the art of moving on. Letting it go. Choosing not
to get tangled up in picking apart the minutiae of everything
you've ever done, everything ever said to you, every interaction
with every person you know. Just . . . move on.

It sounds simple, and really, it is. But even simple things can
be difficult to practice! So have patience with yourself as you
grow in this skill. And since it is a *skill*, that means we can get
better at it over time. We just have to keep working the "moving
on" muscle, until eventually it becomes stronger. Rest assured
that when it does, moving on starts to feel more natural.

REFLECTION Write out some affirmations to help you let go and move
on next time the need arises. For example, if you obsess over things your
friends have said to you, write out truths about your friendships, such as,
"My friends have shown me many times how much they love me. Every
time I need help, they're always there for me."

POISON: LONELINESS

God sets the lonely in families, he leads
out the prisoners with singing.

PSALM 68:6

Sometimes perfectionists feel alone, even when they're surrounded by people. This feeling isn't unique to perfectionists, of
course. But the root cause may be. Often, we feel alone because
there's a sense that if others knew how "bad" we are, how deeply
we miss the mark, they wouldn't *really* want to be around us.

When you read that on the page in black and white, is it
easier to see what a lie it is? How contrary to God's deep love for
you? When we're caught in the vortex of our own emotions and
negative thought patterns, the truth can be harder to see. But
remember, friend, that type of loneliness is not what God wants
for you. He sets the lonely in families—which means he points
supportive groups of people toward those who are lonely—and
these families come in all shapes and sizes. Sometimes we're
born into them. Other times, those families are chosen. The
point is, you are loved!

REFLECTION Do you struggle with feelings of loneliness, even when
you're surrounded by others? Take a few moments to dig into that. Are
you afraid to show others the real you? Are you afraid of being rejected or
found wanting?

ANTIDOTE: FRIENDSHIP

"Greater love has no one than this: to lay
down one's life for one's friends."

JOHN 15:13

Friends are one of the greatest gifts in this life. Those friends
can be found in all corners of our lives, even in our families (if
we're super lucky!). The gospel of John was written by one of
Jesus's best friends. John 13:23 calls John "the disciple whom
Jesus loved." We also know Jesus was close friends with Lazarus
and his sisters, Martha and Mary. Peter was also a friend of
Jesus's. If even our Lord made the time and space in his life for
friends, we probably should too!

And no, we don't need to be perfect like Jesus in order to be
worthy of true, deep friendship. We only need to be willing to
show up, be authentic, and give grace to ourselves and others.
That's it. That foundation will support some pretty awesome
friendships!

REFLECTION Would you like to have more friendships in your life?
Brainstorm a list of ways you might connect with others who share your
interests, your faith, or your desire for greater connection.

POISON: BEGRUDGING FORGIVENESS

"If your brother or sister sins against you, rebuke them; and if they repent, forgive them."
LUKE 17:3

Forgiveness is sometimes a tricky concept for followers of Christ. As imperfect humans, we get it wrong. Sometimes we cling to "eye for an eye" justice, even though Jesus was clear we shouldn't give in to this kind of vengeance (Matthew 5:38–39). Other times, victims of abuse are told to forgive their abusers, even when there's been no repentance. Proper biblical forgiveness is spelled out very clearly in this verse from Luke 17, but it's still tough for us to practice proper forgiveness.

All the more so for perfectionists. When our standards are sky-high, we might read Jesus's words in the next verse—"Even if they sin against you seven times in a day and seven times come back to you saying 'I repent,' you must forgive them"—and balk. We're supposed to overlook *seven* sins in one day! That's tough for anyone. How much tougher when we won't accept less than perfection from those around us? So let's look at how we can start.

REFLECTION How easy is it for you to accept the words "I'm sorry" from someone who has wronged you? Do you have a hard time saying those words yourself? Spend some time in prayer as you think about your answer.

ANTIDOTE: FORGIVE FREELY

"Even if they sin against you seven times in a
day and seven times come back to you saying
'I repent,' you must forgive them."
LUKE 17:4

Did you guess that verse was going to come back to haunt us?
It truly is the antidote to an unforgiving spirit. When we offer
forgiveness freely, in the same way God offers forgiveness to
us, no matter how many times we sin, we can shake loose the
chains of vengeance and human justice that want to bind up our
hearts and trap us in bitterness.

This doesn't mean we overlook sin. In yesterday's verse,
Jesus said we are to rebuke those who sin against us. Offering
forgiveness freely does not mean we become doormats or submit
ourselves to abuse. Instead, it means we are able to recognize
repentance, offer grace, and release bitterness. Doing so benefits
us as much as the one being forgiven! And this type of gracious
love is a very strong foundation for lasting relationships.

REFLECTION Have you been holding a grudge against someone? Did they
sin against you, requiring rebuke? Or was this an offense that can be easily
overlooked? Pray about it!

POISON: BITTERNESS

Day **101**

> Get rid of all bitterness, rage and anger, brawling
> and slander, along with every form of malice.
> **EPHESIANS 4:31**

You may have already noticed we've used the word *bitterness* a
lot. That's because a lot of these relationship poisons eventually cause our hearts to sour and harden. When we feel lonely,
afraid, rejected, or slighted, sometimes we feel the best reaction
is to let our tender hearts calcify. We think this toughness will
protect us from being hurt in our relationships. In truth, it can
cause us to lose relationships that might have otherwise been
supportive and loving, and that hurts us far worse.

Sounds tragic, right? The good news is this isn't a foregone
conclusion in your life. Just because you might be a perfectionist, struggling with the things we've been talking about, that
doesn't mean you have to throw up your hands and assume
bitterness will become part of your life. We can change these
patterns now, friend!

REFLECTION What feelings pop up when you read the apostle Paul's
words in the verse above? Are any of the things he mentioned struggles
for you?

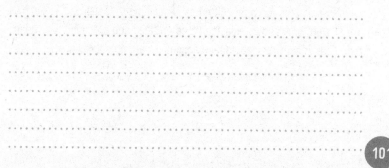

ANTIDOTE: RELEASE

"And when you stand praying, if you hold anything against anyone, forgive them, so that your Father in heaven may forgive you your sins."

MARK 11:25

Are you noticing a theme? Acceptance, moving on, release. If you're picturing an ice princess twirling around on a snowy mountaintop, singing at the top of her lungs, you probably have a good visual for our recurring theme: Let. It. Go. (Though don't get me started on *her* emotional issues . . .)

If we need any greater motivator than the promise of healthier relationships and more inner peace, check out the last piece of this verse: "So that your Father in heaven may forgive you your sins." This is not the only place in the Bible where Jesus drew a parallel between our willingness to forgive others and God's willingness to forgive us (see also Matthew 6:14). The message is not that God refuses to forgive us if we're not perfect in the way we treat and forgive others. But it seems clear Jesus wants us to consider how much grace we've been given when we're tempted to hold on to bitter feelings.

REFLECTION Do you have any grudges in your heart, whether recent or long-standing? Is there any bitterness beginning to fester as a result? As a first step, pray about releasing those grudges and softening your heart, then determine if you should take actions toward reconciliation.

POISON: ALL-OR-NOTHING THINKING

●●●●●●●●

Therefore, with minds that are alert and fully sober,
set your hope on the grace to be brought to you
when Jesus Christ is revealed at his coming.
1 PETER 1:13

It's been a while since our old "friend" all-or-nothing thinking reared its ugly head. But rest assured, this negative thought pattern isn't just harmful to our own hearts. It can also harm our relationships with others.

The biggest danger of all-or-nothing thinking is the tendency to believe that if our relationship isn't completely perfect—if the other person doesn't continuously behave how we'd hoped they would—it means that something is wrong, or even that the other person doesn't really love us. This is another way to project our perfectionism outward, and it's absolutely poisonous to our relationships.

The truth: no one loves perfectly, except God. We can't love others perfectly, and they can't love us perfectly. If we try to hold ourselves and others to this standard, we will never stop being disappointed, frustrated, and lonely.

REFLECTION Take a really honest look at your most important relationships. Have you ever wondered if those treasured loved ones really love you at all? If you step outside the all-or-nothing box, how fair is that question?

ANTIDOTE: EMBRACE THE GRAY

●●●●●●●●○○

"So do not fear, for I am with you; do not be dismayed,
for I am your God. I will strengthen you and help you;
I will uphold you with my righteous right hand."
ISAIAH 41:10

Humans are complicated and messy. Sometimes we hurt the ones we love most. We can be insensitive to those we truly *don't* want to upset. Sometimes we push away the people we want to be closest to.

And yet . . . our love is still true and genuine and real. How can that be? It's because we're all works in progress, walking through various stages of becoming more discerning and closer to God. It's because we're sinful. We live in a fallen world. We're imperfect. And sometimes, we're simply having a bad day. Human beings aren't all-or-nothing, black-or-white, in-or-out. We're gray—created in God's image, yet imperfect in our behavior.

Showing grace—to ourselves and to others—means embracing that gray. This doesn't excuse bad behavior, of course. It just embraces the truth that we can love imperfectly and it's still love.

REFLECTION Sit for a little while with the idea that two things can be true at once—love can be real, even if it's not flawless. Does thinking about this "gray" in your relationships make you feel any better (or freer) in how you approach them? Why or why not?

. . . .

. . . .

. . . .

. . . .

POISON: CLOSED TO CHANGE

"Do not let your hearts be troubled and do not be afraid."
JOHN 14:27

Change is scary. We may feel like we're in better control of our lives when we don't rock the boat, don't step out in faith, and don't go for it unless we're assured of a win. But like most of our relationship poisons so far, being closed off to change is something that hurts both the perfectionist and those around them.

You can probably see how this resistance could affect the perfectionist themself—how it makes their life smaller and duller than it has to be. (Maybe you've even felt boxed in this way yourself.) But have you considered why it would be hard for those around the perfectionist?

Being closed off to change kills spontaneity. It gives rise to rigidity, and it discourages openness, healthy risk, and freedom on both sides of the relationship. This can be really difficult for people in our lives, especially when it makes us less fun to be around. And no one wants that! So let's look at how we can *change* how we approach our thinking.

REFLECTION Are you someone who is closed off to change? Being as objective as possible, can you see ways this may have hurt anyone in your life?

. . . .
. . . .
. . . .
. . . .
. . . .
. . . .
. . . .
. . . .

ANTIDOTE: RELEASE CONTROL

"Peace I leave with you; my peace I give you. I
do not give to you as the world gives."

JOHN 14:27

Change can be good. Risk can be healthy. Releasing control is beneficial for your soul.

Were those things painful to read? Difficult to accept? Cringe-inducing and anxiety-spiking? Do you sense somewhere *way* down in your heart that they're probably true?

When it comes to relationships, sometimes it's better to take the focus off ourselves for a minute and think about the other person. Instead of framing it as "I need to open myself to change, and that's scary," think of it as giving those in your life space to be themselves. If those around you love to be spontaneous and dive in to new adventures, imagine how hard it would be for them to squash those parts of themselves down. And by allowing them to be themselves, you might even find that not only does your relationship become better, the experience is more freeing than you expected—or at least not as scary as you feared.

REFLECTION Do you have a beloved free spirit in your life? Journal about why you love them and how valuable that relationship is to you, then try to think of something new and fun you can do together.

POISON: CONFLICT IS FAILURE

"If your brother or sister sins, go and point out
their fault, just between the two of you. If they
listen to you, you have won them over."

MATTHEW 18:15

When everything is viewed through the lens of "all or nothing,"
and when the standard is absolute perfection, sometimes we get
the (very wrong) idea that any time we experience conflict in a
relationship, it means we've failed.

Friends, no relationship will ever measure up if conflict is
perceived as failure. Conflict happens in any close relationship
to varying degrees, and in some relationships more frequently
than others. If the conflict is constant, that's a sign the relationship may be toxic and perhaps it's time to walk away. But if we
have the erroneous belief that *any* conflict means our relationships have failed or are not good enough, we're setting ourselves
and our loved ones up for a lot of hurt. And healthy conflict
doesn't have to take that path.

REFLECTION What was your most recent conflict with a friend or family
member? What were some of your private thoughts about that conflict?
Did you dip into this type of thinking, wondering if the relationship would
survive or if that person even loved you anymore?

ANTIDOTE: CONFLICT IS GROWTH

● ● ● ● ● ● ● ● ● ●

"Blessed are the peacemakers, for they will be called children of God."

MATTHEW 5:9

If conflict is going to happen sometimes in every close relationship, and if conflict *isn't* a sign that the relationship is a failure, then what does it actually mean?

If conflict is managed in a healthy way—without bullying, name-calling, and other unhealthy communication patterns—it usually just means two imperfect humans are running into differences of opinion, thought process, or communication style. Far from signaling some kind of failure, conflict give us an opportunity to grow in our relationships, both as individuals and in closeness with the other person.

Constructive conflict is a chance to express ourselves and see things from someone else's point of view. It allows us to gain a deeper understanding of this person we love, and that creates a stronger, deeper, truer relationship.

REFLECTION Have you ever thought about conflict in this way—as an opportunity for growth? When framing it that way, how might it change your approach to conflict in the future?

POISON: PROCRASTINATION

Everything should be done in a fitting and orderly way.
1 CORINTHIANS 14:40

Wait just a minute. Procrastination makes us miss deadlines, sure. It sometimes leads us to rush through work we've been putting off, making our finished product sloppier than it should be. But how is procrastinating a poison to our relationships?

If you've ever been close to a procrastinator, you may already know the answer. When a procrastinator puts off important tasks at school or work, perhaps the only person hurt is the procrastinator, as their grades come back disappointing or they get reprimanded by their boss. But when we do this in our personal lives, our loved ones are often left waiting for us, feeling shoved aside or bumped down our to-do list. We can make them feel like they don't matter to us, even when that's the furthest thing from the truth.

REFLECTION Looking back, can you think of a time when your procrastination might have sent the wrong message to someone you care about?

ANTIDOTE: JUST START

Do everything in love.

1 CORINTHIANS 16:14

The antidote to procrastination poison should come as no surprise. Remember the art of "just starting"? We simply have to exercise that new skill here in preserving our relationships too. Don't be afraid—just dive in.

When we're willing to dive in and we make sure not to leave our loved ones waiting around for us, it sends the message that they are a top priority. We care about their feelings. We respect their time.

Not only that, when our procrastination is fear-based, rooted in worry over rejection, just starting gets us past that emotional roadblock. Over time, we will find the fear monster shrinking. He will have less power in our lives, less control over when and how we complete our tasks. Our relationships will be richer for it, and our hearts will find greater peace!

REFLECTION Write some reminders on index cards and place them in the areas you're likeliest to avoid tasks. If you procrastinate on your laundry and it affects your relationship with your mom, stick a card that says "Just start one load!" over your hamper.

RELATIONSHIP HOPE

"Forget the former things; do not dwell on the
past. See, I am doing a new thing!"
ISAIAH 43:18–19

Hopefully you're not feeling too beat up by all these relationship
poisons we've been examining. Ideally, the antidotes we've been
adding to our toolboxes should help us move forward, feeling
empowered and ready to cultivate deeper, stronger, healthier
relationships in our lives. Who doesn't want that?

But if you are feeling a bit discouraged, here's some hope for
us all. *Everyone* has baggage. Whether someone is a perfectionist
or the furthest thing from it, everyone brings their own bits of
unhealthiness and issues into relationships. The goal for anyone
and everyone is to change those patterns, work through those
issues, and be the best version of themselves they possibly can.

Through Christ and the empowerment of the Holy Spirit,
we can overcome even the most ingrained patterns!

REFLECTION Spend some time praying, reflecting, and journaling about
your valued relationships. What are you most thankful for in each? Praise
God for giving you loved ones, whether friends, family, or both!

BOUNDARIES: LOVING LIMITS

●●●●●●●●●●

Like a city whose walls are broken through
is a person who lacks self-control.
PROVERBS 25:28

No discussion of relationships is complete without mentioning boundaries. As we work on improving our relationship skills and uprooting unhealthy tendencies, it's important to understand what personal boundaries are and how to set them up and obey them in godly ways.

Scripture often tells us to exercise *self*-control, but our human nature—especially our perfectionistic nature—sometimes leads us to want to control others instead. Boundaries define the line between "self" and "others." Boundaries say, "These things are my responsibility. These other things are your responsibility." These distinctions help us set loving limits on what we ask of ourselves and others.

When we practice good boundaries, we attempt to control only what's in our own "yard" (the space within our boundary). We also develop a clearer idea of when someone is crossing the line into our yard and when we're crossing into someone else's yard. Boundaries teach us when to say no—whether to our own impulses or to other people.

REFLECTION What are some things in your "yard"—things within your boundary line that are your responsibility? Do you ever feel like you need to control things that are in someone else's yard?

. . . .

. . . .

. . . .

. . . .

BOUNDARIES: OWNING OUR THOUGHTS AND FEELINGS

Fools give full vent to their rage, but the wise bring calm in the end.

PROVERBS 29:11

It's not easy to take responsibility for our thoughts and feelings. Many people struggle with this throughout their whole lives, blaming others for how they feel and letting others' feelings heavily influence their own. While it's certainly true other people's behavior affects us, we get to choose how we respond. Their choices are in their yard. Our choices are in our yards. Their feelings are in their yard. Our feelings are in our yards.

While taking this kind of accountability is difficult sometimes, it's actually empowering when we realize we have control over what we choose to give space in our minds. And we can choose to exhibit the kind of self-control and wisdom the Bible encourages us to have. Good boundaries allow us to own our feelings and create distance between things that often feel far too entangled.

REFLECTION Do you tend to get wrapped up in other people's feelings? Or perhaps you often blame others for the way you feel. Good boundaries take practice! Think about the areas you can grow in when it comes to boundary enforcement and boundary respect.

BOUNDARIES: OWNING OUR CHOICES

Do not be deceived: God cannot be mocked.
A man reaps what he sows.

GALATIANS 6:7

Reaping and sowing is a concept that appears in Scripture a lot. The basic idea is that you will experience the consequences of your actions, whether good or bad. This does not mean there's a cosmic tally of the good and bad everyone does, or that each action is always rewarded or punished. We've all seen good deeds go unnoticed and hurtful actions go unpunished.

Instead, reaping and sowing is about the natural outflow of our actions—and their spiritual consequences. But often, our impulse is to blame others when bad "seeds" grow into a plant we have to deal with. From the very first sin, Adam tried to shift the blame, and we've been following the pattern ever since—trying to justify ourselves, doing everything except taking responsibility. This is especially true for those of us who have a hard time accepting our failures—it's easier to accuse someone else than point our gaze inward to explain what happened.

But part of having good boundaries is owning our choices, particularly our mistakes. It's also important to recognize good choices and see the positive impacts ripple outward!

REFLECTION What kind of "seeds" have you been sowing this week? Are they seeds of righteousness, joy, and peace? Or are they seeds of discord, grumbling, or strife?

BOUNDARIES: YOUR FENCE

Day **115**

Remind the people . . . to slander no one, to be peaceable
and considerate, and always to be gentle toward everyone.
TITUS 3:1–2

When discussing boundaries, we've been using a yard analogy.
The things within your yard are your responsibility. Your yard
protects you and others. But can having a yard like this ever be
a bad thing?

Sadly, yes. Like everything good, boundaries can become
bad if misused. For example, for perfectionists who tend to opt
out as a defense against fear, there can be a temptation to build
strong walls as a way to control what happens around us and
keep ourselves "safe." Over time, it becomes easier to add more
bricks, until the walls become so high and impenetrable, we only
succeed in excluding others and walling off our hearts. And that
is not what any good boundary is designed to do.

So instead, approach your boundaries as a fence with a gate.
You have the right to close your gate to unhealthy expectations
and things that will harm you or others. But when you decide to
open that gate, you let people safely into your life, your heart,
and your world.

REFLECTION When thinking about your boundaries, is your tendency to
wall yourself off or allow people to run amok in your yard? How can you
build a healthy fence around your yard with a gate you choose to open and
close?

115

DANGERS OF PERFECTIONISM: STRESS

●●●●●●●●●●

Yet man is born to trouble as surely as sparks fly upward.

JOB 5:7

Perfectionists are some of the most stressed-out people around. It's impossible to have the kind of recurring thoughts we have, the expectations we set, the standards we chase, without feeling like a frazzled and exhausted mess a significant portion of the time. Peace is hard to come by. Contentment—nonexistent. Joy, hope, patience, happiness—all of these can seem like distant dreams for the perfectionist who feels like they're running on fumes, sparking like a live wire stripped of its protective coating.

As always, friend, there is hope! We are going to talk about stress—what it is and what it leads to—but most importantly, we'll look at how to combat stress using biblical wisdom. Hang in there!

REFLECTION Do you consider yourself a stressed-out person? Quickly brainstorm a list of five to ten self-care activities you can do this week. Even if you are only able to get to half of them, that's an excellent start!

....

....

....

....

....

....

....

....

....

WHAT IS STRESS?

Mortals, born of woman, are of few days and full of trouble.
JOB 14:1

Some people think Job is the oldest book in the Bible. And in this verse from Job, it says mortals' days are few and "full of trouble." It's amazing to have such a relatable statement in a book that's thousands of years old! Job's culture was very different from the world we have today. Our technology is different. Our *lives* are different. Yet we can relate to this statement— our days are full of trouble. And it's comforting to know even ancient people got stressed-out.

Stress can be defined as the emotional strain we experience in very demanding environments. For perfectionists—and for many people, in general—stress is the feeling of never having enough resources to meet the demands placed upon us. It's feeling like we don't have the tools available to complete the task at hand.

Does that sound like your current situation? You may be under stress, my friend. And over the next few days, we'll look at what it does to us—and what we can do about it.

REFLECTION Thinking about the past month, how stressed-out have you been? Have you felt secure in the tools and resources you've had to accomplish the tasks on your plate?

HOW DOES STRESS IMPACT US?

Cast all your anxiety on him because he cares for you.

1 PETER 5:7

Stress can be a helpful motivator in certain situations. When we need to tackle a problem or immediate danger before us, stress triggers our bodies to release an extra boost of adrenaline or cortisol—two hormones that help us better deal with the stress by helping our brains and bodies function.[2]

But when stress becomes frequent or chronic, it begins to negatively impact us. Those same hormones that can be really helpful in the short term wreak havoc on our bodies in the long term. They can cause mental health problems like depression and anxiety, and physical ailments like muscle tension, headaches, and even heart disease. Stomach problems, concentration issues, high blood pressure, and strokes have all been linked to chronic stress.[3] Yikes!

Clearly, our bodies were not designed to sustain high levels of stress for extended periods of time. The good news: If you're dealing with a lot of stress, you don't have to handle it alone.

REFLECTION Have you ever noticed the physical effects of stress in your life—whether they're bad for a short period or chronic? What are some ways you can alleviate these physical symptoms when they arise? Examples to get you started: going for a walk, taking a hot bath, exercising, going to bed early.

BURNOUT

My soul is weary with sorrow; strengthen
me according to your word.
PSALM 119:28

Experiencing chronic stress is bad enough. It's harmful for our
bodies, hearts, and minds. But there's a step beyond chronic
stress that's even worse: burnout. *Burnout* is a state of utter
exhaustion that affects us mentally, physically, and even spiritually. If stress heightens our bodies' awareness and ability to
respond to demands (in the short term, at least), burnout does
the opposite. We become apathetic, helpless, and hopeless, with-
drawing from our social lives and work or school tasks.

That's a dark place to be. The good news is that when we
deal with our stress, we can reverse the beginning of burnout.
One way to do this is to make an effort to connect with others
when you feel the urge to withdraw. Reach out to friends. Talk
to your parents. Engage in social communities. Another important tactic to reverse burnout, especially for a perfectionist, is
to reframe the way you think about your tasks. Focusing on the
positives and releasing unrealistic standards can drastically
reduce your stress levels.

REFLECTION Have you experienced any signs of burnout recently? What
about in the past? Now that you're aware of what burnout looks like, write
down some warning signs you can look for to help you address it in the
future.

COMBATTING STRESS WITH BIBLICAL WISDOM

●●●●●●●●●

Cast your cares on the LORD and he will sustain
you; he will never let the righteous be shaken.

PSALM 55:22

Sometimes people's behavioral struggles are miraculously
healed. God can do anything. But for most of us, it's not going
to instantaneously or completely change, and things like stress
and a tendency toward perfectionism will be a part of our lives
until Earth is created anew.

This truth does nothing to diminish God's goodness in our
lives! But, for those of us who have these challenges, it's important we take the small, daily steps we can to adapt and live our
best lives, grow closer to God, and love others.

How can we reduce stress and navigate our mental health
using biblical wisdom? Keep in mind that God is the source of
our strength. Take care of our God-gifted bodies with proper
sleep, good nutrition, stress-busting exercise, and lots of fresh
air. Cultivate a rich prayer life so we can talk to God when we
need help. Focus on the many blessings in this world, including our loved ones. Serve others with our gifts and talents. All
of these wise habits contribute toward building a less stressful,
more fulfilling life.

REFLECTION Map out a plan for reducing your stress levels over the next
several weeks by building up good habits. If implementing the whole plan
at once feels overwhelming, start small!

DANGERS OF PERFECTIONISM: IT HINDERS REST

"The seventh day is a sabbath to the LORD your God. On it you shall not do any work."

EXODUS 20:10

There are many things perfectionism tries to steal from us. Our self-worth, our identity as children of God, our mental health. Peace, joy, friendship. Clearly, perfectionism is no friend of ours! And one of the biggest things perfectionism tries to steal is rest.

Rest may sound like a small thing, but it's not. Rest is absolutely crucial to our well-being. It's so crucial, the Lord made it part of the law, commanding his people to have one day per week when they simply rested. Having a well-rested mind and body is vital for maintaining many of the other things mentioned at the start of this devotion. It's impossible to have peace when your body is run ragged from getting little rest. It's difficult to maintain strong, healthy friendships when your mind is exhausted because you haven't taken any breaks.

Rest is foundational. And rest is *very* hard to come by for overworked overachievers. We're going to look at several ways to cultivate this important element in our lives.

REFLECTION Thinking back on the last week, how much rest did you get? How did you sleep? When you were awake, did you have any downtime?

PRIORITIZING SELF-CARE

Then they went home and prepared spices and perfumes. But they rested on the Sabbath in obedience to the commandment.

LUKE 23:56

The pressure placed on teens and young adults these days is pretty intense. If you're academically focused, discussions about college sometimes begin in elementary school. If you're into sports and other competitive activities, often the focus on winning is placed above everything else.

School and our outside interests are certainly important. But in the midst of those important things—and the astounding pressure we place on ourselves to do well at them—it's easy to push rest and self-care to the side. It's easy to focus more on achievement and prioritize our bodies' and brains' needs last—or overlook them completely.

Do you need permission to prioritize self-care? If so, I just granted it. If you need some ideas to get started, think about things you find fun and relaxing. Working on creative projects, exercising, focusing on skin care, taking a bubble bath, having a nap, playing a sport (just because, not for competition)—these are all good places to start your self-care journey.

REFLECTION Set a timer for ten minutes and write down every possible self-care activity you can think of. Add a few that are outside the box, such as something you've never done before. Discovering new things you love just for the sake of it is half the fun!

RESTING WITH ALL OUR MIGHT

Whatever your hand finds to do, do it with all your might.
ECCLESIASTES 9:10

Does that seem like a weird idea? Resting with all our might? Self-caring with all our strength?

It does seem a little odd to use our maximum effort to relax, yet that's exactly what the Bible tells us to do. Whatever we're doing, we should do it to the glory of God and with all our strength. And we know God cares about how much we rest. That's why he created the Sabbath for us!

Maybe you think resting with all your might would look like a whole week with no schoolwork or chores bogging you down. (Don't get me wrong—that would be awesome!) But we can bring the spirit of resting well into our everyday lives, even when we're busy with our usual tasks and responsibilities. It's about cultivating a mindset that allows us to rest well, and regularly.

REFLECTION Looking at the list you brainstormed yesterday, what's one thing you can incorporate into your day today? How about something else tomorrow, and something different the day after? It can be one small thing, but over time, those moments of rest and enjoyment make a huge difference.

TURNING DOWN THE VOLUME

The LORD is in his holy temple; let all the
earth be silent before him.

HABAKKUK 2:20

Life is rarely quiet in our modern society. Whether our days are
packed with several extracurriculars and an after-school job or
we're just trying to keep up on our regular schoolwork and maintain a healthy social life, silence can be hard to come by. Our
world buzzes with activity, and it's incredibly easy to get caught
up in it. Sitting in a quiet place can almost feel wasteful. But that
may be exactly what you need to do.

Turning down the volume on the demands of life, tuning
out everything and sitting in silence, and being open to God's
voice is a really important practice. Jesus went away to quiet
places to pray (Mark 1:35) and rest (Mark 6:31). If Jesus found
this to be an important habit in his life, we should intentionally
seek silence in ours too!

REFLECTION Instead of journaling today, take this time to sit in silence
with your thoughts and with the Lord. Pray, meditate on Scripture, or just
enjoy the stillness.

MAKE SPACE FOR RECOVERY

Everyone who competes in the games goes into strict training. They do it to get a crown that will not last, but we do it to get a crown that will last forever.
1 CORINTHIANS 9:25

If you've ever heard elite athletes talk about their training, you may have noticed they have one thing in common, no matter what sport they play. They all allow their bodies to recover within their training cycles. Rest and recovery are an important part of the process.

God didn't create our bodies to run at max speed constantly. In the same way rest allows an athlete's muscles to repair themselves, recovery allows our minds to quiet and our hearts to heal.

Have you been giving yourself space to recover? Have you prioritized self-care and plenty of rest? Or have you been asking your body and mind to run at max speed for far too long? Take a tip from elite athletes: work hard, and then rest hard.

REFLECTION If you had to quantify your work-to-rest ratio, what does it look like? If it's greater than a six-to-one ratio (the model God set out for the Israelites when it came to days), can you think of ways to bring the ratio into better balance?

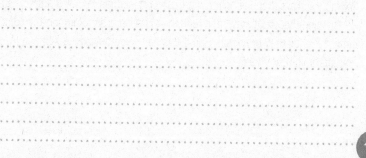

LETTING TASKS GO

You, LORD, hear the desire of the afflicted; you
encourage them, and you listen to their cry.
PSALM 10:17

If I asked to see your planner right now, what would I find? Is every night of the week busy? Is the weekend crammed with activities, chores, and social engagements? Do you have a ton of approaching due dates and deadlines? If something unexpected came up—a health crisis, a relationship hiccup—would you quickly feel overwhelmed?

Overscheduling is easy to do, and sometimes it feels impossible to maintain a less hectic agenda, even without anything unexpected swamping us. There are a lot of cool opportunities out there. It's hard to say no sometimes.

It's true we all have commitments we can't bail on, and some seasons are extra busy. But is there anything on your plate you could remove in order to allow yourself time for rest? Pray about it and see what the Lord shows you. Maybe there's something that *seemed* vital when you added it, but now you realize it's not as important as having some recovery time.

REFLECTION Make a list of the activities on your plate—school, sports, extracurriculars, hobbies, church groups or ministries, etc. Put a star next to anything that must stay, then rank the extras in order of importance and how much joy they bring you. See if this helps you determine some activities that might not make the cut.

DANGERS OF PERFECTIONISM: IGNORING REALITY

●●●●●●●●●

For all have sinned and fall short of the glory of God.
ROMANS 3:23

Perfectionists usually do perform pretty well, by all external standards. In fact, people may be surprised to discover how much we're struggling internally, especially if we're really good at hiding our troubles. Most people would probably describe us as smart and capable. Which is why it's particularly sad that one of the hallmark dangers of perfectionism is that it causes you to ignore reality.

That's somewhat embarrassing to admit at first, but think about it. Perfectionism demands we be perfect in order to be worthy. It doesn't allow for mistakes, flaws, or foibles. And yet . . . we all have these. Many of them. The Bible is very clear about it! If we weren't so prone to mistakes, failures, and wrongness, we wouldn't need a Savior.

There is no need to ignore the reality of our mistakes. When we're able to admit our shortcomings to ourselves and others, we make room for Jesus to step into our weaknesses. We allow ourselves to depend more on God than on ourselves and become more authentic with others.

REFLECTION Are there some parts of your life that are extra hard to be honest about? Spend some time gently drawing out the truth, and allow God to comfort you and reassure you of his love every step of the way.

WHAT IS FAILURE?

●●●●●●●●●

"The LORD himself goes before you and will be
with you; he will never leave you nor forsake you.
Do not be afraid; do not be discouraged."

DEUTERONOMY 31:8

Perfectionists don't usually love to think about failure. So I have to warn you—this next section is about how to fail. But don't close the book yet! I'm not encouraging more failure in your life—instead, we'll be taking a close, honest look at what failure is, some of our unhealthy responses to it, and ways we can learn to better deal with our failures. Because, truthfully, failures *will* happen, as much as we wish they didn't.

So what is failure? It's simply missing the mark. Not meeting the standard that was set. A lack of success. The inability to meet expectation.

How many times did you cringe as you read that? But the fact is we all find ourselves in that position sometimes. Even if we somehow *never* fail at our external achievements, we fail in our hearts. Probably daily. We know this because Scripture tells us so.

REFLECTION How uncomfortable is it to think about your failures? Do you find it easier to accept the ones that happen internally or the ones that occur externally?

. . . .

. . . .

. . . .

. . . .

. . . .

THE URGE TO HIDE

Then the man and his wife heard the sound of the LORD God
as he was walking in the garden in the cool of the day, and
they hid from the LORD God among the trees of the garden.
GENESIS 3:8

Ever since humanity's very first failure, we've been trying to
hide our deeds. This can be true of external disappointments
we find humiliating—failing a test, not making the team,
facing rejection. But it's perhaps even truer when we consider
our moral failures—sins we would rather tuck away and never
openly acknowledge.

That's certainly what Adam and Eve tried. They ate from
the Tree of Knowledge of Good and Evil—the one thing God
told them not to do—and then, when they heard the Lord's
voice, they tried to hide from him. Maybe they forgot who God
really is, or maybe they never fully understood that he could
always see them, always know their minds and hearts. There is
no place to hide from God, no place to run from him.

But we may have an advantage over Adam and Eve. We
know that when we are honest with God, coming to him in
humility and repentance, he is quick to forgive us. There's no
need to hide!

REFLECTION Is there anything you've been trying to hide from God?
Confession and repentance don't mean we escape consequences. But they
do mean spiritual freedom and renewed closeness with God!

THE URGE TO BEAT OURSELVES UP

●●●●●●●○○○

The LORD upholds all who fall and lifts
up all who are bowed down.

PSALM 145:14

We perfectionists tend to want to hide from ourselves, our sins, and our mistakes because . . . well, when we acknowledge them, we might engage in another very unhealthy behavior, which is to beat ourselves up.

Many of us are experts at this. It's practically written on our bones—we are champion, A+ self-critics. When given the option between being expertly hard on ourselves and hiding from the truth of our failures, is it any wonder we sometimes choose to hide?

We're going to learn better habits than *either* of these two urges we may currently experience. For now, remember you're not alone, and the Lord does not ask you to beat yourself up for your mistakes. He is there, ready to freely dispense grace, when you come to him with your heartache.

REFLECTION Are you likelier to hide from mistakes or beat yourself up about them? Or do you do both of these things, depending on the situation? Spend some time in prayer today sharing your thoughts with the Lord, asking him to make you receptive to new habits.

DENIAL

If we claim we have not sinned, we make him
out to be a liar and his word is not in us.
1 JOHN 1:10

Maybe none of us would state it quite like the start of today's verse. It would be a pretty bold claim for a follower of Jesus to say, "I haven't sinned—ever." And yet it can be excruciatingly difficult for perfectionist Christians to acknowledge their sin. We know it's there. Sometimes we even feel haunted by it. But the weight of failure can be so great, it's easier to live in denial, perhaps even getting defensive when we're called out about something we've done.

If you relate to that, you certainly aren't alone. But the apostle John was very clear in this verse and others that denying our sins and failures makes us into liars. Yikes! None of us wants that label, so we have to develop some tools for looking at our sin honestly (without beating ourselves up). And the first step is admitting we need the tools in the first place.

REFLECTION One of the best ways to move past denial is to surround yourself with trusted people who will be honest with—but also supportive of—you. Can you make a list of people in your life who might meet those criteria?

WEARING A MASK

"Who can hide in secret places so that I
cannot see them?" declares the LORD.
JEREMIAH 23:24

Sometimes we hide. Sometimes we beat ourselves up. Sometimes we live in denial and defensiveness. But other times we put on a mask to cope with our failures. This is related to, though slightly different from, the shame-based hiding we already discussed. In fact, wearing a mask can make it appear to everyone around us that we're perfectly fine, thanks. Happy, even!

So what's the problem with that? The "happiness," carefully cultivated to make it look like our failures don't faze us, is plastic. It's not real. When we're putting on a smiley mask, it's usually hiding deep sadness—sadness we don't want to acknowledge or express because it's too painful or embarrassing. Sadness that only grows when we believe we need to keep the mask on, since people think that's the real us.

If this is you, I'm sending hugs through the pages. It's time to remove the mask and get real with our feelings. There's a better, more authentic way to live, and it's ours for the taking! Because we never need to hide our mistakes or who we are—especially as people (and God) will and do accept and love the real, honest, not-always perfect you.

REFLECTION Can you remember the last mistake or failure (real or perceived) that really hurt? How did you respond? Did you put on a mask?

"SHOW NO WEAKNESS"

I know what it is to be in need, and I know what it is to have plenty. I have learned the secret of being content in any and every situation.

PHILIPPIANS 4:12

The last of our unhealthy coping mechanisms takes on a slightly different flavor than the others. The "show no weakness" perfectionist affects a tough-guy or tough-girl persona. Like the "smiley mask" perfectionist, failures don't faze them. Of course not. They're too strong for that!

Except on the inside, they might be beating themself up. Deeply insecure, to the point that they're trying desperately to convince themself as much as everyone else that they don't care. *Who needs anyone's validation anyway?*

The answer to that question for perfectionists, of course, is *us*. We crave validation from everyone! Especially those we trust or respect. But here's the truth, friend: Failures happen to everyone. Mistakes are universal. Pretending to be tough and unfazed by it doesn't help you in your spiritual or personal growth journeys. We only find real strength by accepting and working through what we perceive as failure.

REFLECTION Do you relate to the "show no weakness" response? If so, take a few minutes to write down some of your most vulnerable feelings associated with failure, mistakes, and disappointments. (If you want, you can write it on separate paper and throw it away when you're done!)

CONFESSION FIRST

●●●●●●●●●

"But unless you repent, you too will all perish."

LUKE 13:3

Those are some strong words from Jesus. They should be enough to make us take notice and receive a clear message: repentance is important. Jesus was talking about a person's initial repentance, when they recognize their sin for the first time. But it's also important to do in our daily lives as we continue to sin, even when we wish we didn't. (At least we can take comfort that this is a relatable battle—see Romans 7:15–20.)

Here's the thing about repentance: the first step is confession. We can't turn away from sins we don't acknowledge. If we're hiding from them or living in denial, then we're not looking our failures in the face, seeing them for what they are (no worse, no better), asking for forgiveness, and making a genuine effort to turn away from them in the future.

It all starts with honest confession. Remember, my perfectionistic friend—not all failures are sins in the spiritual sense, and even though we can apply biblical wisdom to any type of failure, it's important not to elevate simple mistakes on your homework to the level of a true sin!

REFLECTION Do you have an easy time with confession? Think through your usual response to failure—both simple mistakes and actual sins—and write out a prayer, asking God to touch this area of your life.

. . . .

. . . .

. . . .

. . . .

BIBLICAL FAILURE: DAVID

Then Nathan said to David, "You are the man! . . . Why did you despise the word of the Lord by doing what is evil in his eyes?"
2 SAMUEL 12:7, 9

If you thought sin-level failure was something experienced only by "bad" people, think again. The Bible is extremely clear that *all* people have sinned, and I don't mean in the ways we might consider small, like a bad attitude or a white lie. I mean in major, life-shattering, would-land-you-in-prison ways. And sometimes those sins were committed by heroes of faith.

Like David. The Bible calls him a "man after [God's] own heart" (1 Samuel 13:14; Acts 13:22). He was handpicked from among all God's people to be king, and eventually Jesus came from his line.

Yet David committed adultery and murder, abusing his power so grievously, the prophet Nathan harshly called him out in the verses above. David failed in spectacular fashion, and the Lord did not spare him from consequences. But still he had a special relationship with God. David penned many of the most beautiful psalms in the Bible. He loved God—but he wasn't perfect.

REFLECTION How does it feel to read David's story in Scripture? Is it puzzling? Encouraging? Does it seem weird that someone with such a special relationship with God still sinned in this way?

BIBLICAL FAILURE: ABRAHAM

But the LORD inflicted serious diseases on Pharaoh and his household because of Abram's wife Sarai.

GENESIS 12:17

If we want to talk about special relationships with God, we have to mention Abraham, the father of nations. Here he was called Abram, and despite having the kind of one-on-one discussions with God many of us dream of, here he had gone into Egypt and lied to Pharaoh about his wife, Sarai (later called Sarah). He told the Egyptian king that Sarai was his sister, not his wife, because he was afraid Pharaoh would kill him in order to have Sarai. Because of this, the Lord judged Pharaoh and inflicted diseases on his household for taking Abram's wife, even though Pharaoh didn't know she was married to Abram at the time.

Whew. What a mess. Looking back at this thousands of years later, we might shake our heads at Abram, wondering why he didn't just consult with the Lord or ask for his help. After all, Abram was a man of faith, and the Lord spoke directly to him frequently. But Abram is just like us—full of faith but sometimes insecure. And, you guessed it, imperfect!

REFLECTION We may not always hear God's instructions audibly like Abram did, but can you remember a time you really felt God's leading via the Holy Spirit? Take a few minutes to thank God for still speaking to his people, after all these years!

BIBLICAL FAILURE: PAUL

> Meanwhile, Saul was still breathing out murderous threats against the Lord's disciples. . . . Suddenly a light from heaven flashed around him. He fell to the ground and heard a voice say to him, "Saul, Saul, why do you persecute me?"
>
> **ACTS 9:1, 3–4**

If we want a stark illustration of a biblical hero being imperfect, a verse that begins with "breathing out murderous threats" might be a good place to start. It's hard to believe this was the origin story of the great apostle Paul, author of many books in the New Testament. But it is, back when he was Saul, the great persecutor of Christians.

As much as many other New Testament heroes, Paul's life shows us that God can use *anyone*, no matter how imperfect their past. Not only can he use us, he can do so in ways we'd never imagine. Saul's violent opposition to Jesus's followers didn't disqualify him from being saved. He continued to wrestle with his past (more on this later), but it didn't stop him from ministering to others, planting churches all over the ancient Near East, and continuing to encourage those churches for the rest of his life.

REFLECTION Was there a time in your life when you would have considered yourself an enemy of the gospel? Or perhaps there's another area of your life where God turned a great weakness into a surprising strength. He has a way of doing that!

BIBLICAL FAILURE: PETER

Then [Peter] began to call down curses, and he swore
to them, "I don't know the man!" Immediately a rooster
crowed. Then Peter remembered the word Jesus had
spoken: "Before the rooster crows, you will disown me
three times." And he went outside and wept bitterly.

MATTHEW 26:74–75

This one actually hurts. Peter was one of Jesus's closest friends.
His disciple. Someone deep in his confidence. Peter felt so sure
of his faith in the Savior that he didn't believe Jesus when he
said Peter would deny him three times before the rooster crowed
(Matthew 26:35).

Yet that's exactly what happened. Despite his years of walking by Jesus's side. Despite his confession that Jesus is the
Messiah (Matthew 16:16). When Jesus was approaching his
death, Peter didn't hold fast. He didn't admit to being a follower
of Christ, a friend of the crucified man. He messed up. Hugely.

But this mistake did not define Peter. He went on to witness
Jesus's resurrection. He had a big hand in spreading the gospel
message in the church's early years. His life story, thankfully,
did not end with this mishap.

REFLECTION Think about one of your biggest mistakes (I won't make you
write it down). How would you say it compares with Peter's? If you've ever
felt disqualified because of your past mistakes, how do feel now?

BIBLICAL FAILURE: ELIJAH

He came to a broom bush, sat down under it and prayed
that he might die. "I have had enough, Lord," he said.
"Take my life; I am no better than my ancestors."

1 KINGS 19:4

Poor Elijah. His ministry was tough—constantly having to call
out some of the most wicked rulers Israel had ever seen—and
he was still faithful to the Lord. He performed many miracles.
He was the Lord's vessel his entire life, and in the end, he was
taken up in chariots of fire, rather than dying in a more typical
fashion. One can assume the Lord was pleased with his work.

Except here . . . well, here we don't catch him in his finest
moment. His life was in danger, yes, but God had kept Elijah
safe many times before. Couldn't Elijah have had some trust?
Some faith that God would not let his enemies capture him?

Elijah's failure to trust is deeply relatable. God has proven
himself to us many times over, and still we struggle to believe,
especially when we're afraid, discouraged, or sad. Thankfully,
God didn't give up on his discouraged prophet here. He provided
food and a nap (who doesn't need that?), and afterward, Elijah
carried on with his work. God doesn't abandon us in our dis-
couragement either!

REFLECTION Have you ever had an experience like Elijah's "broom bush"
moment? How did God show up for you? Write about it so you'll remember
it better the next time you're feeling discouraged.

BIBLICAL FAILURE: RAHAB

> By faith the prostitute Rahab, because she welcomed the spies, was not killed with those who were disobedient.
>
> **HEBREWS 11:31**

It's kind of a bummer that Rahab is always called "Rahab the prostitute." Even here, where she's mentioned in the Heroes of Faith chapter in Hebrews—as though this is the major hallmark of her identity.

Even though it's sad this label has followed her through the millennia, there's a blessing in it for us. The writers of the Bible didn't shy away from the truth. They didn't sugarcoat Rahab's past or try to make it more palatable. She was a prostitute *and* she acted in faith, welcoming Israel's spies and keeping them safe. She was a woman with a past, and she was a hero. They are not mutually exclusive.

Rahab may not have made the most moral choices before becoming part of the Israelite community, but that past did not define her whole story.

REFLECTION Do you have mistakes in your past that felt story-defining for you, either at the time or today still? Take heart! You have so much story left to write. Journal about your biggest hopes for the future, keeping your eyes facing forward, toward all the many wonderful things yet to unfold.

BIBLICAL FAILURE:
THE WOMAN AT THE WELL

The woman said, "I know that Messiah" (called Christ) "is coming. When he comes, he will explain everything to us." Then Jesus declared, "I, the one speaking to you—I am he."
JOHN 4:25–26

There are many things on the résumé of the woman at the well that might, at first, suggest she isn't going to be a great role model for us. She was a Samaritan, for one, and though that designation doesn't mean much to us, it would have for the Jews of Jesus's time. Many viewed the Samaritans as their enemies. This woman had been married to five men and was currently living with a man she wasn't married to.

And yet, she had an exchange with Jesus where he confronted her with the truth of her life. Then he told her the truth of who he is—one of his earliest proclamations that he was the Messiah everyone was waiting for. The failures of the Samaritan woman's life did not disqualify her from hearing these blessed words!

REFLECTION Who do you consider "outsiders"? How comfortable are you interacting with those outsiders? What do you think this story tells us about Jesus's view of them?

●●●●●●●●

But Paul did not think it wise to take him [John Mark], because he had deserted them in Pamphylia and had not continued with them in the work.

ACTS 15:38

There's a lot of backstory (and a lot of drama) surrounding this verse. We really shouldn't be shocked to see disagreements—even a little fighting—among the apostles. They were human, after all. We see them as faithful servants, but they weren't perfect. Here, the disagreement is actually between Paul and his close friend Barnabas, and it's concerning John Mark.

While Paul and Barnabas disagreed sharply about whether or not to take John Mark with them on a missionary trip, one thing was certain: John Mark had previously messed up. He had abandoned their missionary work in Pamphylia, leading Paul to mistrust him. Because of that mistrust, Paul didn't want to bring him along again. Barnabas, however, thought John Mark deserved the chance to redeem himself.

Who was right? Both of them, really. God used the disagreement for good, launching two missionary journeys instead of one. And, importantly, John Mark *did* work through his issue—quite spectacularly—which we'll explore tomorrow.

REFLECTION Have you ever had a sharp disagreement with a friend? Did you make up eventually? Were there good things God brought about from something that was initially a painful experience?

FAILING WELL

She who is in Babylon, chosen together with you, sends
you her greetings, and so does my son Mark.
1 PETER 5:13

There's some question as to which Johns and Marks are which in
the Bible, but most scholars believe the Mark mentioned by Paul
in this verse is the same John Mark mentioned in Acts—and
that the same Mark is the author of the gospel of Mark, written from Peter's eyewitness testimony. When we consider that
the man who abandoned Paul and Barnabas in Pamphylia later
wrote an important book and worked closely with Paul to spread
the good news about Jesus, it begins to paint the complete arc
of his life. From division-causing deserter to faithful servant
of God.

But a person can't ever have that type of comeback story if
they can't boldly face their failures and shortcomings and use
them as opportunities to grow. When we ignore or hide from
our mistakes, it robs us of the opportunity to fail well. Failing
well is exactly what John Mark must have done. He owned up to
his earlier mistake and matured into a better version of himself.

REFLECTION Can you think of a time when a bad experience was later
redeemed for good? Maybe it happened quickly. Maybe it took years to see
the good in it.

HOW TO RESPOND

With the help of Silas, whom I regard as a faithful brother, I
have written to you briefly, encouraging you and testifying
that this is the true grace of God. Stand fast in it.

1 PETER 5:12

You might be asking yourself *how we fail well*. The very first step
is honesty. Some unhealthy perfectionists tend to hide or deny
the truth, refusing to face it. We already know that's not healthy.
But others engage in a brutal form of self-criticism, thinking
they are looking at themselves honestly, since they aren't living
in denial of their sins and failures.

But that's not honesty, friend. It's a harsher-than-true lens
to view yourself, so if that's you, I want you to really hear what
I'm saying. Looking at ourselves honestly is important, but that
means seeing the *truth*—no more, no less.

And what is the truth? That we are imperfect, yes. But also,
even in the midst of our imperfections, we are loved by God. The
God of the entire universe looks at us and says, "You are worth
loving." We must rest in that truth, even when confronting our
failures!

REFLECTION How clearly do you think you usually see yourself? Do you
err on the side of brutal "honesty" or denial? How might you find a healthy,
accurate self-image?

GOD, OUR STRENGTH

"'If you can'?" said Jesus. "Everything is
possible for one who believes."
MARK 9:23

When we have a catastrophic failure, it can be humiliating. It
can make us want to give up. Stop trying. Never attempt anything new again. When we have these feelings, two things are
usually true. One, we are pretty concerned about what others
will think of us (it's human to care how the rest of the world
perceives us). Two, we are forgetting the source of our strength.

Following a crushing loss, taking moments of tenderhearted
mourning is an excellent way to remember that the world
doesn't rest on our shoulders. Perfectionists easily fall into the
trap of thinking it does. Like the world will spin off its axis if we
don't perform well, win the prize, save the day.

But in truth, God is the source of our strength. He is the
one who gifts us, enables us, sustains us. Without him, nothing
is possible. With him and through him, everything is possible.

REFLECTION When things are going well, how often do you acknowledge
God as the source of your strength? How about when things aren't going
so well? Consider ways to make a regular practice of remembering where
your strength comes from.

CHRIST, OUR RIGHTEOUSNESS

●●●●●●●●●●

"For even the Son of Man did not come to be served, but
to serve, and to give his life as a ransom for many."
MARK 10:45

Perfectionists don't always have the easiest time with the truth
that because Jesus was perfect and died in our place, we are
spiritually covered by his perfection. In other words, he was perfect so we don't need to be.

To be fair, most of us are deeply grateful for this, but we
don't always live as though we *really* understand it. Sometimes,
especially when dealing with our failures, we live as though our
salvation depends upon our own achievements and excellence.
And that's one reason failure can feel so catastrophic.

The way we live *does* matter. Scripture wouldn't be filled
with directives, advice, and admonishments if God didn't care
how we behave or what we choose to do in our lives. But there's
a fundamental difference between something being important
and our salvation depending on it. Take some of that pressure
off yourself! Jesus has you.

REFLECTION When you think about the fact God's judgment of you
depends upon Christ's life, not yours, what emotions come up? Pay attention to what arises first, then second and third. What do these feelings
tell you about how well you're grasping the idea of resting in Christ's
righteousness?

. . . .

. . . .

. . . .

. . . .

. . . .

REFRAMING FAILURE: LEARN SOMETHING

My fellow prisoner Aristarchus sends you his greetings, as does Mark, the cousin of Barnabas. (You have received instructions about him; if he comes to you, welcome him.)

COLOSSIANS 4:10

As we work on reframing our failures, looking at them in a healthier manner, and using them to move forward, we circle back to our friends John Mark (likely the Mark mentioned here) and Paul, the author of Colossians.

Mark had previously failed pretty miserably, leading to a rift between two early church giants, Paul and Barnabas. It's hard to say if Paul also failed—he may have lost his temper or been unforgiving, though the text doesn't specifically say that. Either way, it appears by this point, the two men had reconciled. And we already know Mark went on to do some pretty important work for the kingdom.

The failure and ensuing conflict were used as learning and growing opportunities. Everyone involved became stronger on the other side of it. Failure sometimes creates friction in our lives, but friction is also what polishes a rough gem.

REFLECTION Take some time to visualize a rough gemstone. (If you've never seen one before, look it up so you have the correct visual.) Now imagine the process of polishing those rough edges, producing a glittering jewel. Can you think of a time when a moment of friction led to self-improvement?

REFRAMING FAILURE: RELEASING PRIDE

●●●●●●●●●●

When pride comes, then comes disgrace,
but with humility comes wisdom.

PROVERBS 11:2

Failure is an important part of growing for everyone, not just perfectionists. Failure reminds us we're human. We're not perfect. Sometimes we're not even that good at whatever we're attempting.

These blunders can help keep us humble. Again, it's important to avoid the mindset where we beat ourselves up, but acknowledging our failures and releasing our pride is an important part of seeking the actual truth about ourselves.

Humbly seeing the truth—the good and the bad—without clinging to our pride allows us to grow in wisdom. Perhaps next time, knowing we're going to be participating in an activity that isn't our strong suit, we will set our expectations in a reasonable place. We will still try our hardest, but our newfound humility won't allow us to set ourselves up for an emotionally crushing fall.

REFLECTION On a scale of 1 to10, how much of a struggle is pride for you? Some clues may be how hard it is for you to admit when you were wrong, how quickly you become defensive, and how easily offended you are.

REFRAMING FAILURE: GOD'S PROVISION

God is our refuge and strength, an ever-present help in trouble.
PSALM 46:1

Failure provides us with a lot of opportunities. (Wait—don't close the book! I promise this is good!) It's painful, and we might even hate it at first, but we often grow more from our failures than we do from our successes.

We're able to become humbler, more compassionate individuals. And we can use these difficult experiences to lean on God. I know, I know. Can't we lean on God *and* succeed? Yes, of course we can. But oftentimes people feel closest to God when they have their usual supports stripped away; when they feel small and vulnerable, they hear God's whisper clearer than in moments of triumph.

No matter our outcomes, God is providing for us. But the next time you find yourself in that small, vulnerable place, remember to listen hard for God's whisper, and lean on his provision and strength to help you overcome.

REFLECTION When do you feel closest to God in your life? Is it during your highest highs or your lowest lows? Maybe both? Or is it neither, and you feel close to him in all your day-to-day moments? Contemplate this for a while!

REFRAMING FAILURE:
TRUSTING THE PROCESS

Yes, my soul, find rest in God; my hope comes from him.

PSALM 62:5

Perfectionists like trophies. We like As—better yet, 100 percents. The end goal, the achievement, the prize. These things often become our focus when we're working on something. And when we've got our eye on the prize, falling short doesn't sit very well.

But what if we took our eyes off the prize for a second? What if we reframed the entire way we look at our projects, tasks, and goals? What if, instead of looking toward the finish line, we pay attention to the race as we run it? When we're focused on the race, we're thinking about how our run time has improved over the past year. We're thinking about how strong our legs feel. Maybe we're noticing the neatly clipped grass or the beauty of the blue sky overhead. We're thinking about the many hours of pre-race practice spent with our friends and fellow runners.

There is more to be had in a race than what awaits us at the finish line. Trust the process, and grow throughout the entire journey!

REFLECTION Are you an eyes-on-the-prize runner? What would it look like for you to slow down, observe, and experience your journey in a different way?

DANGERS OF PERFECTIONISM: SQUASHING CREATIVITY

●●●●●●●●●

He has filled them with skill to do all kinds of
work as engravers, designers, embroiderers . . .
all of them skilled workers and designers.

EXODUS 35:35

God created us to be creative. It's no surprise. This is one of
the unique ways human creation reflects him. Unlike most of
the animal kingdom, we create art for the sake of its beauty.
Throughout human history, we've built elaborate structures,
fashioned fine crafts, and constructed beautiful ornaments. It's
a shadowy reflection of the work our Father did when he created
the world and everything in it.

Perfectionism can rob us of this precious gift of just doing
something, dampening our creativity. Being creative requires
risk, and perfectionists are often afraid of taking risks. What
if the artistic experiment fails? What if other people don't like
or understand it? What if we can't get all the angles just right?
These questions can plague us to the point we decide the artistic
risk isn't worth it.

If you like to create, don't let negative thought patterns and
oppressive doubts rob you of this gift!

REFLECTION What's your favorite way to be creative? Has it been a long
time since you've created something for the sake of it? Brainstorm a list of
ways you could lean into your creativity this week.

DANGERS OF PERFECTIONISM: IT SQUASHES LEAPS OF FAITH

Now faith is confidence in what we hope for and assurance about what we do not see.

HEBREWS 11:1

When we are insecure, afraid of potential failure, it really puts a damper on our willingness to take leaps of faith. Sometimes when God asks us to do something, he's not guaranteeing success. He's simply asking us to be obedient. And that can be really scary for a perfectionist. No guarantee of success? Are you sure, God?

But there's good news for perfectionists and timid faith warriors everywhere. You can be afraid and still be a mighty man or woman of God. You can be afraid, even doubt yourself, and still take leaps when directed to. We have many examples of this in Scripture—Moses, Gideon, and Isaiah, to name a few. Being afraid does not disqualify us from God's service. We simply have to leap despite our fear.

REFLECTION Have you ever shied away from something you knew God wanted you to do because you were too afraid to move forward? Was there a time you were afraid but did it anyway? Reflect on what you learned through those experiences.

TOXIC SUCCESS: SELF-SUFFICIENCY ILLUSION

Surely the lowborn are but a breath, the highborn are but a lie. If weighed on a balance, they are nothing; together they are only a breath.
PSALM 62:9

We've discussed our failures and shortcomings. But what about the success perfectionists tend to crave? Can it ever be bad for us? In short—*yes*. We will look at a number of ways success can actually harm us, especially when we pursue it at the expense of all else, ignoring our spiritual, mental, or physical health or anything that truly matters in life. Let's call this "toxic success"—when we have the success we think we want, but it actually isn't the best thing for us.

One of the major potential downfalls of toxic success for Christians is that it's really easy to mistakenly believe we are self-sufficient. Don't get me wrong—it's important that we work hard, and God grants us the gifts, talents, and strength to carry on in our pursuits. But it's even more important we continuously recognize that, without God, we would have none of those things. We *need* him.

REFLECTION Have you ever fallen into the trap of feeling like you're totally self-sufficient? Is it easy for you to see that God is the one enabling your success? What are some things that make this acknowledgment easy or difficult?

TOXIC SUCCESS: PERFORMANCE TRAP

●●●●●●●●○○

For it is by grace you have been saved, through
faith—and this is not from yourselves, it is the gift of
God—not by works, so that no one can boast.

EPHESIANS 2:8–9

The performance trap is a biggie for perfectionists. Particularly when we are high performers and we've lived a life of repeated successes—whether in school, sports, the arts, or something else. It's *very* easy to get the mistaken impression we have now set the bar for ourselves and can reach it. Anything that falls short means a loss of love, joy, peace, affection, and standing. We are in danger of feeling this way about our human relationships, but even worse, we sometimes get the mistaken impression we must perform, perform, perform in order to hold on securely to God's love too.

Ouch. It hurts to think about—the idea that God would love us less if we don't get straight As or win first place. And yet, sometimes without being completely aware of it, this is exactly the kind of thinking we fall into. But remember this: grace is free. We did not earn God's favor. He gave it to us, not because of who we are or what we do but because of who *he* is. A tall bar for salvation doesn't exist.

REFLECTION Have you ever fallen into the trap of doubting God's love for you? Have you ever tied his love to your performance? Pray about breaking those negative thought patterns and embracing God's love for you!

TOXIC SUCCESS:
EVER-MOVING GOALPOSTS

"Do not store up for yourselves treasures on earth. . . .
But store up for yourselves treasures in heaven."
MATTHEW 6:19–20

You did it. You won first place. Part of you hadn't dared hope it would happen—but it did! Elation fills your spirit. You're absolutely soaring—for approximately three minutes. Because that's when you realize you won regionals. But what about state? And then nationals? Suddenly, the big win seems small. The finish line—the goal, the prize—has magically extended a hundred yards away, and you're still standing in the same spot.

Sound familiar? If a win has ever felt hollow to you, you might have experienced the phenomenon of the ever-moving goalposts of success. This happens when our mindset is auto-focused on chasing the biggest prize, the best trophy. We can't help but think, *What's next?* no matter what we've accomplished, and as far as toxic success goes, it's a biggie! The good news is, we can start to reboot our mindsets by allowing ourselves to be more present in each moment.

REFLECTION Have you experienced ever-moving goalposts before? If so, I want you to reframe that whole experience by focusing not on your next goal but on your amazing accomplishment. Thank God for enabling you to achieve such a wonderful thing!

TOXIC SUCCESS: ARROGANCE

But he gives us more grace. That is why Scripture says: "God opposes the proud but shows favor to the humble."
JAMES 4:6

Perfectionists' sense of self takes a big hit when they fail. But what about perfectionists who haven't experienced a ton of failure in life yet? What about those who seem to be charmed, breezing through their blessed existence from win to win to win, never having to wrestle with the crushing weight of loss?

First, it won't last forever. It can't. But even if they somehow avoid failure, that too can be toxic for a perfectionist who hasn't done the hard work of breaking the harmful thought patterns we've been learning about. These folks are in danger of becoming arrogant, puffed-up on their success and convinced of their own invincibility. Aside from the danger to their spiritual lives—since we know God wants us to be humble and filled with gratitude, not arrogance—the arrogant, successful perfectionist is setting himself up for a big fall when that inevitable loss occurs. And if you fall into this "charmed" camp, remember that failure—or lack of it—doesn't define who you are.

REFLECTION Whether you've dealt with a lot of failure in the past or not, do you think any arrogance has crept into your heart? If so, think about some humbleness traits you'd like to cultivate in your life (e.g., listens well, admits mistakes, focuses on growth, serves others).

HEALTHY SUCCESS: HUMBLE CELEBRATION

Praise him with the clash of cymbals, praise him
with resounding cymbals. Let everything that
has breath praise the LORD. Praise the LORD.
PSALM 150:5-6

If success can be so toxic, should we avoid it? Can success ever be
healthy? *Yes!* Of course there are healthy ways to succeed! First,
we should always give praise to God. He is the one who enables
us to reach our goals, whether through the brains and bodies
we were born with, the opportunities that have come into our
lives, or the inborn talents and aptitudes he's given to us. He is
the source of all these things, and our praise should reflect that!

Second, we can embrace joyful, humble celebration when
we meet a goal that's important to us. When our focus is on
God and what *he* has done in our lives, no amount of joy or
excitement is too much. So celebrate those wins! Just remember
where your focus belongs.

REFLECTION What was your last big win? How did you celebrate? If you
didn't stop to applaud your accomplishment at that time, throw yourself a
little party now, keeping the focus on God as your source.

HEALTHY SUCCESS: PROGRESS AS SUCCESS

Stand firm. Let nothing move you. Always give
yourselves fully to the work of the Lord, because you
know that your labor in the Lord is not in vain.

1 CORINTHIANS 15:58

Another way to embrace healthy success is to steer our minds away from unhealthy, perfectionist thought patterns, reframing the way we look at success. The first way we can do this is measuring our success by how much progress we've made.

When we shift our focus in this way, our goals become less and less about the big pot of gold at the end of the rainbow and more and more about the small, sustainable steps we take toward improvement. For example, a runner who previously was only satisfied with first place instead focuses on improving her personal time. Winning is out of her control. The race result doesn't depend only on how well she performs but who else shows up to race that day and how well they perform.

Deciding to consider progress a key measure of success is a healthier way to strive for self-improvement. It also takes pressure off our shoulders when we don't believe we need to be the very best all the time!

REFLECTION What's one area of your life where you generally have big goals? Take a minute to reframe your idea of success in that area so that it measures your progress, rather than your wins.

HEALTHY SUCCESS: LEARNING AS SUCCESS

Instruct the wise and they will be wiser still; teach the righteous and they will add to their learning.

PROVERBS 9:9

Measurable progress isn't the only healthy measure of success. Sometimes we can have a very big success that didn't involve advancement *or* winning a prize. How is that possible?

It has to do with how we see learning—because learning things along our journeys is a huge success that often goes unnoticed. When we train our brains to think of learning as a win, it puts success into much healthier perspective. Perhaps our runner didn't make much progress on her personal time, but she learned new techniques that will protect her joints in the future. Maybe she discovered she prefers distance running to sprinting. Maybe she found she enjoys helping others get into running, and decided to help coach a kids' running league.

All of those are big successes, even if they're not how we'd traditionally define *success*. Learning new things is such an important part of life—let's not overlook it!

REFLECTION With this new mindset that learning is success, can you think of a time when you may not have won or made personal progress, but you learned something really important? Reflect on that experience for a bit.

"The kingdom of heaven is like a mustard seed. . . .
Though it is the smallest of all seeds, yet when it grows,
it is the largest of garden plants and becomes a tree."

MATTHEW 13:31–32

Some experiences help us grow in a specific way that's vitally important, and this growth should be thought of as success: for example, when we grow closer to God, become more like Jesus, or take a leap in maturity, that's a big win.

Maybe our runner was in the middle of training, sprinting with all her might, and she tripped. *Boom.* Season-ending ankle injury. How can this possibly be considered a success? There's no win, no progress, and nothing new to learn now. Except she can continue supporting her team. She can work hard on rehabbing her ankle. She can trust that God is able to heal her so she can come back strong.

All of these things help her grow into a more mature, God-loving person—one who knows there's value in these experiences, even if she has no shot at winning this time. That's character growth—and that's success!

REFLECTION Character growth often comes during seasons in life that don't feel successful. Instead, they just feel hard! Can you think of a time like that? How does focusing on how you grew as a person change how you look back at that experience?

DANGERS OF PERFECTIONISM: LAW AND GOSPEL

The promise comes by faith, so that it may be by grace and may be guaranteed to all Abraham's offspring—not only to those who are of the law but also to those who have the faith of Abraham. He is the father of us all.

ROMANS 4:16

One of the basic principles in Christianity is the relationship between the law and the gospel—with *basic* meaning that it's fundamentally important, not that it's always simple. The law, given to the Israelites through Moses, showed God's people the requirements for having a relationship with him. It taught the Israelites (and us) about sin. It showed them God's heart and his holiness, and it offered promises to the faithful.

The gospel—the good news of Jesus Christ—is the fulfillment of the law. Through Christ, we are offered forgiveness of our sins. He perfectly lived the law and died in our place.

It's easy to get this fundamental truth twisted-up in our minds. When we become performance-obsessed, we drift into a law-based mindset—both literally in our relationship with God (this is known as legalism) and in a more abstract way, believing our worth is based on our performance in all areas of life. We'll look more closely at this over the next few days.

REFLECTION Have you heard teachings about the law and gospel before? Do you feel you tend to drift away from a balanced understanding of those principles?

LEGALISM: SELF-RIGHTEOUSNESS

●●●●●●●●●●

Since they did not know the righteousness of God and sought to establish their own, they did not submit to God's righteousness.

ROMANS 10:3

A legalistic mindset can be harmful to our spiritual walk and emotional health in many ways. One of the most frequent is the legalist's tendency to become self-righteous. To be clear, pursuing righteousness itself is a *good* thing. It's important to pay attention to the way God tells us to live and to align our hearts and our actions as closely with Scripture as possible.

The difference between humbly pursuing righteousness and being *self*-righteous is probably best illustrated in the difference between Jesus's disciples and the Pharisees. The disciples were far from perfect, but their lives were built around following Jesus (literally!), learning about God from him, and using what they discovered to grow in their relationship with God. The Pharisees focused on keeping the letter of the law, to the point following the rules became the thing that mattered. And because they ignored the spirit of the law, they made following God seem difficult for others and didn't see how the law showed God's love for his people. They missed the point entirely! When you look at it this way, which mindset would you rather have?

REFLECTION Write two columns, one titled "Righteousness" and one titled "Self-Righteousness." What sort of things belong in the Righteousness column? How about Self-Righteousness?

LEGALISM: FALSE HUMILITY

The Pharisee stood by himself and prayed: "God, I thank you that I am not like other people—robbers, evildoers, adulterers—or even like this tax collector."

LUKE 18:11

Oof. This prayer. It feels pretty gross to read it on the page. Yet . . . if we think about it really hard, how often have we felt whispers of this ourselves? *God, thank you that I'm not like that broken, lost person over there.* Or, *God, thank you that I'm so blessed—unlike that person over there.*

There's nothing wrong with thanking God for how he's made us, how he's blessed us, or even the fact he has redeemed us or spared us from some bad things. It can be a dark, scary world out there, and there's nothing wrong with being grateful that the Lord pulled you out of that, into the light.

The problem comes—and legalism enters the picture—when we believe we are better than someone who is struggling, doesn't have the material blessings we do, or doesn't yet know Jesus. And in the process, we can often lose track of where our blessings came from in the first place, and what we're meant to do with them.

REFLECTION What is a Christlike response to "that person over there" who is struggling? The Pharisee chose judgment and false humility. What would Jesus do?

LEGALISM: SELF-FLAGELLATION

A person is not justified by the works of the law, but by faith in Jesus Christ.
GALATIANS 2:16

Self-flagellation (extreme self-criticism) is, perhaps, more common in perfectionists than the arrogant, self-righteous flavors of legalism, since we tend to struggle deeply with our sense of worth and value. *Flagellation* literally means flogging (or whipping). So when you hear the phrase "beating yourself up," that's what it's getting at. When we believe our standing with God is based on our ability to uphold the law, we can become very down on ourselves when we (inevitably) fail.

Even though at first this sounds like a politer form of legalism, it's just as harmful. First to ourselves, but secondly, believing this lie—that our justification before God is based on our performance—eventually spills out onto our view of those around us when we apply our views to others as well. It's bad for our hearts and for how we treat the people we encounter.

REFLECTION Have you struggled with this type of legalism before? A good way to tell is by asking yourself if you ever worried about losing God's love because of a mistake. Pray for the love of God—and the warmth of his grace—to wash over you now.

LEGALISM: THE IMPOSSIBLE TASK

●●●●●●●●●●

Therefore no one will be declared righteous in
God's sight by the works of the law; rather, through
the law we become conscious of our sin.

ROMANS 3:20

As with the Pharisees, legalism puts us in danger of missing the most fundamental truth of all: we couldn't earn salvation on our own, so Jesus died for us.

It's the essence of our faith. The foundational truth of Christianity. Jesus came to Earth, lived a perfect life, and willingly died for us so we could be reconciled with the Father. The law was good—it *is* good—because it shows us where we fall short. It points to our need for a savior. But trying to keep the law through our own power is an impossible task. Attempting to do so leaves us either in a state of false moral superiority, like the Pharisees, or in a state of despair, knowing we fall short but are unable to do anything about it.

And how freeing is it to know that even when we do mess up, God has already forgotten the things we've repented of and sees us as his excellent children . . . and that's not going to change.

REFLECTION If you have time, read Matthew 5 today, paying attention to how Jesus revealed the very heart of the law. As you read, consider how often we fall short of this ideal. How does it make you feel gratitude for Christ's sacrifice?

LEGALISM: SHAME

Day **166**

For we maintain that a person is justified by
faith apart from the works of the law.
ROMANS 3:28

Ah, shame. The old "friend" of perfectionists everywhere. If
there's one thing we don't need, it's more shame!

But that's exactly what legalism can lead to. If you're focused
on keeping the law, and if you're self-aware enough to see how
you fall short, it can lead you down a path of deep spiritual
shame, feeling unable to stand before the Lord. This can effec-
tively kill our prayer life, nudge us out of community with other
believers, and force us into hiding—from God, from others, and
from ourselves.

So what's the solution? Understanding that we are justified
through Jesus's works, not our own. Embracing the free gift of
grace. Truly grabbing hold of the idea that our redemption does
not rest on our shoulders.

REFLECTION Read the last sentence of the devotion again, then shout,
"Amen!" Or if you're not the shouting type, write out a prayer of thanksgiving for the life and work of Jesus Christ—and the freedom it gives God's
people.

GRACE: UNMERITED FAVOR

What then? Shall we sin because we are not under the law but under grace? By no means!

ROMANS 6:15

We've covered the goodness of the law and the dangers of legalism, but what about the gospel side of that law-and-gospel equation? What actually is *grace*, anyway? If you've spent any time in church, you've probably heard this word a lot! It has a few different meanings.

In the context of this discussion, *grace* means unmerited favor—favor we didn't earn. We have God's approval, even though we couldn't keep the law perfectly. That's grace. But something important to note, as Paul did in his letter to the Romans, is that just because we do not live "under the law" (needing to keep it perfectly to receive God's favor), that doesn't mean we should run around sinning on purpose. Grace is not an excuse to do what we want. It's a pardon extended to followers of Jesus who are dedicated to living their lives for him. We're supposed to live according to the principles Jesus taught—which never included willful sin!

REFLECTION When you think about the concept of grace, what's the first picture that comes to mind? (For me, I always imagine standing before a throne, bowing to a king who has every reason to throw me in a dungeon but instead extends his hand to me.)

GRACE: MERCY

Let us then approach God's throne of grace with
confidence, so that we may receive mercy and
find grace to help us in our time of need.

HEBREWS 4:16

An important aspect of God's grace is his mercy. We experience
God's mercy first in the fact that he offers us forgiveness instead
of judgment. And that alone is pretty cool! But his mercy doesn't
stop there.

We need God's compassion beyond our initial salvation
experience. The Greek word translated as *mercy* suggests
pity. But it's not a sad kind of pity—it's more like sympathy.
God patiently deals with us, offering favor we didn't earn and
compassion we desperately need as we move through this life
imperfectly, managing life's hardships and the effects of sin
(ours and others').

When we receive God's ongoing compassion, it should
inspire us to extend that compassion outward to others who are
in need. This world is lost and hurting, and followers of Jesus
can demonstrate God's great love by showing mercy to others.

REFLECTION What are some ways you've experienced God's mercy in
your life? Think of a few big moments and a few small ones. Sometimes
the small ones are so specific, they're a good reminder of how clearly God
sees us and how much he cares!

GRACE: ATONEMENT

"He himself bore our sins" in his body on the cross, so
that we might die to sins and live for righteousness;
"by his wounds you have been healed."

1 PETER 2:24

Peter referenced Isaiah 53:5 at the end of this verse, which reads,
"by his wounds we are healed." He was not speaking about our
physical bodies here. He was talking about our spiritual condition.

Jesus physically died so that we might live spiritually. He
took our sins onto his body, paying the price we owed, and
because of that, we're free. In short, that is atonement. The perfect Lamb of God who takes away the sin of the world allows us
to be reconciled to (reunited with) the Father.

Have you ever thought about what it means to be reconciled
to God? There is no more barrier between him and us. Sin no
longer separates us from our holy God. Jesus was a once-and-
for-all sacrifice that undid the brokenness that began in the
garden with Adam and Eve. That means we are restored into
close relationship with the Father. We can approach his throne
with confidence, assured we're in standing with him. Hallelujah!

REFLECTION When you learn about atonement, does it sound very legal or
clinical? How about when you add in what we learned about grace and mercy?

GRACE: OUR WORKS

Day **170**

All of us have become like one who is unclean, and all
our righteous acts are like filthy rags; we all shrivel up
like a leaf, and like the wind our sins sweep us away.

ISAIAH 64:6

This verse can be a little tough for perfectionists to swallow,
particularly if we're still wrapped up in a performance-based
mindset. We might easily admit that our sins are like filthy rags.
We might readily agree that our failures are worthless. But our
righteous acts are like filthy rags? How?

This verse doesn't suggest that our work is meaningless to
God or that he doesn't care about how we live or what we do. But
in the *spiritual* sense, yes, even our good deeds and righteous
works are like filthy rags. Why? Because they have no power
to save us. Only the Messiah has the power to do that. Only
he could have lived a life free of sin. Only he could become that
perfect sacrificial lamb. We lack the ability.

Instead of discouraging you, this idea should fill you with
joy! Jesus made a way for us all.

REFLECTION How does it feel knowing our righteous works are like filthy
rags? Do you find it easy to distinguish between something that has no
spiritual power and something that is truly worthless? If this is hard for you,
stay tuned! There is more to come on how to serve God well.

MARTHA WORKED

●●●●●●●●●

As Jesus and his disciples were on their way, he came to a
village where a woman named Martha opened her home to him.
LUKE 10:38

We know our works are worthless in a spiritual sense. They don't
save us. But what does Scripture say about our works otherwise?
Are we meant to do good for the kingdom? Of course! But it's
important to dig into some of Jesus's key teachings in this area.

Martha is a great place to start. She is a woman in the Bible
who is often remembered for her work—and not always in a
flattering way. We may wonder why she has this reputation.
Here, we see her doing something really good. She was showing
hospitality (an excellent thing) to Jesus and his disciples (even
better!). So what's the issue?

It will become apparent as we get a little further into the
story. For now, we can note that Martha's work was good. Who
knows—she may have even been a fellow perfectionist. She
seemed to manage a lot, working hard to ensure everyone was
looked after and her home was an inviting place for those she
hosted.

REFLECTION If you don't know the story of Martha and her sister, Mary,
do you have any guesses about what's going to go wrong with this good
work Martha was doing? Knowing what you know about the parts of the
law Jesus emphasized, what might be the impending problem?

MARY LISTENED

> She had a sister called Mary, who sat at the Lord's feet
> listening to what he said. But Martha was distracted
> by all the preparations that had to be made.
>
> **LUKE 10:39–40**

Ah, now we meet Mary, and a fuller picture of what's happening in this household begins to take shape. Martha was busy with her many hosting duties. Mary was sitting at the Lord's feet. We have the benefit of perspective, two thousand years after the fact. We know that this was *the* Jesus Mary was listening to—the Savior of the world. Surely the hosting duties could wait, Martha?

But in the moment, Martha didn't have the benefit of this perspective. At least not to the degree we do! She was taking care of all the things she was culturally obligated to take care of. She was working hard, making sure everything was perfect. She was doing what she thought she needed to do.

And Mary just . . . sat. And listened. Learned. Absorbed. Can you feel the tension brewing? If you have siblings, perhaps you felt it from the very first moment Mary was mentioned!

REFLECTION Stepping back from this Bible story for a moment, what do you think of the dynamic taking shape between Martha and Mary? Does it seem fair that Mary wasn't helping her sister?

MARTHA WAS BITTER

She [Martha] came to him [Jesus] and asked,
"Lord, don't you care that my sister has left me to
do the work by myself? Tell her to help me!"
LUKE 10:40

If you have siblings at home, have you ever felt like you're the one who "does everything"? It's a common feeling. If you're like my family, every kid feels they are the one who does the most! Even though I'm not sure how that's possible . . .

Honestly, Martha is relatable in this moment. It's frustrating to feel like you're shouldering the load, doing all the work. Maybe you don't have siblings, but have you ever worked on a group project at school? If you're a high-achieving perfectionist, chances are you've been in a group at some point where others were happy to let you do more than your fair share.

And let's be real, it stinks. It's easy—understandable, even—to become a little bitter when it feels like everything falls to you and no one is helping. But . . . what did Jesus have to say about the matter?

REFLECTION What do you think of this story as it's unfolding? Who is more relatable to you, Mary or Martha?

MARY WAS PRAISED

"Martha, Martha," the Lord answered, "you are worried
and upset about many things, but few things are
needed—or indeed only one. Mary has chosen what
is better, and it will not be taken away from her."

LUKE 10:41–42

Few things are needed. Mary has chosen what is better. We can
imagine this stung a little. After all, Martha had been looking
after the needs of Jesus and his friends. Did that matter to him?
Didn't he see how hard she was working?

Yes, of course he did. Jesus and Martha were good friends. I'm
sure he noticed and appreciated the work she was doing for him.
However, he is uncovering an important truth for Martha here—
not to hurt her feelings but because he loved her. He was actually
removing the heavy burden she and her culture had placed upon
her shoulders. He said *only one* thing is truly needed—to hear his
words, to listen to his teachings. To love him, to follow him. This
was what Mary had chosen, and, though Martha was doing good
work, Mary's choice was the one that had *eternal* significance.
Therefore, it will not be taken away from her.

REFLECTION How do you feel about this turn the story has taken? Do
you think Jesus was being unfair, or do you understand the lesson he was
teaching Martha?

MARTHA, STILL FAITHFUL

"Yes, Lord," she [Martha] replied, "I believe that you are the Messiah, the Son of God, who is to come into the world."
JOHN 11:27

Martha gets beat up on a lot. Many commentaries compare her unfavorably to her sister, and it's understandable why. It seems Jesus did that very same thing (though it's important to note that he did not condemn Martha—he was still kind to her!).

But the story of Martha hosting Jesus and his disciples is not the only time we see this family in Scripture. In fact, we have this profound, stunning confession from none other than our super busy, semi-bitter, possibly perfectionistic sister Martha. Here, she made a confession on par with the confession of Jesus being Christ that the apostle Peter is (rightly) praised for.

Martha, despite her moment of frustration and bitterness directed toward her sister, *got it*. She understood who Jesus truly was. Her understanding may not have been perfect or complete, but she got it even better than some of the men who traveled with Jesus.

REFLECTION Have you ever felt judged based on one small part of your story? How does it feel when people make judgments about your character based on one mistake? Or perhaps when they judge you based on who you were three, five, or ten years ago?

HOPE FOR MARTHAS

Now Jesus loved Martha and her sister and Lazarus.

JOHN 11:5

Ah, this is a wonderful verse. This is the same Martha we've been looking at, and yes, this is *that* Lazarus, the one Jesus resurrected from the dead. John took the time to let us know without question: Jesus loved this family.

Including Martha. The one who boldly demanded Jesus *do something* about her sister not helping with the work around the house. If you found Martha at all relatable in that moment—and I think many of us probably did—this should be an encouragement to you. Like Martha, it's easy for us to get wrapped up in our work, concerned with many things. Troubled, worried, easily irritated. And Jesus would likely say to us what he said to Martha: Few things truly matter—indeed, only one.

But we don't need to feel condemned by that rebuke. Jesus loved Martha. He loves us. He rebukes us for our benefit, to reorient our perspective and remind us what's really important.

REFLECTION If you were to create a list of the top priorities in your life right now, where does your relationship with God land on that list? Does it feel like other things are trying to crowd it out? Take a few minutes to think about how you can shift things around to better reflect the priorities of your heart.

OUR STRENGTHS: WORKS PREPARED FOR US

For we are God's handiwork, created in Christ Jesus to do good works, which God prepared in advance for us to do.
EPHESIANS 2:10

We know our relationship with God is the most important thing in our lives—the only thing that matters in an eternal sense. We know our works cannot save us. So do we kick up our feet, recognizing that we're saved by grace and that knowing Jesus is the most important thing we can do in life?

Nope! Here the apostle Paul said we are "created in Christ Jesus to do good works." Our works may not save us, but they are still pretty important! And what Paul wrote next is very cool: God prepared these tasks in advance for us to do.

You were created with a specific set of gifts, talents, and interests. You were born in a particular time, place, and culture. There are works laid out just for you that are going to help build the kingdom of God. Wow! That's an amazing calling we each have placed on our lives and in our hearts.

REFLECTION Brainstorm a list of things you're good at—things you love, things that interest you. Maybe it seems like some of them don't have much to do with the kingdom of God yet, but that's okay. Write them down anyway.

GLORY TO GOD

●●●●●●●●●●

Not to us, LORD, not to us but to your name be the
glory, because of your love and faithfulness.
PSALM 115:1

We've spent a lot of time talking about failure (sorry!). We've
spent time talking about owning our mistakes and being real
with ourselves and others about the fact we don't measure up.
We've even talked about how toxic it can be when we succeed
(sorry again!). These are important things to understand, rotten
roots we need to dig out so we can replant healthy trees.

But now we're going to talk about godly ways to operate in
our strengths. Because *yes*, we have them. Of course we do! And
we're each called to use the strengths God has given us. The
number one, most important thing to remember is that—as we
operate in our strengths, doing the work God has prepared in
advance for us—we must acknowledge God as the source of our
strength. He is the source of our gifts, and he is the reason we
work hard—everything is for his glory. Amen!

REFLECTION When you think about all your work being done for God's
glory, what feelings come up? Is it freeing? Scary? Daunting?

. . . .

. . . .

. . . .

. . . .

. . . .

. . . .

. . . .

. . . .

STRENGTH: OLDER IS HAPPIER

Gray hair is a crown of splendor; it is attained in the way of righteousness.

PROVERBS 16:31

Did you know research shows getting older increases happiness?[4] That may sound like a wild idea in our youth-obsessed culture, but it's true!

We don't know for sure why this happens. Some people theorize that older adults appreciate how far they've come in life—and that they're still hanging on. Or, perhaps for the perfectionists among them, they've let go of things that used to seem so important, like striving for accolades. Perhaps they have shifted priorities to things that feel more enjoyable or more meaningful.

When we think about the works God has prepared for us in this life, maybe we can start "living like an older person" now. Maybe it's time, no matter your actual age, to let go of the more trivial things and find joy in the lasting, meaningful work God is calling you to.

REFLECTION What are some things that may seem important but aren't actually that meaningful in your life? Can you rearrange your priorities to make more time for the things that really matter to you?

STRENGTH: BEING THERE FOR A FRIEND

●●●●●●●●●

When Moses' hands grew tired, they took a stone and put it under him and he sat on it. Aaron and Hur held his hands up . . . so that his hands remained steady till sunset.

EXODUS 17:12

We may think of being strong as handling everything on our plates. Or perhaps we equate strength with excellence, thinking we're strong when we achieve at a consistently high level (yeah, I see you . . .). But truly, one of the most wonderful ways we can display strength is by being there for someone who is in need.

Even Moses, who is one of the most prominent figures of the Old Testament, was a person in need of help. He was God's chosen prophet, the appointed leader of Israel, and yet he got to a point he couldn't hold his hands up anymore. In that moment, as long as he held his hands up, Israel was winning the battle before them. But when his hands would drop, they would begin to lose. When Moses got tired, Aaron and Hur literally held his hands for him.

Like Aaron and Hur, we can step into the gap for a friend who needs us. (And like Moses, we can accept help when we need it.)

REFLECTION Is there anyone in your life who may need their hands held up right now? Perhaps they're carrying a particularly heavy load. How can you share their burden?

BIBLICAL STRENGTH: ESTHER

● ● ● ● ● ● ● ● ●

"For if you remain silent at this time, relief and deliverance
for the Jews will arise from another place, but you and your
father's family will perish. And who knows but that you
have come to your royal position for such a time as this?"

ESTHER 4:14

The Bible gives us many wonderful examples of people using
their strengths for the sake of God's kingdom. Esther is perhaps
one of the most famous of these.

She was a young Jewish woman exiled with her people during the reign of Xerxes of Persia (also called Ahasuerus). She was
somewhat reluctantly put in a position to speak to the Persian
king on behalf of the Jews. Her people were being persecuted,
and though she risked her own life to do so, Esther spoke up for
them so they would not be killed.

Esther is a role model for us when we feel like we're stepping into the role we were born for. Remember when I said you
were born when, where, and who you are exactly on purpose?
We don't all get a story as dramatic as Esther's. But you, too,
were born for "such a time as this."

REFLECTION Have you ever needed to be bold like Esther? How did you
handle the situation? If it was a struggle for you, think of some ways you
can bolster your courage the next time something like this comes up.

BIBLICAL STRENGTH: JOHN THE BAPTIST

●●●●●●●●●●

Then Jesus came from Galilee to the Jordan to be baptized by John. But John tried to deter him, saying, "I need to be baptized by you, and do you come to me?"

MATTHEW 3:13-14

John the Baptist was Jesus's forerunner. He spent years proclaiming God's Son was coming. He traveled from place to place, preaching repentance and baptizing people. He had followers of his own, and he is regarded as a prophet, holy man, and important religious figure.

John the Baptist did a great job at executing the task set before him with excellence. We might even call him a high achiever, though not in the way his society would have viewed it. In fact, people probably thought he was a weirdo—a zealot who wore strange clothes, ate strange food, and preached an unexpected message.

Yet we recognize him for who he was. The one who foretold Jesus's earthly ministry and humbly baptized his Savior. John is an example of doing the work God sets before you, even if others don't get or appreciate you in the moment.

REFLECTION What are some positive traits you think John the Baptist displays? Write out ways you might cultivate those traits in your own daily life.

. . . .

. . . .

. . . .

. . . .

. . . .

. . . .

BIBLICAL STRENGTH: JOSHUA

"Choose for yourselves this day whom you will serve . . .
But as for me and my household, we will serve the LORD."

JOSHUA 24:15

There's a good chance you've come across this verse before, whether at church or on a piece of artwork in someone's home. It's a great quote from Joshua. "But as for me and my household, we will serve the LORD." It's a declaration that, no matter what anyone else may choose to do, in this house, we will serve God.

Joshua, Moses's right-hand man who became Israel's leader after Moses's death, had been faithfully serving God for many years at this point. He began his life as a slave in Egypt, then was with the Israelites through years of desert wandering. At this point, Joshua had conquered Canaan and distributed the land, as dictated by God, for the Israelites to settle in. When we look at the parts of Joshua's story recorded in the Bible, he goes from strength to strength.

He is an excellent example of someone using their gifts—and the moment of history they were born into—to serve God.

REFLECTION Have you ever had to take a stand for your faith the way Joshua did here? What do you like about the way Joshua stated his intention?

BIBLICAL STRENGTH: DANIEL

"My God sent his angel, and he shut the mouths of the lions. They have not hurt me, because I was found innocent in his sight. Nor have I ever done any wrong before you, Your Majesty."

DANIEL 6:22

Daniel was definitely a high achiever. Was he a perfectionist? It's impossible to say. But he certainly excelled at everything he did. He was taken to Babylon by King Nebuchadnezzar because of his decency, and intellect. There, Daniel remained faithful to God despite being in a difficult environment. God blessed Daniel and his friends, and they found favor with the king in all they did. In fact, they outlasted several kings in Babylon.

Daniel faced some truly terrifying situations, but each time his unwavering faith shone through. When Babylon's wise men could not interpret the king's dreams, the king ordered all the wise men (including Daniel) be put to death. Daniel quietly saved the day by asking for—and receiving—an interpretation of the king's dream from the Lord. Later, King Darius threw Daniel into lions' den because of a decree the king couldn't legally take back. God saved Daniel, shutting the lions' mouths so they wouldn't attack.

REFLECTION Daniel's story shows us how acting on our faith can reflect the Lord back to those around us. What do you notice about how Daniel went about this?

GIFTED FOR HIS KINGDOM

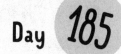

> Now to each one the manifestation of the
> Spirit is given for the common good.
>
> **1 CORINTHIANS 12:7**

Maybe perfectionists don't have a hard time believing everyone has strengths and gifts and talents in this life. If we're high achievers, we might even be aware of what some of our own talents are. But something that might be a little harder for us to grasp is exactly *why* each of us is gifted.

The world dangles a lot of rewards in front of high achievers. It promises success, money, accolades, and plenty of other bright, shiny things in exchange for us using our gifts to excel. And there's nothing wrong with using your sharp intellect to pursue higher education. There's nothing wrong with being great at a job and earning an excellent salary. But what does the Bible say about why we're gifted?

Paul made it clear that the gifts of the Spirit are given to us for the common good and to build up the church (1 Corinthians 14:12). In other words, we are supposed to use our gifts in service of others for God's glory, not our own.

REFLECTION Think about some of your gifts and talents. What are a few ways you could use each of these gifts to serve others for God's glory?

GIFTS: EVERYONE HAS THEM

There are different kinds of gifts, but the
same Spirit distributes them.

1 CORINTHIANS 12:4

Maybe you've never thought of your gifts in the way we're talking about them here—for building the kingdom of God, serving him and others. That can be a little daunting at first, especially when you've mostly used your gifts in quite a different context, like in school or on a sports field. Or even worry you'll somehow use them wrong or not have gifts that "fit."

If you're feeling that way, don't worry. I have two pieces of good news. First, gifts that you haven't thought of in a kingdom-building way before may be more useful than you think. Maybe you're excellent at math but can't see how it could be helpful to the kingdom. But have you ever thought about how important it is to have numbers-minded people helping with a church's finances?

Second, every single Christ follower has been given spiritual gifts in addition to natural talents. We're going to take a small detour from focusing on perfectionism in order to go over the gifts mentioned in the Bible, but even that won't be a complete list. There are probably a thousand different ways the Holy Spirit might gift believers—and that includes you!

REFLECTION Which of your gifts seem more obviously connected to serving the church? How about those that might not be as obvious at first?

GIFTS: ACKNOWLEDGE THE SOURCE

There are different kinds of service, but the same Lord.
1 CORINTHIANS 12:5

It's okay to celebrate the unique ways in which we're each gifted. Scripture does. It's noted more than once how many different kinds of service there are, how many different ways we can be part of the body, and that while we all do different work, each part is necessary.

But it's equally important to acknowledge we all are gifted from the same source—God, specifically the Holy Spirit (1 Corinthians 12:7). No matter what our individual gifts are, they are given to us through the Spirit. This is freeing, in one sense, because it allows us to acknowledge we're not relying on our own strength when we're using our gifts. We should be relying on the Holy Spirit.

It's also an important reminder to stay humble about the gifts God has given to us. Spiritual gifts aren't about us at all, really. They are about serving others with the tools God has handed to us.

REFLECTION Take a few moments to write out a prayer of thanksgiving for your specific gifts. Can you think of some ways God has enabled you to use them in the past? What are some ideas for using them in the future?

GIFTS: DEPENDENCY AND UNITY

There are different kinds of working, but in all of
them and in everyone it is the same God at work.

1 CORINTHIANS 12:6

God has created a wonderful dynamic. Everyone in the church
(a group of believers) is gifted in a unique way, and each type of
gift is required to build up the church. This makes us depend
upon each other in a way we wouldn't otherwise.

Churches, of course, are also buildings where the group of
believers meet, worship collectively, and grow in their faith. But
a local church in both senses of the word serves as a community
home base, even for people who don't regularly attend services.
A lot of people rely on local churches for ministries of mercy—
food, shelter, medical care, or mental health and counseling
services.

All of those functions are varied, requiring several different skill sets. There isn't one person who could handle all of
those tasks—and God didn't design it to be so! Instead, we each
rely upon others to meet our common goals, dependent on one
another and unified in purpose.

REFLECTION Have you ever thought about what gifts you definitely
don't have? For example, I'm really shy, so anything requiring speaking
to strangers is not my natural gift! Spend some time thinking about areas
you're not gifted in and thanking God for those who are.

GIFTS: PRACTICE

Each of you should use whatever gift you have received to serve others, as faithful stewards of God's grace in its various forms.
1 PETER 4:10

Sometimes we have a certain mental picture when we think about God giving us something. It can sound almost magical, like God has handed us a superpower to use for his kingdom, and we need only to grab the gift he extends and run with it.

There's a tiny bit of truth to that—the gift is not from ourselves, so it is like something God is handing to us and saying, "Run! Use this for the good of my kingdom!" But we can sometimes mistakenly believe gifts are handed to us fully formed with nothing required of us to use them.

Instead, these gifts are more like the talents elite athletes receive. Like the runner who is born with all the right genetics to be the fastest sprinter at the Olympics, we still have to train so the gift develops and grows into what it's designed to be. We have to practice and be diligent with the gifts bestowed upon us.

REFLECTION Think about one of your gifts. What are several ways to sharpen or train that gift? Make a list!

GIFTS: THE MOST EXCELLENT WAY

Are all apostles? Are all prophets? Are all teachers? Do all work miracles? Do all have gifts of healing? Do all speak in tongues? Do all interpret? Now eagerly desire the greater gifts. And yet I will show you the most excellent way.

1 CORINTHIANS 12:29–31

These verses have been interpreted in a fascinating number of ways among theologians and pastors alike. What are the "greater gifts," exactly? Some people say Paul was referring to the gift of prophecy. Others say he was referencing apostles. Still others say he was referring to the gifts that serve the church—meaning, all of them!

But perhaps the final sentence is a clue as to what we should focus on when it comes to gifts—the "most excellent way." Immediately following that sentence, 1 Corinthians 13 begins—the famous love chapter of the Bible. Perhaps Paul was telling us that, no matter what gifts we have, we must use them with love. If we can perform miraculous healings but don't have love, we're missing the point. If we have excellent faith and stellar administration skills but we don't have love, we have nothing.

REFLECTION When you're serving with your gifts, how often do you stop and think about love? It sounds weird to say it that way, but think about it! Love should be at the center of everything we do, so brainstorm some ways to bring love into how you share your talents with others.

GIFTS: MESSAGE OF WISDOM

To one there is given through the Spirit a message of wisdom.
1 CORINTHIANS 12:8

Maybe you have a good handle on which talents you were been born with, but the idea of spiritual gifts is a little fuzzier. We're going to look at each of those mentioned in the Bible—what they mean, and what they might be used for today. Remember, these are not thought to be an exhaustive list of all the gifts the Holy Spirit might bestow, but it's an excellent place to start.

"A message of wisdom" has been interpreted many ways over the years, but someone who has this spiritual gift is probably someone people go to for advice. They may be able to help resolve conflicts between believers, and they might be particularly good at applying spiritual truth to any given situation. They are probably judicious—sensible and careful, able to sort through facts, opinions, and feelings to help decide the best course of action.

REFLECTION On a scale of 1 to 10, where would you rate this gift for yourself? If it's high on your list, what are some ways you could help sharpen this gift? (Hint: To be truly wise, someone needs to be deeply rooted in God's Word.)

GIFTS: MESSAGE OF KNOWLEDGE

To another [is given] a message of knowledge
by means of the same Spirit.

1 CORINTHIANS 12:8

Have you ever met someone who seems insatiable in their thirst for knowledge? Perhaps they spend lots of time reading non-fiction books to learn more about the world. Maybe they're known for deep dives into niche subjects or the nitty-gritty details of how things work. Maybe their grasp of theological concepts—even the rather complex ones—seems effortless. Or at least easier than it is for most!

If this describes someone you know or if it describes you, it means these interests may point to the spiritual gift of knowledge. It doesn't mean someone is born knowing everything (if only). It means they have a great capacity for learning and understanding, and they may also have a desire to share that knowledge by teaching or mentoring. If you're curious, analytical, and good at synthesizing information, consider whether message of knowledge is your spiritual gift!

REFLECTION On a scale of 1 to 10, where would you rate this gift for yourself? If it's high for you, what's something you can do to sharpen this gift over the next year? No matter where you land on the scale, what's something you can do to encourage growth in this area of your life?

GIFTS: FAITH

To another faith [is given] by the same Spirit.
1 CORINTHIANS 12:9

If you're a follower of Jesus, you already have faith. That's true for all Christians. But some are specially gifted in this area. These people have a deep, supernatural trust of God's will. They are able to jump into his plan, even if they don't have a sense of where it's ultimately leading. They believe in God's goodness. They have faith he is working everything for his glory and our good, and they don't often hesitate in moving forward and leaning into his plan.

People with the gift of faith tend to be open and optimistic. They probably have strong prayer lives. They are encouragers, helping us be our best selves for God's kingdom. They are wonderful people to have in your inner circle and in your church family. And you may be one of them.

REFLECTION On a scale of 1 to 10, where would you rate this gift for yourself? If it's high for you, how can you encourage this gift to grow? If it's not as high, what are some aspects of this gift you'd like to cultivate in your life, even if it's not your spiritual gifting?

GIFTS: DISCERNMENT

To another [is given] distinguishing between spirits.

1 CORINTHIANS 12:10

Do you have a knack for seeking God's will in any given situation? This is something every one of us should do, but some people have an especially keen insight into God's plans and purposes. They are able to apply that insight on an individual level and also in a church setting.

People with the gift of discernment—or distinguishing between spirits, as it's called here—are also good at differentiating between good and evil. That may sound basic. Shouldn't we all have an idea of what's good and what's evil? But it's not always obvious. Evil can be deceptive. Sometimes things considered good or normal in our culture are contrary to the life Jesus would have us live. It can be hard to sort through the various influences pressing in on our lives and voices vying for our attention and loyalty. But those with this gift are able to tap into what Scripture says and how the Holy Spirit guides them, and apply it to what we experience today and help guide themselves and others in that truth.

REFLECTION On a scale of 1 to 10, where would you rate this gift for yourself? If it's high for you, what's something you can do to sharpen this gift over the next year? If it's lower for you, do you have trusted people in your life who are gifted in this area?

GIFTS: APOSTLE

●●●●○○○○○○

And God has placed in the church first of all apostles . . .

1 CORINTHIANS 12:28

Some of the spiritual gifts mentioned in the Bible are a little controversial today—not all Christians believe the gifts operate the same way now as they did in the early church. The gift of apostleship is one of these controversial gifts, if we're thinking of it as an office of the church.

But if we broaden *apostleship* to think about the term more generally, most Christians would probably agree there are people gifted in some of the things the early church apostles did. These are people who take an interest in taking care of people emotionally, spiritually, and physically—from making sure others have supportive people to talk to, to ensuring they have their needs met, to spending time talking to them about God and questions they might have about him and faith. Someone with a gift like this might someday help start a new community church where there's a need, or even become a pastor or head of a nonprofit organization. Or they may simply be called toward situations that allow them to take a leadership position and use their gift to spread God's love.

REFLECTION On a scale of 1 to 10, how much does this gift resonate with you? If it's on the higher end for you, this is likely the kind of gift you'll have to grow into as you get older. But what's one way you could begin to sharpen this gifting now?

GIFTS: PROPHECY

And . . . to another [is given the gift of] prophecy.

1 CORINTHIANS 12:10

This is another controversial gift, as there are Christians who believe prophecy was a skill given to the early church, and once direct prophecy wasn't needed anymore, this gift ceased. Others believe this gift still works similarly to how it did in the Old and New Testaments. Still others believe prophecy still exists, just in a different way than it used to.

We certainly won't solve a problem here that theologians have debated for many years, but we can look at a definition of prophecy that *everyone* can agree is still relevant for today.

Some people would describe this gift as God spontaneously bringing something to mind for you to share with another person. Today, this might look like praying for someone and having a message to share with them that may not even make sense to you . . . but *they* understand the meaning. This isn't the same as Old Testament prophets who spoke the authoritative words of God, but you can see how this view of prophecy would be an encouraging gift!

REFLECTION On a scale of 1 to 10, how much does this gift resonate for you? If it's on the higher side, how comfortable are you sharing the things that spontaneously come to mind? What are some ways you can continue to develop this gift, and what are some things you might want to be extra cautious of while you use this gift?

....

....

....

GIFTS: TEACHING

And God has placed in the church . . . third teachers.
1 CORINTHIANS 12:28

Even though teachers are listed right alongside two of the more controversial spiritual gifts—apostles and prophecy—everyone today agrees that the church still needs teachers and that some people are especially gifted in this area.

If this is your gift, you might already be well aware of it! Perhaps you like volunteering to help in Sunday school classes. Maybe you've taught children (or assisted those doing so) how to do new things for years. But even if you haven't done any of these things yet, you might be gifted in this area if you are especially able to share the things you've learned with others. As you've read this book (or others), have you ever felt excited to share what you read with someone else? Have you found joy in explaining a truth you uncovered or sharing an insight that encouraged you? Especially when it comes to spiritual things?

Spiritually gifted teachers tend to be disciplined and practical. Often they are organized, which helps them convey information to other people. They also get excited about sharing!

REFLECTION On a scale of 1 to 10, where would you rate this gift for yourself? If it's high for you, how can you volunteer at your church using this gift?

GIFTS: HEALING

And God has placed in the church . . . gifts of healing.

1 CORINTHIANS 12:28

The gift of healing is another controversial one. Jesus and the disciples performed miraculous healing, and at the time Paul wrote this letter to the Corinthian church, this gift still seemed to be operational, since he mentioned it as a casual fact here. Most Christians today believe God can perform miraculous healings. Whether or not he specifically gifts some to do this as the apostles did is the debate. It doesn't help that people have used the promise of having healing powers to manipulate sincere followers into giving them financial support, which further muddies the waters.

No matter what you believe when it comes to the gift of healing, we can all agree our faith can help bring God's healing into the world. So if you have ever prayed for someone's miraculous healing and that healing came to pass, you might want to research more about this gift! The gift of healing could also be interpreted as ministering to the health care needs of others. If you have a heart for this type of work, you may have a spiritual gifting in this area.

REFLECTION On a scale of 1 to 10, where would you rate this gift for yourself? Do you think the gift of healing operates today as it did in the Bible?

GIFTS: HELPING

And God has placed in the church . . . gifts . . . of helping.
1 CORINTHIANS 12:28

Helping is a spiritual gift everyone recognizes as vital to the function of any church community. People who have the gift of helping tend to volunteer for support roles. They often work behind the scenes, making sure all tasks are completed in a timely manner, events run smoothly, and everything is functioning the way it's supposed to. Churches (and pretty much anything that needs organizing) would have a much harder time getting things done without those who have the gift of helping.

Those with the gift of helping are especially skilled at bearing others' burdens in the way we're all called to (Galatians 6:2). They are often friendly, dependable, reliable, and humble individuals. They don't usually seek the spotlight and are happy to work quietly, so sometimes they don't get the recognition they deserve. But anyone who has ever planned an event or had to make a church service run smoothly knows how vital gifted helpers are.

REFLECTION On a scale of 1 to 10, how much does this gift resonate for you? If it's high on your list, I'm guessing you already volunteer a lot, but is there a way to up your level of responsibility to continue growing in this gift?

GIFTS: GUIDANCE

●●●●●●●●●○○

And God has placed in the church . . . gifts . . . of guidance.

1 CORINTHIANS 12:28

The gift of guidance is also translated as management, leadership, or governance. Basically, that means people born with this spiritual gift have the ability to figure things out and be the one in control. They are probably good at strategizing, delegating, and organizing events. We often find those with this gift on leadership teams, or we might find them at the head of the line when someone asks for volunteers to help with an event. People with this gift are vital to many church functions.

In order to carry out the many ministries of a church, or even carry out things outside the church, it's important to have both leaders and helpers. Those with the gift of guidance often have the vision for planning and directing, while those gifted as helpers are able to execute the work required to make those plans come to life. It's another example of how God harmoniously equips his followers to work together!

REFLECTION On a scale of 1 to 10, where do you think your administrative gifting lands? If the number is on the higher end of the scale, can you think of a few ways you might grow this gift over the next several months?

GIFTS: TONGUES

●●●●●○○○○○

To another [is given the gift of] speaking in different kinds of
tongues, and to still another the interpretation of tongues.
1 CORINTHIANS 12:10

Of all the spiritual gifts mentioned in the New Testament,
tongues is probably the most controversial of all. This gift has
been understood to mean many different things over the centuries, and there is little agreement among Christians about
whether it's still operational in the modern church.

First Corinthians 12:30 mentions interpretation of tongues
alongside speaking in tongues, so that seems those two things
worked together in the early church. The Greek word translated
"tongues" here literally means *languages*, so many people take
this to mean someone is supernaturally able to speak a language
they don't otherwise know in order to share the gospel (like in
Acts 2). Some also take this gift to mean being especially adept
at translation work or learning other languages with the purpose of sharing the gospel.

If you're interested in the subject, or think it might apply to
you, there are many commentaries that can help you explore the
various viewpoints surrounding the gift of tongues.

REFLECTION What do you think about the controversy around some of
these spiritual gifts? If we think of tongues as having a gift for languages,
do you think this is a gift you possess? How might you use it to further the
kingdom of God?

GIFTS: EVANGELISM

●●●●●●●●●○

So Christ himself gave the apostles, the prophets, the evangelists, the pastors and teachers, to equip his people for works of service, so that the body of Christ may be built up.

EPHESIANS 4:11–12

The gift of evangelism is crucial to the health and growth of the church. Someone who has evangelism as a spiritual gift is particularly good at sharing the good news of Jesus with other people who don't yet know him. They are often able to meet people right where they're at, not shying away from those living a life of unrepentant sin. They may also have a knack for explaining things in an approachable yet profound, life-changing way.

Those who have this gift are often very good at building relationships with others. They usually don't mind talking to strangers, and they usually aren't overly worried about offending people if they talk about Jesus (not that they're rude!). Evangelists are often open and bold individuals, with a warm personality. And even if this isn't one of your core gifts, it's one we can all try to use in some way with the people we get to know!

REFLECTION On a scale of 1 to 10, how much does this gift resonate for you? Have you used this gift much in the past? If not, what are some ways you can expand your evangelistic reach?

. . . .

. . . .

. . . .

. . . .

. . . .

. . . .

GIFTS: SERVING

If [your gift] is serving, then serve.
ROMANS 12:7

Serving is a gift that, like the closely related gift of helping, sometimes goes unnoticed. In fact, those without this gift might find service-related tasks boring. But those with the gift of serving understand doing small tasks and making sure things get done is important. For example, getting clearly worded invitations out on time is vital, preparing food and entertainment for everyone coming is important, and cleaning up afterward is essential. Or if we think about the church, there needs to be someone who cleans the building, or does office work, or makes sure there are caretakers in the nursery and refreshments for communal time after the service. Those with a gift of service not only volunteer to help, they find joy in the work.

These kinds of tasks may not look spiritual on the outside because they're so practical. But it's the spirit with which a server approaches these tasks that makes them as spiritual as any other work we've discussed. It's the Christlike attitude of humility the server brings into their work that elevates it. Those with this gift are hardworking, reliable, and willing.

REFLECTION On a scale of 1 to 10, how highly would you rate this gift for yourself? Even if it's not high on your list, we're all called to have a servant's heart in the church. What are some ways you can cultivate this in your life, no matter how highly you rate it for yourself?

GIFTS: EXHORTATION

If [your gift] is to encourage, then give encouragement.
ROMANS 12:8

The gift of encouragement—or *exhortation*, as it's sometimes called—is really important to the health of the church body, and to humanity in general. Encouragement isn't just about being everyone's cheerleader, though encouragers are definitely good at cheering others on. It's also about dialing in to the emotional needs of others. When people need comfort, someone with the gift of exhortation can meet that need. When someone needs to be challenged or held accountable, an encourager is often the right person for the job.

A person with the gift of exhortation is supportive but challenging. They're empathetic and trustworthy, unafraid to call someone out in biblical love, but they're also sensitive. These supportive brothers and sisters in Christ are essential to the emotional and spiritual well-being of a church body.

REFLECTION On a scale of 1 to 10, how much does the gift of encouragement resonate with you? If it's high on your list, what's one way you can use your gift to show love to a fellow believer this week?

GIFTS: GIVING

●●●●●●○○○○

If [your gift] is giving, then give generously.
ROMANS 12:8

Everyone is called to give, but did you know giving is a specific spiritual gift some people have? Those with this gift probably don't even need to be reminded of the second half of this verse. Giving generously comes naturally (or supernaturally!) to them. They may even manage their resources specifically so they can give to others as much as possible. In a world that places a lot of importance and security on our material possessions, this is an amazing gift!

Givers are not only great at picking out the right present or helping support charities, many are also particularly good at planning ministries and outreaches that meet the physical needs of the communities around them. Meeting physical needs is important, as it often paves the way for spiritual needs to be addressed next. These ministries show those who don't yet know Jesus that Christ's followers care about the whole person—physical, emotional, and spiritual.

Those with this gift are often generous, charitable, and responsible. They are usually sensible in their planning but extravagant in their willingness to share.

REFLECTION On a scale of 1 to 10, how would you rate this gift for yourself? Do you have an easy time giving and sharing, or is it really difficult for you? What's one way you can give generously over the next week?

GIFTS: LEADERSHIP

If [your gift] is to lead, do it diligently.
ROMANS 12:8

This gift is pretty self-explanatory! We know exactly what leadership looks like—helping to determine a vision for the group, directing others in how to reach those goals, and encouraging those under your care to be the best they can. Leadership positions also come with a lot of responsibility, as the health and well-being of the group rests on your shoulders. It can be daunting, even for those called into leadership roles.

It's interesting to note that Paul told leaders to lead diligently. So if we get the idea that being a leader is about being the loudest and pushiest person in the room, we need to think again. True leaders are to be careful, judicious, and concerned with the flock they're shepherding, making sure everything is in accordance with God's will. Those with this spiritual gift tend to be visionaries who are persuasive and inspiring but also trustworthy. Many leaders are also gifted administrators, though some are called more into pastoral care, or similar positions in the corporate world where they can lead well and make a positive difference.

REFLECTION On a scale of 1 to 10, where would you rate this gift for yourself? Have you ever felt like you might be called to a leadership position in the future? What's something you can do now to grow your skills as a leader, or lead in some way today?

GIFTS: MERCY

If [your gift] is to show mercy, do it cheerfully.
ROMANS 12:8

Those with the gift of mercy are blessings to the people around them, both in the church and outside of it. That's because they have a special ability to notice others' pain. Not only are they aware of the pain and suffering around them, they seek to take action. As Paul's encouragement here suggests, they do this cheerfully, meeting the physical, emotional, or spiritual needs of people who need it most.

People with the gift of mercy are compassionate and kind. They care about the disenfranchised and marginalized. They don't flinch away from circumstances that make others uncomfortable. You might find them caring for those who are sick or recovering in the hospital. They might attend to the needs of people who are terminally ill. They might minister to individuals who are unhomed or are unable to feed or clothe themselves. Anywhere there is a great, pressing need, you are likely to find someone with the gift of mercy.

REFLECTION On a scale of 1 to 10, how much does this gift resonate for you? If it's high on your list, have you ever thought about joining a ministry in your community or looking into a career that supports others? If this isn't a natural gifting for you, what are some ways you can grow in your compassion and displays of mercy?

GIFTS: HOSPITALITY

●●●●●○○○○

Share with the Lord's people who are
in need. Practice hospitality.

ROMANS 12:13

Hospitality was very culturally important in the ancient Near East of the Bible, but it's also a specific spiritual gift some people have. These people cheerfully, willingly open their homes to others, hosting gatherings and making others feel welcome. It's not about being the perfect host or hostess. It's about making people feel valued, seen, and wanted. It's giving others a sense of home away from home.

Those with this gift are often outgoing, inviting, and sociable. They have a knack for making others feel at ease, even if the situation would normally be uncomfortable. This gift can also extend beyond someone's own home into places like the church. Hospitable people make good greeters. They're excellent on teams designed to help new members of a church, community, or any type of group feel welcomed.

REFLECTION On a scale of 1 to 10, how well does this gift resonate for you? Is your house often the place where all your friends congregate? Is your family everyone else's "second family"? If so, consider whether this might be your spiritual gift!

TABITHA: ALWAYS DOING GOOD

In Joppa there was a disciple named Tabitha (in Greek her name is Dorcas); she was always doing good and helping the poor.
ACTS 9:36

If we're looking for a prime scriptural example of someone who used her gifts for the glory of God, we need look no further than Tabitha. She was a devout follower of Jesus, and she spent her time making clothes for widows and the poor—two marginalized groups in her society.

Tabitha might have had the gift of helping or serving. It seems clear she had the gift of mercy, looking after those whose position in society was tenuous. When Tabitha died suddenly, people who had received her kindness and mercy mourned deeply, and Peter was compelled to raise Tabitha from the dead. Imagine the rejoicing when she got up from her deathbed!

Tabitha is a wonderful example of serving those in need and showing love through our works. Our actions don't save us (nor do they have to be big or perfect), but they do show people the heart Jesus has for them. And learning this truth might help lead someone else on the road to salvation.

REFLECTION Do you have a practical gift like Tabitha's (such as making clothes) that can be used to express one of your spiritual gifts (like mercy)? Think about the ways some of your talents and interests might work together with your spiritual gifts.

TABITHA: HUMBLE SERVICE

When he [Peter] arrived he was taken upstairs to the room. All the widows stood around him, crying and showing him the robes and other clothing that Dorcas [Tabitha] had made while she was still with them.

ACTS 9:39

Something else that's cool about Tabitha is she seems to have put a lot of time and care into her work. The widows mourning her death made a point to show Peter Tabitha's craftsmanship as they explained the loss of their friend. She didn't simply distribute castoffs or hand-me-downs (though there's nothing wrong with clothing donations, of course!). She took time and care to make new garments for those in need.

Tabitha shows us how to strive for excellence while keeping our hearts in the right place. Surely the quality of her work mattered to her. But she didn't make clothing to feel more accomplished, to prove her worth, or to win favor with influential people. She didn't even do it to make a profit. Instead, she served like the hands and feet of Jesus, humbly but with excellence, using her talents as best she could so people saw how much they were valued and loved.

REFLECTION If you read Tabitha's whole story in Acts 9, you might note Luke never recorded anything she said. Instead, we know her character from what those who knew her say about her. What do you hope others might say about you?

STRONG IN WEAKNESS

●●●●●○○○○○

But we have this treasure in jars of clay to show that this
all-surpassing power is from God and not from us.
2 CORINTHIANS 4:7

We have talked about our weaknesses—admitting them, owning them, understanding our worth is not impacted by them.
We've talked about our strengths—acknowledging the source,
keeping our hearts in check, and using our God-given gifts for
building the kingdom.

But there's another concept that is perhaps unique to
Christians: we are strong *in* our weakness. Huh? How can that
be possible? By definition, weaknesses make us weaker, don't
they? In one sense, yes, of course that's true. But in another very
real sense, our weaknesses allow God to shine brighter.

When we acknowledge our weaknesses and ask God to fill
our gaps—to help us with something we know we can't do—it
allows his glory to be displayed even better than when we're
able to do something using our own power. Not only does it
allow wonderful things to be accomplished, when God operates through our weaknesses, there is no question about who is
doing the work, and all glory goes to him—appropriately!

REFLECTION Can you think of a time when God shined brightest through
your gaps? Or is this the first time you've considered asking him to work
that way in your life? If he were to work through one of your weaknesses
today, what might that look like for you?

FLAWED HUMANS

"The greatest among you should be like the youngest,
and the one who rules like the one who serves."

LUKE 22:26

If we need encouragement to allow God to work through our weaknesses, we don't have to look any further than our Bibles. We're going to examine a few specific stories in days to come, but needless to say, every single one of God's heroes in the Bible was a flawed human (except Jesus). They were all loved and used by God. But not a single one was perfect. In fact, God often called them to work they *didn't* feel particularly equipped for.

If you read the Hall of Faith chapter (Hebrews 11), you'll see a list of some biblical heroes. If we had only those snippets about them, we might get the impression these people were angelic beings whom God loved and used because they were so awesome. And they *were* awesome in many ways. But we also get a fuller story about each of them when we read the Old Testament. And every single hero in Hebrews made big mistakes. God used them all mightily anyway, and that should be a big encouragement to us!

REFLECTION Have you ever thought about how flawed many of our biblical heroes are? Do you have a favorite figure from the Bible? If so, who and why does that person's story appeal to you so much?

GRATITUDE AND HUMILITY

Humble yourselves before the Lord, and he will lift you up.

JAMES 4:10

Our weaknesses allow God's glory to shine all the brighter, but they can help us grow in other ways. Being aware of our weaknesses encourages gratitude for the strength God provides. When he shows up in a big way to work through our weakness—wow! We have no question he's shown up in our lives and cares, and our usual response is thankfulness. Being weak in some areas also provides a contrast to the areas where we're strong, and that can also encourage gratitude in our hearts for what we've been given. Praise God that he's both gifted us *and* reminded us to rely on him!

Recognizing our weak areas also continuously reminds us we depend upon God. We can't do it all on our own, no matter how much our perfectionistic hearts might love that! We need his grace, his power, his ability to help us—in our own lives and as we work to build his kingdom.

REFLECTION What are some ways your weaknesses have helped you grow in gratitude or humility?

LOOKING TO NEW EARTH

●●●●●●●○○○

"And I confer on you a kingdom, just as my Father conferred one on me, so that you may eat and drink at my table in my kingdom and sit on thrones, judging the twelve tribes of Israel."

LUKE 22:29–30

Christians often spend a lot of time thinking about and talking about heaven. And with good reason. Heaven is a somewhat mysterious, intriguing concept—God's dwelling place, where his will is done completely.

But sometimes in our wondering about heaven, we overlook new earth—when heaven and Earth will be renewed at the last resurrection, the final state of redeemed humanity. We don't have a ton of info about new earth either, but we know it will be amazing. There will be no pain or tears. No illness, no sin, and no weakness. Only perfect worship of God for eternity.

Here on Earth, we recognize the importance of our weaknesses, where we have growing to do. We have suffering to endure here. But our weaknesses in this life can also prompt us to remember we have a better future ahead. While we might not enjoy having weaknesses (or pain or suffering), we can rest in the knowledge that someday we'll be in a place with no pressures or worries, and that's a wonderful future to look forward to!

REFLECTION Have you thought much about new earth before? Imagine our world renewed and restored—sin-free and saturated with worship of God. What are you most looking forward to?

INCREASING TRUST

But he said to me, "My grace is sufficient for you, for
my power is made perfect in weakness." Therefore I
will boast all the more gladly about my weaknesses,
so that Christ's power may rest on me.

2 CORINTHIANS 12:9

Boasting about our weaknesses?! Paul mastered what many perfectionists hope to achieve someday—truly not being ashamed of our weaknesses and understanding how they can magnify God's glory when we allow him to work through us.

But even if we find it a struggle to feel so secure in our weaknesses (at least for now!), we can still learn to allow our weaknesses to increase our trust in God. We can appreciate the opportunities God puts in our laps—those that use our gifts and play to our strengths, but perhaps even more so those that fall outside our comfort zones. Often those are the experiences that prompt us to trust God the most, encourage us to grow the most, and nudge us farther down the path of sanctification.

REFLECTION Is there a time you can remember God placing an opportunity in your lap that felt uncomfortable—like it was something you might not be fully equipped to do? How did you respond? How do you think you would respond if that same opportunity were placed in your lap today?

THE LEAST OF THESE

If anyone has material possessions and sees a brother or sister in need but has no pity on them, how can the love of God be in that person? Dear children, let us not love with words or speech but with actions and in truth.

1 JOHN 3:17–18

The Bible is very clear about how we should treat those in need. The marginalized and disenfranchised, the desperate, the forsaken—we are to show these people special care. We shouldn't look past them, as is often our instinct. We shouldn't ignore their needs or overlook their pleas. Instead, we should pay extra attention to them and how we can offer help and support.

Maybe you've been in need in the past. Maybe you still are. But even if you've never counted yourself among the groups Paul is referring to, your weaknesses should help you empathize with them. That's right—being weak within ourselves not only increases our dependence on God, it helps us to show mercy to those who need it. There's no room for feeling superior when we recognize our own frailty, and this allows space for compassion to grow in our hearts.

REFLECTION Do you have a gift for showing compassion and mercy to those in need, or is that a more difficult habit for you to practice? What's one way you can help the needy in your community this week?

ENDURANCE

●●●●●●○○○○

You need to persevere so that when you have done the
will of God, you will receive what he has promised.
HEBREWS 10:36

Physical, emotional, and spiritual weaknesses can be exhausting. It's easy to become frustrated with ourselves and our
inability to feel better, do better, *be* better. Especially when all
our perfectionist wiring is telling us we not only need to be better, but absolutely perfect. It's a draining merry-go-round—one
we'd like to jump off, please and thank you.

But this exhausting merry-go-round actually serves a purpose in our lives. Though it may feel like we're moving in circles,
if we are focused on continuing to grow in Christlikeness and
building God's kingdom, all while dealing with our various
weaknesses, we are actually gaining strength and endurance.
Not the kind of strength that erases our weaknesses, but the
kind of strength that reminds us we can be used despite our
weaknesses. That we are valued by God. That he loves us and
sees us, even as we struggle. When we persevere and don't give
up, it builds a whole new kind of inner strength.

REFLECTION Have you ever been through a hard time and now, looking
back, you can see it was important in building your endurance? What were
some things you learned or ways you grew during that time?

....

....

....

....

....

....

I can do all this through him [Christ] who gives me strength.

PHILIPPIANS 4:13

This is a verse Christians love to quote, and who can blame us? It's a great verse, and it seems like such an empowering statement. In fact, sometimes people alter it a bit to say, "I can do all things through him." But Paul was actually pretty specific. He said he can do all *this*. So what is *this*? The answer lies in the previous verse.

Paul said in verse 12 that he lived in plenty and in want. He learned to be content in every situation, no matter the circumstances. The key, he discovered, is to rely on God's strength. Rather than a blanket statement that Paul could do anything he wanted because God was on his side, he was instead stating he could be content in any situation because God gave him the strength to do so.

Paul had his priorities straight. And we can too. When we rely on God's strength, not our own, we can face any circumstance and find contentment.

REFLECTION Is there a situation in your life right now that feels really overwhelming or scary? Maybe there's something that's simply uncomfortable or less than ideal. Today, pay for God's strength to fill you and help you find peace in that situation.

BEING THERE

Rejoice with those who rejoice; mourn with those who mourn.
ROMANS 12:15

No one is born an invincible superhero. We all have struggles, challenges we must overcome, and other things we will never accomplish in this life. When we're in the midst of battling through those trials, we might think about how much better off we'd be if we *had* been born invincible and invulnerable.

And yet, there is a beauty in the way God has knitted our broken world back together. In our weaknesses and struggles, we simply have to rely on others for support. We long for—and desperately need—community. We need other people who will support, encourage, and challenge us. Similarly, we need to be that person for others. God made us dependent on each other and on him. He created beauty from our broken, needy state.

REFLECTION Can you remember a time where you relied on the strength of those around you to get you through? Or have you been that person for someone else? What did these experiences show you about community?

But Moses said, "Pardon your servant,
Lord. Please send someone else."

EXODUS 4:13

Confession: my perfectionist heart feels bad doing this. I'm going to be calling out some of our biblical heroes and quoting their moments of greatest doubt, biggest failures, hugest mistakes. And it feels *wrong*. I'm sorry, guys!

But the truth is these moments are included in Scripture for a reason. We're taught an important lesson when we look at Moses—arguably the most important figure in the Old Testament—and note how he begged God to send someone else to do the work. God had just instructed him to speak to Pharaoh, promising it would result in freedom for Moses's people. And Moses said, "Please, not me. I can't."

It's so . . . relatable. Especially because it's tempting to view Moses as far above us, not relatable in the least. It's easy to view him as someone who was strong, who had a special relationship with God and could handle difficult people. And he did have those qualities, yet he had this moment where he felt too weak for the task God set before him. And God still saw the task accomplished (sending Moses help via Aaron) and continued to have a special relationship with Moses for years to come.

REFLECTION When you think of Moses, what descriptors come to mind? How would you describe his life story?

....

....

....

STRONG IN WEAKNESS: GIDEON

"Pardon me, my lord," Gideon replied, "but how can I save Israel? My clan is the weakest in Manasseh, and I am the least in my family."
JUDGES 6:15

Gideon was a great leader during the era of the judges. We know him as someone who was courageous in battle, and as a judge who delivered his people from the Midianites. So it might seem unbelievable that the verse above was Gideon's response when the Lord first called him.

Not only did he tell God he'd called the wrong person, Gideon then requested multiple miracles before he was ready to embrace what God was asking him to do. And when Gideon relented (hesitantly), God trimmed down the size of Gideon's army before allowing them into battle. It seems he was really driving home the point that as long as Gideon was faithful in doing what God asked of him, the victory would surely come—through God's strength. Gideon is a perfect example of God showing his power through the weakness of a flawed but faithful human—and that human then relying on God and his power to overcome their doubts and go on to do great things.

REFLECTION How would you feel if God asked you to do something that made you nervous and then stripped away the majority of the resources you thought you needed to complete the task? Even though Gideon showed doubt, what does he also demonstrate in this story?

STRONG IN WEAKNESS: PAUL

But for that very reason I was shown mercy so that in me, the worst of sinners, Christ Jesus might display his immense patience as an example for those who would believe in him and receive eternal life.

1 TIMOTHY 1:16

Paul wrote these pretty profound words to his protégé, Timothy. He said God selected him to do immense work (evangelism, church planting, pastoral care—with mortal danger at every turn) *because* he was the worst of sinners.

Paul had adamantly persecuted Christ-followers before his conversion experience. He was an unlikely choice for the work he would end up doing on behalf of the kingdom. Yet Paul said he was chosen for precisely this reason. Paul's weakness allowed God's patience and grace to be on full display. His weakness became a strength when God displayed his power through it. And because of this weakness-turned-strength, Paul said his living example of God's goodness would bring others to faith, allowing them to receive eternal life.

REFLECTION Has God ever powerfully met you in one of your weak spots? Has there been a moment when he shined through those weak places and used your vulnerability to build his kingdom?

STRONG IN WEAKNESS: ABRAHAM

By faith Abraham, when called to go to a place he would later receive as his inheritance, obeyed and went, even though he did not know where he was going.
HEBREWS 11:8

This verse highlights Abraham's great faith. He walked closely with God, and he obeyed when God told him to go. He believed, even when God's promises seemed impossible. He was and is the father of many nations. He is the spiritual father to Jesus-followers. If Moses is arguably the most important figure in the Old Testament, Abraham certainly makes the top five.

But Abraham had a problem with lying. He twice told powerful men his wife was just his sister because he was afraid he would be harmed if they knew the truth. In doing so, he actually put her at risk and brought a whole cascade of consequences down on other people. Not a great move.

Abraham later made other mistakes when it came to his family. He wasn't perfect. And though God wasn't pleased with some of Abraham's choices, he still maintained a special relationship with this man who would become the father of our faith. This is a powerful testimony to us, Abraham's fellow imperfect humans. God still chooses us, and God will still use us!

REFLECTION How does it feel to know the Bible sometimes points out the weaknesses of our greatest heroes? How does that affect the way you feel about your own imperfections?

●●●●●●●●●

David burned with anger against the man and said to
Nathan, "As surely as the LORD lives, the man who did
this must die! He must pay for that lamb four times
over, because he did such a thing and had no pity."
Then Nathan said to David, "You are the man!"

2 SAMUEL 12:5-7

Oof. This moment in David's life is painful to read. He was a
man after God's own heart—a forerunner of Jesus himself. And
yet David did a terrible thing. He had one of his most trusted
soldiers killed to cover up the fact that he'd taken this man's
wife and gotten her pregnant. He compounded sin upon sin, and
it cost an innocent man's life. Later it cost the life of David and
Bathsheba's infant son.

When the prophet Nathan confronted David, David
repented, but he did not escape consequences. This moment of
great weakness in his life serves as a powerful example to us,
millennia later. Through David's sin, the Lord shows us we can
be deeply imperfect and still loved by God. We learn about God's
forgiveness, even as we see that forgiveness does not always
erase the repercussions.

REFLECTION Have you ever sinned in such a way you wondered if you'd
be defined by it? Know that forgiveness is available for the truly repentant!
Think about the ways God has shown up in your life since the sin you worried might mark you forever.

"Just as the Son of Man did not come to be served, but to serve, and to give his life as a ransom for many."
MATTHEW 20:28

Now, before anyone panics that Jesus is showing up in a section on weakness, I'll explain! Jesus did not have moral weakness in the way Abraham or David did. He did not doubt like Moses or Gideon. He certainly was never "the worst of sinners," like Paul, since he never sinned. And still, he is perhaps the best, strongest, clearest example of strength in weakness.

I'm talking, of course, about the weakness of a human body. Jesus, fully God in his nature, chose to clothe himself in a human body with all its frailty, vulnerability, and feebleness. Imagine *being God* and making that choice. But he did what was necessary to reconcile humanity, and taking on physical human weakness was part of that. He had to be vulnerable to death so that we might live.

REFLECTION Have you ever considered the fact that God himself became human? This doctrine is called the *incarnation*, and it's wild to think about! What does it say about God that he chose to do this?

EMBRACING OUR WEAKNESS

●●●●●●●●●

Trust in the LORD with all your heart and lean not on
your own understanding; in all your ways submit
to him, and he will make your paths straight.

PROVERBS 3:5–6

Here's an important truth: you don't have to have everything
figured out. I know—this is *shocking* to the perfectionist's soul.
But it's true. We can and should embrace our weaknesses.

Not only is it okay, it's *necessary* to acknowledge we don't
have it all figured out. Of course we should give our best effort
to the tasks set before us. We're called to do good works in God's
name, and we're supposed to be living, breathing reflections of
God's love. But we are limited. Small. Imperfect. No matter how
much planning, training, or (over)thinking we do, there's still
a good chance there's something we missed or a mistake to be
made. Or it's a situation that we simply can't overcome ourselves
because it's just not humanly possible.

That truth is empowering. Because it means God doesn't
expect us to *be* him. He simply expects us to *trust* him.

REFLECTION Imagine inhaling all your insecurities. Hold that breath, that
heavy weight, in your lungs for a few seconds. Now release the breath
and imagine handing control over to God. Write down your biggest current
concerns—the things you definitely don't have figured out—and give them
over to God. Put them in his wise, powerful hands.

EMBRACING WEAKNESS, BANISHING SIN

"If my people, who are called by my name, will humble themselves and pray and seek my face and turn from their wicked ways, then I will hear from heaven, and I will forgive their sin and will heal their land."

2 CHRONICLES 7:14

There is a fine line when it comes to acknowledging our weaknesses. It can easily lead to throwing up our hands and adopting a powerless stance against sin. There is perhaps less danger of this happening when I'm speaking to perfectionists—those with a predisposition to try their very hardest and who sometimes struggle to cope when something isn't flawless.

But still, we are all human, and humans are vulnerable to sin. It's important we search our hearts on this matter. *Not* to condemn ourselves but to draw closer to God and allow him to continue shaping us to be more and more like Jesus. When we sin, God wants us to repent so he can forgive us, because he is merciful and loving.

REFLECTION We know everyone sins. Is there a sin that's become such a habit, you're barely aware of it anymore? Ask God to reveal any areas that need your special attention.

HEALTHY PERFECTIONISM

Whatever you do, work at it with all your heart, as working for the Lord, not for human masters, since you know that you will receive an inheritance from the Lord as a reward. It is the Lord Christ you are serving.

COLOSSIANS 3:23–24

At this point, we've talked a lot about the ills of perfectionism. So how can I put *healthy* and *perfectionism* next to each other?

That's a great question. One way to approach it is by knowing God created you, me, and anyone reading this book with a certain set of traits. But because we live in a broken world, how you use those traits may have gotten twisted up. They may have led you down a path of perfectionism, but that doesn't mean the traits themselves are bad. For example, it's a safe bet you care about excellence. I'd also guess you're a hard worker—diligent and thoughtful. These are wonderful traits, and we can use them in healthy ways that benefit ourselves and those around us.

"Healthy perfectionism" may be an oxymoron. But the pursuit of excellence to God's glory is certainly not. You can be *you*, using your traits well, and reject the toxicity of perfectionism at the same time!

REFLECTION When you think about who you are as a student (or as an athlete, artist, or whatever you do), what qualities come to mind? What have your teachers, coaches, and mentors said about you over the years? Write out a list and think about the positive sides of those traits.

ISAIAH THE HIGH ACHIEVER

Then I heard the voice of the Lord saying, "Whom shall I send?
And who will go for us?" And I said, "Here am I. Send me!"
ISAIAH 6:8

While the Bible gives us many necessary, important examples of
people's great failures, highlighting the fact we're all imperfect,
it also gives us several examples of individuals who were high
achievers. They embody traits we've looked at—diligence, con-
scientiousness, hard work—and they're faithful servants of God
on top of it. These examples give us a blueprint for biblical high
achievers, and they remind us it's okay to be us!

Isaiah is one example. He was one of Judah's greatest
prophets. Many of the messianic prophecies we know well were
given to Isaiah. He served God during the reigns of some wicked
kings, and he remained steadfast and faithful.

One of his most amazing moments of excellence was his
response to hearing the Lord call him to prophetic ministry.
God asked, "Whom shall I send?" And unlike Moses or Gideon
(sorry, guys!), Isaiah immediately responded, "I'm here! Send
me!" His willingness is a shining example of how to respond to
God's prompting in our lives.

REFLECTION We don't often get moments as dramatic as Isaiah's calling. But was there a time you felt God prompting you to do something to
serve him or those around you? How did you respond? How do you hope
to respond next time?

KING JOSIAH

> Josiah was eight years old when he became king, and he
> reigned in Jerusalem thirty-one years. . . . He did what was right
> in the eyes of the LORD and followed completely the ways of
> his father David, not turning aside to the right or to the left.
>
> **2 KINGS 22:1–2**

This endorsement of Josiah is pretty amazing when you consider how few kings have things like that said about them in Scripture. Most of Judah's kings (and all of Israel's) are said to have done "evil in the eyes of the LORD." It's safe to say we can think of Josiah as a high achiever when it comes to ruling God's people.

We're going to look at several lessons from Josiah that should be particularly encouraging to recovering perfectionists. The first is that our heritage doesn't dictate our future. There were some good kings in Josiah's family line, but the last good king, Hezekiah, ruled several generations back. In fact, Josiah's grandfather, Manasseh, is singled out as the king who led Judah away from God. In spite of wicked rulers for two generations before Josiah took over, he broke the cycle and returned the nation to worshiping God.

REFLECTION Sometimes familial pressure—whether intentional or not—can lead us to develop perfectionistic tendencies. Do you think this has played a role for you? If so, how?

JOSIAH'S REPENTANCE

When the king heard the words of the Book of the Law, he tore his robes.
2 KINGS 22:11

This moment is so relatable. Perhaps it's weird to imagine we can relate to an ancient king who ruled thousands of years ago. Though do you recall the moment you first became aware of your own sin? Perhaps you were very young when this happened. Maybe it's been more recent. But that moment—recognizing our need for reconciliation with God—is what Josiah was experiencing here, and we've all been there.

This healthy, high-achieving king shows us a wonderful example of humility and proper response when we encounter our own sin. Josiah clearly wanted to do the right thing and was what we might call a "good person." But he didn't react defensively here, insisting he was doing well for himself and didn't need God's law. He recognized he fell short of God's standard, and he mourned. Then he made some big changes in his kingdom to correct course! Likewise, recognizing our errors and being repentant is part of keeping a healthy mindset.

REFLECTION Can you remember the moment sin first became real for you? Have you generally understood this concept as long as you can remember, or did you have a big *whoa* moment like Josiah?

JOSIAH'S SUCCESS

●●●●●●●●●

Neither before nor after Josiah was there a king like him who turned to the LORD as he did—with all his heart and with all his soul and with all his strength, in accordance with all the Law of Moses.

2 KINGS 23:25

Examples like Josiah, beautifully highlighted in Scripture, teach us something really important: success in itself is not bad or wrong.

Josiah had a very specific, important job set before him. He was to lead the kingdom of Judah, taking over at a time when Judah had strayed from the Lord for two generations. The task set before him was huge, and the consequences of failure would have echoes into eternity. Josiah's success was crucial and, with the Lord's help, he accomplished the task set before him.

Josiah's story teaches us that when our hearts are bowed before God and we're setting ourselves to the tasks he puts before us, we don't need to fear success. We can reject perfectionism while pursuing excellence in a healthy manner, just like Josiah did.

REFLECTION When you think about the things in your life right now, are there some that stand out as tasks God has placed before you? We all have tasks we simply must do, but which ones feel like they could have significant meaning in your life?

JOSIAH'S LEGACY

Jehoiakim was twenty-five years old when he became
king, and he reigned in Jerusalem eleven years.
He did evil in the eyes of the LORD his God.

2 CHRONICLES 36:5

Jehoiakim was Josiah's son, and succeeded him on the throne.
We might wonder how the son of one of Judah's very best kings
could turn away from the Lord so completely. After all the work
Josiah did to return God's people to his proper worship, why
would it last for only one generation?

    We learn a hard but crucial lesson from this next chapter in
the story. Josiah could only do his very best at *his* own work. He
was not responsible for his son's choices. As much as Josiah was
able to reject the wicked heritage handed to him, Jehoiakim was
able to reject the godly one handed to him. While it would have
been wonderful for Jehoiakim to follow in his father's godly
footsteps, Josiah's legacy as a faithful king—based on his own
choices—remains intact, no matter what happened with those
who came after him.

REFLECTION Have you ever considered what kind of legacy you'll leave
behind? What sort of things will you want to be said of you? What are some
steps you can take now to build that kind of legacy?

Finally, brothers and sisters, whatever is true, whatever is noble, whatever is right, whatever is pure, whatever is lovely, whatever is admirable—if anything is excellent or praiseworthy—think about such things.

PHILIPPIANS 4:8

Maybe we're convinced pursuing excellence is a good thing. And hopefully we're convinced toxic perfectionism is a bad thing. But perhaps you're wondering how we can become high achievers without falling into a perfectionistic trap.

First, hear this truth: God created *you* on purpose. Your unique personality traits, gifts, and strengths were created by God when he knitted you together. Second, he made you wonderfully. Nothing in creation is perfect anymore, but many things are wonderful, including you.

As we pursue excellence *and* health, think about those wonderful traits. That attention to detail that used to notice every flaw? Work on using that trait to detect the beauty and goodness around you, to recognize your growth, to see things others do and thank them for work others may not notice. If we keep everything true and praiseworthy in view, we can shift our entire focus while proudly embracing who we are.

REFLECTION What are some traits you've struggled most with? Make a list, and then think of a positive way you can use each one. If you get stuck, flip back to the start of this book, where we compared perfectionists to high achievers.

HOW GOD SEES US: FALLEN

As for you, you were dead in your transgressions and sins.
EPHESIANS 2:1

When reframing our view of ourselves—working on crafting a truthful, healthy self-image—it's important to ask ourselves how God sees us. In fact, this may be the *most* important question we ask ourselves. There are plenty of self-help books out there that will encourage us to work on our self-esteem. But if they don't square up with what Scripture says about our identity, then we've missed the point by a mile.

Now, this first aspect of the way God sees us might sound negative. He sees us as fallen creatures. That's not a good thing, of course, but it's really important to understand so we can fully grasp everything else God says about us.

We're sinners. We have fallen short. We are not the perfect creations God originally intended us to be. This should bring us to a place of humility, but not shame and hopelessness. There is such good news to come in the next few days!

REFLECTION When you contemplate this important part of how God sees us, how does it make you feel?

A LOSING BATTLE

Day 236

You who are trying to be justified by the law have been alienated from Christ; you have fallen away from grace.

GALATIANS 5:4

More than anyone else—more than any of us could possibly imagine—God sees and understands the losing battle we human beings face in trying to be perfect. The weaknesses we try to conceal? He knows them all. The failures we wish we could forget? He knew about them before they even occurred. There is no picture we can paint, no image we can try to put forth, of our own efforts that will ever fool God.

Attempting to justify ourselves by our works is a war we'll never win, and God alone sees the depths of how fruitless it is to try. Because he is so intimately familiar with each of us, he would be the first to tell us that striving for perfection under our own steam is only going to result in stress, feelings of failure, and a negative view of the good things we *are* capable of.

I know I promised it would get more hopeful. We're almost there!

REFLECTION Spend a few moments in prayer today speaking to the God who sees you. Nothing is hidden, so whatever you want to confess or ask him, whatever praise you'd like to shout, go for it!

HOPE

●●●●●●●●●●

Day 237

For in Christ Jesus neither circumcision nor uncircumcision has any value. The only thing that counts is faith expressing itself through love.
GALATIANS 5:6

Okay, we've gotten to the good part. Because of how God rightly sees us—fallen, deeply imperfect, with no hope of changing that on our own merit—he sent Jesus to redeem us and the Holy Spirit to help us change. His perfect and complete insight into our spiritual brokenness is why he has countered with a perfect and complete plan for salvation.

Which is faith expressing itself through love. Not "trying our hardest until we collapse." Not "stressing ourselves out until we can't sleep or find joy." Not even "winning everything we can and becoming a shining star." Instead, it's simply having faith in Jesus's work and expressing that faith to the world through our love of God and those around us.

It's an easy burden, friend. It's an expression of God's love and kindness. It's a plan that satisfies his justice and offers weak, fallen, desperate humans a way out of the storm.

REFLECTION How has your faith impacted your life? That's a big question! But think about who you were before your relationship with God became real to you, and think about who you are now.

CHRIST'S RIGHTEOUSNESS

●●●●●●●●●

But now he has reconciled you by Christ's physical
body through death to present you holy in his sight,
without blemish and free from accusation.

COLOSSIANS 1:22

If you thought the good news was going to stop at the fact we're
saved by faith, think again! Don't get me wrong—that is excellent news. But God takes his love one step further. We are not
only reconciled to God (brought back into relationship with
him, ending our separation); we are *holy* in his sight.

Wait, what? Haven't we said multiple times now that we're
all sinners, we make tons of mistakes, and we need to own our
weaknesses? How can we be holy in God's sight?

Easy. Because it's not *our* holiness God sees when he looks at
us. Yes, he sees our good works. He plans them for us, sets them
in our paths, wants us to do them. He sees our sanctification
journey. But that's not what Paul meant in today's verse when
he talked about our holiness. What God sees when he looks at
us is Jesus's perfect, blemish-free righteousness.

REFLECTION The next verse continues Colossians 1:22 with, "if you continue in your faith, established and firm, and do not move from the hope
held out in the gospel." What do you think this says about how we are to
live, even though God sees Christ's righteousness when he looks at us?

....

....

....

....

....

HIDDEN IN HIM

●●●●●●●●●

For you died, and your life is now hidden with Christ in God.
COLOSSIANS 3:3

Paul was writing to church members who were very much alive at the time. So we can be sure when he said "for you died," he didn't mean it literally. He meant we died to ourselves—our old, pre-Jesus self is gone, and we have been raised again with him. After this process, our lives are now "hidden with Christ in God," which means our sins died with Jesus and were buried, and our future isn't weighed down by our sinful nature.

Our new self—the realest and truest version of ourselves—is united with Christ. Our worldly labels don't matter (Colossians 3:11). We should free ourselves from the things that belong to our earthly nature (Colossians 3:5). We are connected to the risen Savior, and our minds are meant to be set on holy, heavenly things.

This is an important part of how God sees us because it lets us know our job is not done. We now have the easy weight of grace through faith, but we also have directives in the Bible that remind us how we're supposed to live. This is a core piece of who we are as Jesus-followers.

REFLECTION If you feel overwhelmed by this idea, don't worry. God sent the Holy Spirit to help us! Consider how these verses can inspire you. What is one thing you can do today to set your mind on heavenly things?

GET HEALTHY: HIGH BUT REACHABLE STANDARDS

I have fought the good fight, I have finished the race, I have kept the faith. Now there is in store for me the crown of righteousness, which the Lord, the righteous Judge, will award to me on that day—and not only to me, but also to all who have longed for his appearing.

2 TIMOTHY 4:7–8

The healthy pursuit of excellence for God's glory is an idea we can get behind. When we think about the excellent examples in Scripture, we rest assured that we can embrace who we are while shooting for high—but reachable—standards.

Love who God made you to be, with your unique set of strengths. Remember the truth about how he sees you—fallen but redeemed, clothed in Christ's righteousness, and hidden in him. Keep all these things in mind, and then . . . *go for it*. Stretch for the big goal. Take a risk and try something new. Banish the idea of perfection and just *live*—for God, for his kingdom, for his people.

Shine by using the gifts God gave you. Let *his* light shine through your weak spaces. Remember that he uses all things— our successes and failures, our highs and lows.

REFLECTION Think about two or three key areas of your life. How can you set high but reachable goals in those areas? If you're not sure what's truly reachable, think of a small goal. Once you reach that goal, set another! See how far you can go.

PROVERBS 31: IMPORTANT RELATIONSHIPS

Her [the wife of noble character's] husband has full
confidence in her and lacks nothing of value. She
brings him good, not harm, all the days of her life.

PROVERBS 31:11–12

The Bible has some excellent examples of high achievers, like
Isaiah and Josiah. But it also has some helpful advice in books
like Proverbs. For thousands of years, Proverbs 31 has been
used as an ideal for wives, outlining several wonderful traits.
But we don't need to be wives or even women to glean wisdom
from these passages, because they set forth a high standard we
can all learn from.

First, the wife of noble character devoted herself to the
important relationships in her life. In this case, it's her husband. But we can similarly support, encourage, and do good for
our parents, siblings, friends, and other treasured people in our
lives.

Then we can take this one step further. What if we tried to
bring a little bit of this kindness, concern, and care to everyone
who crosses our paths? That doesn't mean we deeply devote ourselves to every person we meet, but we can bring compassion,
goodness, and joy to those around us.

REFLECTION Have you recently expressed your love to your treasured
people? What's one way you can show them how much you care for them
today?

PROVERBS 31: DELIGHTFUL WORK

●●●●●●●●●

She selects wool and flax and works with eager hands.
She is like the merchant ships, bringing her food from
afar. She gets up while it is still night; she provides food
for her family and portions for her female servants.

PROVERBS 31:13–15

The wife of noble character took delight in her work. This idea may be a familiar one to you, as most perfectionists like to work. Toxic perfectionism can quickly suck the fun out of our work, but buried underneath the stress, anxiety, and twisted-up sense of never measuring up, there's some joy to be found in a job well-done.

The Proverbs 31 woman felt this too. She carefully selected her materials, then eagerly got to work. She started early in the morning to provide food for her household. She worked hard, and we can imagine it brought her great joy to see those around her enjoy what she made.

When looking at these verses, it's always important to balance the ideal put forth here with grace. No one *loves* their work all the time. But we can aim to approach our various tasks with a sense of delight and gratitude—and satisfaction when the job is completed, the work well-done.

REFLECTION Does this trait of taking joy in tasks resonate for you? How do you usually feel about your work? You may not delight in your least favorite subject in school, but what about your favorites?

PROVERBS 31: WISE USE

She considers a field and buys it; out of her earnings she plants a vineyard. She sets about her work vigorously; her arms are strong for her tasks. She sees that her trading is profitable, and her lamp does not go out at night.
PROVERBS 31:16–18

Here we note a point often missed when the Proverbs 31 woman is discussed—she was a businesswoman. See how she bought a piece of land and turned it into profit? How she worked hard to support her loved ones? Pretty cool!

This passage also highlights how wisely she used the resources at her disposal. The Bible does not promise us we will have riches (in fact, in Matthew 6:19–24, Jesus taught us not to value our worldly possessions). But we do see a principle repeated over and over when it comes to material goods. We are meant to be wise stewards of whatever we have been given, whether it's a lot or a little (see Matthew 25:14–30).

This doesn't only apply to our material resources. We should use other resources wisely too—our time, our energy, our gifts.

REFLECTION Do you feel like you make good use of the resources you've been given? Do you find managing your money difficult? How about other resources, like time? Think of a few ways you can make wise choices in this area.

PROVERBS 31: GENEROUS AND KIND

●●●●●●●●●●

She opens her arms to the poor and extends her hands to
the needy. When it snows, she has no fear for her household;
for all of them are clothed in scarlet. She makes coverings
for her bed; she is clothed in fine linen and purple.

PROVERBS 31:20–22

The wife of noble character was certainly blessed. Her family
didn't fear the cold, as they were dressed in scarlet (which many
theologians think means "warm garments" here), fine linen, and
purple. Purple was a very expensive dye, which is why it was
often associated with royalty. This is quite a statement about
how comfortably this woman's family lived.

However . . . did you notice what the first verse said? Before
we get into the security—riches, even—of the woman's own
household, her generosity and kindness to the poor and needy
are noted. She wasn't worried *only* about herself and her family.
She recognized her duty to care for those in need. The number
of times Scripture tells us to look after those in need is stag-
gering! And this help being mentioned first may also hint at
what aspect of the gifts God gave her is most important—her
willingness to simply be there and do what she can when she
notices a need.

REFLECTION What are some ways you can bless those in your community who are in need? We don't have to be wealthy to do this. Remember,
we have other resources at our disposal—time and energy!

....

....

....

PROVERBS 31: FEARS GOD

Charm is deceptive, and beauty is fleeting; but a
woman who fears the LORD is to be praised.
PROVERBS 31:30

Perhaps the most important trait in the entire passage about
the woman of noble character—her whole reason for working as hard as she did, being as kind and generous as she was,
approaching her life with joy and laughter—is the love this
woman had for the Lord.

Often when we see the word *fear* in the Old Testament,
it doesn't mean fear in the sense of being trapped in a horror
movie, terrified and running for our lives. Instead, it means
reverence, awe, and yes, trembling. It means love and respect
so deep, it might cause us to quake. This is how the Proverbs 31
woman felt about God. He is so good, so holy, that she quaked
before him. She sought to honor him in her life, serve him in her
work, and devote her whole self to him.

That's a tall order, of course. But it's a wonderful ideal to
shoot for. Putting God first in our minds and hearts is the most
important work we will ever do!

REFLECTION Does the Old Testament idea of fearing the Lord resonate
for you? Do you feel like your fear of God is a healthy, reverential trembling
or a terrified hiding?

GET HEALTHY: PROCESS *AND* OUTCOME

Day 246

> Remove the dross from the silver, and a
> silversmith can produce a vessel.
>
> **PROVERBS 25:4**

As we focus on banishing perfectionism in favor of healthy high achievement, one of the most important things we can do is learn to appreciate the process. Perfectionists naturally fixate on outcomes. We want to know what the result will be, and we're eager to make sure it'll be excellent. Perfect, even.

When we reframe this fixation into something healthier, it's okay to keep the end results in mind. We don't have to entirely let go of caring about the outcome. Remember, we're doing all things for God's glory, so it's wonderful to shoot for excellence. But becoming healthier means we must learn to not only *see* the process but truly appreciate it.

Have you heard the saying "The journey is more important than the destination"? A former perfectionist may never fully agree with that statement, but we can fully embrace the idea that *both* the journey and the destination are worth celebrating.

REFLECTION Do you naturally fixate on the prize while ignoring your journey to get there? Think about your last big achievement. Now rewind and write down some of the cool things that happened along the way.

. . . .

. . . .

. . . .

. . . .

. . . .

. . . .

GET HEALTHY: REBOUND FROM DIFFICULTY

We are hard pressed on every side, but not crushed; perplexed, but not in despair; persecuted, but not abandoned; struck down, but not destroyed.

2 CORINTHIANS 4:8–9

Another key consideration when we're pursuing a healthier mindset is learning how to rebound from failure. This is such a big, important, and *hard* thing for perfectionists, we're going to do a deep dive into it for several days.

Building resilience is crucial, friend. Life will always throw curveballs our way. Things don't always go to plan. And— *ugh!*—we make mistakes. When those unexpected detours happen, when hardship presses in on us, and when we royally mess up, bouncing back is necessary. Otherwise, we'll be crushed.

The good news? Resilience can be learned. We can choose to cultivate it in our lives. Even if we aren't naturally springy in this way, we can develop tools that help us recover.

REFLECTION Would you say you bounce back quickly when life knocks you down? Does it depend on the circumstance (for example, maybe you handle hardship out of your control well, but struggle when you've made a mistake)?

MANAGING MISTAKES: HONESTY WITH YOURSELF

●●●●●●●●●●

Jesus Christ is the same yesterday and today and forever.

HEBREWS 13:8

Maybe your self-reflection after yesterday's reading was a little discouraging. Maybe you answered that question, "No, I don't bounce back quickly, and *yes*, it's a million times worse when the mistake is mine." If so, never fear. Help is here. We're going to look at several ways to help our recovering perfectionist brains manage mistakes.

First, it's really important to be honest with ourselves when we make a mistake. If you remember back to the beginning of our time together, we discussed how perfectionists often respond: either by beating ourselves up severely, or by getting defensive and living in denial.

Honesty helps to counteract both of these unhealthy responses. If we're focusing too much on the negative result, we need to ease up and remind ourselves we're human. Mistakes happen. If we're more prone to denial and defensiveness, we need to let down that guard and accept reality, even when it's painful.

REFLECTION When you make mistakes, what is your usual reaction? Do you have a hard time being honest and objective about it? If so, do you tend to beat yourself up, seeing the mistake as much larger and more catastrophic than it is, or do you slip into denial, pretending the mistake never happened or wasn't your fault?

....

....

MANAGING MISTAKES: HONESTY WITH OTHERS

"For there is nothing hidden that will not be disclosed, and nothing concealed that will not be known or brought out into the open."
LUKE 8:17

Once we've learned how to face the truth ourselves, we have to level up: it's time to be honest with others. This may sound like it's all one thing—simply being honest about mistakes—but it's a lot harder for most perfectionists to admit to other people when they fail or flub.

Certainly when our mistakes have hurt other people, it's important we acknowledge them honestly (more on this in a bit). But sometimes, developing a practice of honestly confessing our mistakes to trusted people in our lives, even when the mistake doesn't affect that person, can be really healthy.

Why? Because perfectionists tend to feel outsized shame about our mistakes, and confession brings things into the open. We can get helpful feedback and comfort from an outside perspective. And it proves to our anxious hearts that those we love won't abandon us at the first sign of imperfection.

REFLECTION Do you have a trusted person in your life with whom you would feel comfortable being honest about your mistakes? A trusted parent or mentor is a great option, as is a close friend. Just make sure you're choosing a high-trust person! This can be a vulnerable exercise.

MANAGING MISTAKES: VISUALIZATION

As far as the east is from the west, so far has he removed our transgressions from us.

PSALM 103:12

After we've been honest with ourselves and others about our mistakes, often the heavy weight of "failure" lifts. Being honest, open, and authentic has a freeing effect.

But sometimes, that weight still feels heavy. Sometimes the feeling of freeness is fleeting. We feel better initially, but then we start second-guessing ourselves, allowing anxiety to take hold. In these moments, it's time to whip out another helpful tool: visualization.

Imagine the mistake or overly self-critical thought is a feather in the palm of your hand. Now gently blow that feather away. We don't have to pretend the feather doesn't exist—it's there. It happened. But we also have the power to simply blow it away, as far as the east is from the west.

REFLECTION Can you think of another visualization that could help you in the moments you find yourself dwelling on past mistakes? Maybe you can set your mistakes in a boat and nudge them down a river. Or set them on the wings of a butterfly and watch it fly away. Be creative!

MANAGING MISTAKES: WHEN YOU CAUSE HARM

Therefore confess your sins to each other and pray for each other so that you may be healed. The prayer of a righteous person is powerful and effective.

JAMES 5:16

Mistakes are not always sins. If you accidentally tell someone it's Tuesday but it's Wednesday, that's a mistake, not a sin. There are time mistakes *can* be sins, of course, and sometimes those kinds of errors harm others. Even when that wasn't our intent.

That's a hard truth to swallow. If we find the idea of making any mistakes difficult, the idea of causing harm to someone due to our error may be almost unbearable. But it happens, and we need to train ourselves to respond well.

The first step is to repent. The moment you become aware of the sin, turn away from it! Resolve not to do it again. Second, confess the sin to God. He's always ready and waiting to hear from his children. Third, confess to the person who was harmed. Remember, you can't control how they'll respond, but it's still an important step. Finally, seek their forgiveness. Again, you can't force them to forgive you, but when you've followed these steps, you can rest assured you've done what is within your control to rectify the situation.

REFLECTION Have you ever made a mistake that hurt someone else? How did you handle it? Would you do anything differently if that situation were to happen today?

MANAGING MISTAKES: CONFESSION

●●●●●●●●●●

Whoever conceals their sins does not prosper, but the one who confesses and renounces them finds mercy.
PROVERBS 28:13

Maybe I'm hammering on this point a little too much . . . but you can never have too much confession! Indeed, becoming excellent at confession is important for everyone but imperative for perfectionists who are getting healthy. Confession forces us out of hiding. It demands we bring others into the process of working through our mistakes, and that's so valuable if you have a hard time seeing things as they really are (since anxiety and insecurity will do that).

And it's equally important to keep the goals of confession in mind. The first goal is forgiveness and reconciliation with others. This is particularly important when an error has caused harm. But it's also helpful for fostering supportive, authentic relationships. The second goal of confession, though, is healing for you. When we hide our sins, they begin to fester inside, eventually becoming like poison. Confession helps us draw out that poison and heal, so we can have a healthier mindset.

REFLECTION Does confession come easily to you? How does it feel when you get something off your chest, especially if it's something you felt ashamed of and held inside for a long time?

MANAGING MISTAKES: LET GO OF "WHAT IF?"

●●●●●●●●●●

"If the miracles that were performed in you had been performed in Tyre and Sidon, they would have repented long ago in sackcloth and ashes."

MATTHEW 11:21

Some mistakes lead us to rumination—dwelling on negative feelings, their causes, and their consequences. It can feel like we're caught in a loop, wondering why we made a mistake, and what it would be like if we'd done something differently.

One aspect of God's mind that's hard for us to understand is that God knows all possibilities. God's omniscience means he knows everything that happened in the past, what's happening now, and what will happen in the future. And yet, multiple times in Scripture, God mentions things that could or would have happened but didn't come to pass. This shows us that not only does God know all things actual, God knows all the *possible* facts that will *never* come to pass. That's why Jesus could say Tyre and Sidon would have repented if they'd seen his miracles.

We may think this sounds awesome—something we'd love to be able to know. But this knowledge belongs to God alone. Imagine breaking the loop of *why* and *what-if*. Hand those questions over to God and release a burden that isn't yours.

REFLECTION Have you ever felt like you were caught in a rumination cycle? If you feel yourself going down a path of "What if I'd . . . ?" how will you break that thought process?

. . . .

. . . .

. . . .

. . . .

MANAGING MISTAKES:
NOT YOUR IDENTITY

But you, Lord, are a compassionate and gracious God,
slow to anger, abounding in love and faithfulness.

PSALM 86:15

Want to hear a wonderful, glorious, soul-freeing truth? No matter what mistake you made, whether a small error or a huge
blunder that caused harm to others and must be repented of,
you are not your mistake.

I'll say it again: *you* are not your mistake. That error is not
your identity. Your identity is that you are a beloved child of
God. Your identity is all your wonderful qualities and unique
traits and gifts and talents.

We all mess up. God knew we would mess up from the start,
and so it comes as no shock to him. If he doesn't see you as a
living, breathing mistake, you shouldn't see yourself that way
either. Your mistake is not your identity.

REFLECTION Have you ever made a mistake so big you felt like it sucked
all the air out of the room? Became your whole identity in an instant? If
you have, use the visualization technique we learned earlier to release that
mistake—turn it into a feather and blow it away.

MANAGING MISTAKES: GROWTH

Your beginnings will seem humble, so
prosperous will your future be.
JOB 8:7

An important part of learning to manage mistakes in a healthy
way is getting into the habit of asking ourselves, "What did I
learn?" That can be hard to do in the moment. At the time, we
might not even have the correct perspective to be able to answer
that question.

But we should always look back for learning opportunities, perhaps after we've dealt with the consequences of the
mistake. First, asking ourselves what we learned from a painful experience helps us realize how much we've grown from it.
And second, it helps us reframe our mistakes. Calling mistakes
"learning opportunities" may sound kind of cheesy (I admit it!),
but reframing in that way helps get us out of a negative mindset.
It helps us not repeat the errors of our past.

REFLECTION Think of the last big mistake you made (I know, it can be
painful!). Looking back, can you see what you learned from that experience? What about the last small error you made? Were there any lessons
learned there?

MANAGING MISTAKES: FORGIVE YOURSELF

"This is my blood of the covenant, which is poured out for many for the forgiveness of sins."

MATTHEW 26:28

After we have acknowledged our mistakes, repented, confessed, and sought forgiveness from others (when appropriate); after we've analyzed the situation objectively enough to determine what we learned; and maybe even after we've engaged in some visualization to help release the guilt and negative emotions, then we might be ready to do something that can be *really* hard for perfectionists.

Forgive yourself. It happened. You owned it. You grew from it. You're a wiser, more mature *you* now. It won't be the last time you mess up. (If only we could banish mistakes entirely!) But we're human, and that's okay. We can work to avoid repeating the same mistakes, and we can let our mistakes lead us to increased closeness with the Lord.

Forgive yourself. God already has.

REFLECTION Are you still holding on to any past mistakes? Search deeply to answer this question. If you find something important, revisit some of the devotions from the past week, and then . . . forgive yourself.

GET HEALTHY: GROWING CLOSER TO GOD

Come near to God and he will come near to you. Wash your hands, you sinners, and purify your hearts, you double-minded.
JAMES 4:8

Reworking our mindset from toxic perfectionism into healthy excellence isn't always easy. Okay, it's *never* easy. But it's deeply rewarding. There are positive benefits for your mental, physical, and spiritual health. Throughout the process of improving our mindsets, we can take the opportunity to grow closer to God.

In fact, that's a necessary step when it comes to pursuing health. When we talked about the traits of toxic perfectionism, you might have noticed we didn't focus too much on the perfectionist's relationship with God. That's because a toxic cloud of perfectionist static sometimes fills up our brains so much, we're thinking more about our performance and achievements than we are about our Lord.

Ouch. If this sounds like you, don't worry. We're going to take an in-depth look at how we can draw closer to God as we reshape the way we view ourselves and the world around us.

REFLECTION If you could rate your current closeness to God on a scale of 1 to 10, what would it be? That's hard to quantify, I know! Have you felt closer to God in the past than you do now? Or do you feel like you've been growing closer to him lately?

DRAWING NEAR

> Let us draw near to God with a sincere heart and with
> the full assurance that faith brings, having our hearts
> sprinkled to cleanse us from a guilty conscience
> and having our bodies washed with pure water.
>
> **HEBREWS 10:22**

Did the last reflection question make you feel discouraged? I hope not. But if it did—if you're feeling far from God right now, and you're wondering why you used to feel closer to him—know you're not alone. Times of closeness and feeling distant come and go for most followers of Jesus.

But just because it's common doesn't mean it's not hard! All we want is to go back to the times when we knew with our hearts and minds that God was right beside us.

Don't despair, friend. God is always there, whether we think we feel him or not. And there are ways to reconnect—to jump-start our sensitivity to God's presence again. We're going to take a look at those next, but stay encouraged. He's there. Don't stop searching!

REFLECTION Are there times in your life you've felt closest to God? Have they been big events, or do you feel him in the quieter moments? What activities make you feel God's presence the most?

STEP ONE: LOOK FOR UNCHECKED SIN

●●●●●●●●●●

Search me, God, and know my heart; test me and know
my anxious thoughts. See if there is any offensive
way in me, and lead me in the way everlasting.
PSALM 139:23–24

Ugh, *why* did we have to start here? I know. But self-examination
is an important first step to drawing closer to God. Since God is
always near to us, when his presence feels far away, it's usually
because of something we're doing differently. It could be that
we've gotten so busy, we've forgotten to focus on God. It could
be due to some heartache we haven't processed yet.

Or it could be because we've sinned and, like Adam and Eve
in the garden, we're hiding from God. Sometimes we're not even
doing this consciously. Sometimes we've allowed a bad attitude
to creep in, and the more we lean into that bad attitude, the
farther away God feels.

First and foremost, we have to deal with these unchecked
sins in our lives before we can continue on to the next step.
Remember, even though we might have made a big blunder (or
have been making continuous blunders!), God is always ready
and waiting to accept us back and pull us close to him.

REFLECTION Spend some time in prayer today, asking God to reveal
whether there's any unchecked sin in your life. There may not be, but make
sure you're listening for the answer and responding appropriately.

STEP TWO: REMIND YOURSELF OF GOD'S PROMISES

●●●●●●●●●

Through these he has given us his very great
and precious promises, so that through them
you may participate in the divine nature.

2 PETER 1:4

Sometimes it's not sin or shame or hiding that makes us feel far
from God. Sometimes it's just the busyness of life that makes us
slowly drift away from that feeling of connectedness.

In these times, we have, sadly, forgotten who God is. We've
forgotten his goodness and the promises he's made—and
kept—in our lives. There are a lot of specific things we can do
to help us remember God's promises, and several of them will
be explored shortly, because they are all also excellent ways to
draw closer to God!

But here are some ideas to get you started: Write your
favorite verse on an index card and place it in a visible location
in your room. Spend time in prayer every day. Attend church
services and Bible study whenever possible. Memorize some of
God's promises in Scripture. Each action helps God's presence
feel a little closer.

REFLECTION Do you feel like it's easy to forget God's goodness if you're
not careful to focus on it every day? What are some ways you like to stay
connected?

THE PROMISE TO SAVE

For God so loved the world that he gave his
one and only Son, that whoever believes in him
shall not perish but have eternal life.
JOHN 3:16

God's biggest promise to people who follow Christ is that he
will save us. In fact, he *did* save us already. Grabbing hold of
this truth, allowing it to sink down into our bones, is enough
all on its own to draw us right back into God's arms, warm in
his presence.

He *saved* us. He gave his one and only Son to offer us a way
out of the mess of sin. God would have been perfectly within
his rights—perfectly just—to give humanity over to its sinful
desires and leave us there. He didn't have to save us.

He *chose* to. He loved us so much that he chose to throw a
lifeline to all of humankind. Wow. That's incredible love. That's
an incredible promise.

REFLECTION When was the last time you thought about Jesus's sacrifice
for us? It's something we often think about during the Easter season, but
then it's easy to let it to drift to the back of our minds. What is something
you can do to keep God's (fulfilled!) promise to save you closer to the front
of your mind?

THE PROMISE TO STAY

"Be strong and courageous. Do not be afraid or terrified
because of them, for the LORD your God goes with
you; he will never leave you nor forsake you."

DEUTERONOMY 31:6

God saving us is an incredible act. It's an incredible promise he kept and will continue to keep when Christ returns. But on top of that incredible promise, God has also promised he will not leave us. He will not abandon us. He sent the Holy Spirit to not only be *with* us but *in* us.

The Holy Spirit will never leave us. If we are Christians, we have the Spirit (who is one part of God), and that won't ever change. Jesus said he would send the Spirit after he went away, to teach us, comfort us, and nudge us with reminders of God's will when we're on the verge of sin. We have the Spirit of God within us, and it's no wonder that this Spirit is sometimes called the Advocate, as it is always looking out for us and guiding us along the way.

REFLECTION How have you experienced the Holy Spirit in your life? (Big question!) Have you felt him more as a comforter? A guide? An advocate? All of the above, or something else?

THE PROMISE TO HELP

What, then, shall we say in response to these
things? If God is for us, who can be against us?
ROMANS 8:31

God is not going to leave you stuck. He has promised to help. And sometimes that help comes through the Holy Spirit working inside of us. Sometimes the help comes in miraculously getting us out of a tough situation. Other times, his help comes as a boost of endurance, enabling us to weather the storm and get to the other side (and probably grow a lot in the process, even if we'd rather simply be rescued most of the time).

No matter how he shows up, God has promised he will help us. It doesn't mean we will not suffer. In fact, Jesus has pretty much promised we will at times (sorry!). But it does mean we can rest assured in the fact we don't face that suffering alone. We don't face hardship without an advocate, helper, and loving Father by our sides.

REFLECTION Have you been through a really hard time in your life? How did God show up for you in that situation? Did he help you get out of it, or did he help you endure it?

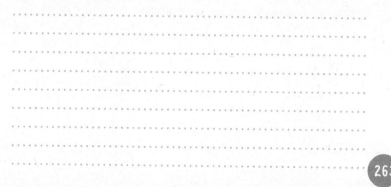

THE PROMISE TO LOVE

Because of the LORD's great love we are not
consumed, for his compassions never fail. They are
new every morning; great is your faithfulness.

LAMENTATIONS 3:22–23

God's love is what prompted him to save us. God's love sent the
Holy Spirit to be with us—which is such a gift! His love prompts
him to help us. Out of his great love, all his promises flow out.
But his love in itself is a promise too.

He will not remove this love from us. How can we be sure?
Because his love was never based on our performance. Read that
back again: His love is not dependent on us. Sure, we change our
behavior in many ways once we have faith in our hearts. We live
for him, aiming to please him in our lives. But he loved us *first*,
before we did any of that. He *still* loves us when we fall far short
of the ideal.

God's love isn't going anywhere, my friend, no matter what.

REFLECTION Sit in silence for a few moments today, thinking about God's
love for you. Consider the utter bigness of God . . . and now think about how
much he has promised to love you. Even if we took a hundred moments of
silence, we could never wrap our minds around it. But it's fun to try!

STEP THREE: REFLECTION AND PRAYER

Day **265**

"Therefore I tell you, whatever you ask for in prayer, believe that you have received it, and it will be yours."
MARK 11:24

This has already been said, but it's worth repeating: God never leaves us. When we feel far from him, it's because we have changed something. We've drifted away or lost touch or we're hiding. God is always *right there*, ready and waiting for us to return to him.

Reflection and prayer are a key step in regaining that closeness with God. We've already looked for unchecked sin. We've already reminded ourselves of God's goodness and his promises. Now it's time to rebuild the close relationship we may have once had—or to start working on it for the first time!

The idea of reflection and prayer can be a little overwhelming. Or even intimidating. We know we're supposed to do these things, but . . . how? How do we build closeness with God in this way? I have three specific ideas for you. Read on!

REFLECTION Do you feel like you're regaining closeness with God or working on it for the first time? Either way is awesome! Spend a few minutes looking back at your relationship with the Lord, then think about where you'd like it to be over the next few months or years.

REFLECTION AND PRAYER: TURN DOWN THE NOISE

Day 266

> Then, because so many people were coming and going that they did not even have a chance to eat, he said to them, "Come with me by yourselves to a quiet place and get some rest."
>
> **MARK 6:31**

Our modern world is busy. Noisy. Distracting. There are so many things vying for our attention. From an entertainment perspective alone, there are hundreds of different voices shouting for us to take notice, hoping to make a sale, a fan, a devotee. And that's to say nothing of our actual responsibilities. Our lives wouldn't look the least bit relatable to our ancestors.

Yet we see in this verse Jesus and his disciples had a similar problem. Perhaps they didn't have modern distractions pulling their focus. But they still needed to get away from the crowds—the people who were pressing them for attention—and go to a quiet place to rest.

Sometimes we need to turn down the noise to allow ourselves to hear God. Perhaps literally. Maybe we need to take out our earbuds and embrace quiet time. Or maybe it's more figurative and we need to step away from some demands and responsibilities to carve out a peaceful moment to commune with God.

REFLECTION Try it right now. Put away distractions and spend time talking to God. Tell him about your day. Tell him what you're working on. Tell him about your journey as a recovering perfectionist.

> For the word of the LORD is right and true;
> he is faithful in all he does.

PSALM 33:4

For a lot of people, the teen years are when their relationship with God becomes real to them. Maybe like them, you went to church as a kid because your parents did. Maybe you even accepted Jesus as your Savior during your childhood years. But in these cases, something changes as we get older and our capacity to understand increases. We *get* it on a different level.

Or maybe like other teens, you are just now discovering God for the first time and still figuring it all out. But whether your time with the Lord has been short or long, there are likely several moments where God has been faithful to you on your journey.

Journaling is an excellent way to remember what the Lord has done in your life. Even if you don't journal every day, writing and reflecting when big things happen in your life will help you look back on God's faithfulness over the years. It's an excellent way to deepen your reflection and prayer time.

REFLECTION Think back to the most recent time God was faithful to you. Maybe it was something that was for you, specifically, or maybe it was something he did for your whole family.

REFLECTION AND PRAYER: STUDY HIS WORD

For the word of God is alive and active. Sharper than any double-edged sword, it penetrates even to dividing soul and spirit, joints and marrow; it judges the thoughts and attitudes of the heart.

HEBREWS 4:12

There's nothing that helps us know God better than studying his Word, the Bible. The Bible is such a deep, layered, multi-faceted book (if we can even simplify it enough to call it a book!). You can spend an entire lifetime studying it, researching the cultural and historical context in which it was written to better understand the messages, and you still couldn't fully grasp *everything* Scripture has to teach us.

But don't let that overwhelm you. The point isn't that we have to gain total and complete understanding. The point is that through our study, prayer, reflection, and learning, over time we understand better and better who God is, how much he loves us, and his history with his people. It's like a treasure hunt with layers upon layers of discovery.

REFLECTION What's a challenge you can give yourself when it comes to reading Scripture? It's okay to start small, like reading through one book of the Bible in a month. Or reading one chapter every day for a few weeks.

STEP FOUR: COMMUNE WITH HIS PEOPLE

"For where two or three gather in my name, there am I with them."

MATTHEW 18:20

Maybe this sounds weird at first. If you want to grow closer to God, you should . . . hang out with people? But it's true. Repeatedly in the Bible, both in the Old and New Testaments, togetherness and community are emphasized. God built us for himself and for each other.

Communities of all kinds are important. It's great to be close with your neighbors or involved in your local town or city. It's awesome to have friends at school and online communities with people who share your interests.

But there's something special about having community with other followers of Jesus. We need people who share our faith to encourage and instruct us so we can grow in our faith and help them to do the same. It's been an essential part of the Christian life since the early church!

REFLECTION Do you make a regular habit of meeting together with other believers? How do you feel when you're spending time with other followers of Jesus?

INTERCEDE FOR OTHERS

●●●●●●●●●

Be joyful in hope, patient in affliction, faithful in prayer.
ROMANS 12:12

Gathering together with other Christians is important when we're drawing closer to God, but there's another element to communing with his people that deserves its own mention—interceding—or praying—for others.

Again, that may sound weird at first. If we want to grow closer to God, shouldn't we pray for ourselves? Of course that's true too! You should definitely make a habit of talking to God frequently—all day long, if you like—and we can be sure he cares about every detail of our lives.

But praying for others is a crucial piece of our prayer life as well. In this way, we can make a habit of thinking of others' needs. We increase our empathy and compassion. We get out of our self-focused bubbles and notice those around us. It's healthy for us *and* for them.

REFLECTION Do you currently spend much time praying for others? Is there a system you could use to help remember the requests and needs of others (like a special notebook or section in your journal, index cards, sticky notes)?

GET HEALTHY: RESPOND WELL TO CRITICISM

●●●●●●●●●

> "You stiff-necked people! Your hearts and ears are still uncircumcised. You are just like your ancestors: You always resist the Holy Spirit!"
> **ACTS 7:51**

Ouch! Talk about some harsh criticism. In this verse, Stephen was pulling no punches in his speech to the Sanhedrin (honestly, it was a valid approach in this case). Hopefully we never hear criticism this harsh, but even less-spiky critiques can be excruciatingly difficult for perfectionists to stomach.

However, learning to respond well to criticism is an important part of breaking out of our perfectionist mindsets and becoming healthy high achievers and pursuers of excellence. Maybe you can't even imagine being able to receive a critique and not take it personally. But don't worry! There are several steps we can take to work through criticism in a healthy way that help maintain boundaries while helping us grow as much as possible.

REFLECTION How well do you usually respond to criticism? If your answer is "abysmally," don't worry. But be honest with yourself about where you're starting now so you can celebrate your growth as you learn new habits!

WHY DOES IT HURT?

The human spirit can endure in sickness,
but a crushed spirit who can bear?

PROVERBS 18:14

Most people don't love criticism. Some people are good at taking constructive comments and using them to improve (which is excellent), but for the most part, people don't like to be told, "You're doing it wrong."

This is doubly, triply, quadruply true for perfectionists. And it makes sense. For a perfectionist, receiving criticism means someone else noticed our shortcomings. We didn't get it right the first time. And as we know, anything that isn't perfect, we perceived as a total failure. Not only that, we take failure as a personal rejection of our very selves.

So someone might think they are providing constructive criticism (and they might be correct!), but a perfectionist hears, "You are a failure." That small comment about how we could improve our work becomes an outsized rejection of who we are as humans. The good thing is, God understands that, and he's here to help us through it.

REFLECTION Have you experienced a painful criticism before? Did it feel like the person said, "You are a failure" or "You are worthless"? Looking back, can you see their points more objectively, or is it still very painful?

LOSS OF LOVE

> Why, my soul, are you downcast? Why so
> disturbed within me? Put your hope in God, for I
> will yet praise him, my Savior and my God.
> **PSALM 43:5**

Some of the criticism we receive happens in comments from our teachers on assignments. Or over text messages. Or on social media. But sometimes it happens to our faces, and those moments can be especially hard to manage.

Whatever the format, criticism delivered to a perfectionist can be seen as an attack. It certainly *feels* that way, even when that's not the intent. And, in our skewed perfectionist perception, this "attack" signals a loss of love. We wonder about the relationship. Have we lost their esteem? Their respect? We may even begin to feel like we've lost our identity if our sense of self has been wrapped up in our performance.

Does it sound a little crazy when it's spelled out like that? It's definitely one area where our feelings don't truly reflect reality!

REFLECTION If you get a less-than-stellar grade on an assignment you worked really hard on, how does that feel? When a friend comes to you and says, "This thing you said hurt my feelings," how do you respond? Spend a while analyzing your response to being told you aren't perfect—dig deep!

SEEK PEACE

If it is possible, as far as it depends on
you, live at peace with everyone.
ROMANS 12:18

Now that we've established perfectionists don't always respond
to criticism in healthy ways (ahem), let's turn to the most important questions: How can we do better? How can we learn to
process criticism in ways that will help us mature and grow, as
well as protect our relationships?

First, it's important to seek peace. If you're dealing with a
face-to-face criticism that feels like an attack, it can be tempting
to respond defensively. This is usually done to protect yourself
from the big hurt you're feeling. But instead, what if we trained
our brains to think *peace* in this situation?

It's important to seek peace both with others and within
yourself. Focusing on the word *peace* can help calm our frazzled
nervous system that wants us to think *Attack!* instead. If we can
calm ourselves, it will make all further communication much
more productive, and we can begin to unravel the lie that tells us
this criticism means we've lost the love of the person standing
before us.

REFLECTION What are some ways you can make *peace* a word that sits
right at the front of your mind? How might focusing on peace help you in a
moment of conflict, crisis, or criticism?

QUICK TO LISTEN

My dear brothers and sisters, take note of this:
Everyone should be quick to listen.

JAMES 1:19

So we've told our brains, *Peace! It's not an attack!* We've convinced ourselves this criticism does not mean a loss of love or relationship with the person critiquing us. Now what?

Listen. Hear what the other person is saying. And, importantly, make sure you are hearing what's *actually* being said, not your worst fears about what they might be trying to communicate. If your English teacher says, "You need to brush up on your grammar," don't allow your brain to turn that into, "You are a terrible writer—why did you even bother?" If your mom says, "Your room is a mess, and I've already asked you to clean it twice," don't hear, "I regret ever having children!"

Remember, if you're a sensitive perfectionist, your mind wants to throw a magnifying glass over what's being said and turn it into something much larger and scarier than it really is. But you have a choice! You don't have to entertain those thoughts. Instead, hear what is actually being said.

REFLECTION How well are you able to hear the words being spoken to you in a moment of criticism? Do you relate to the idea of a magnifying glass blowing everything out of proportion?

SLOW TO SPEAK

[Everyone should be] slow to speak and slow to become angry.
JAMES 1:19

After we have heard what's being said, the next step is to decide how we will respond. James told us to be slow to speak, slow to become angry. That's excellent advice.

During this moment of reflection and processing, we can ask ourselves if a response is even necessary. Sometimes it is, especially if someone is expressing their hurt or frustration toward you. Other times, we simply need to take the note and quietly process it ourselves (most of our feedback in school is like this).

Something that's important in every case is to consider where this person sits in your own personal bull's-eye. The people in the highest trust positions in your life are right in the center. Their criticism should be weighted more heavily. Someone in the very outer ring—or off the target entirely— does not need to be given the same space in your mind and heart. Often, their criticism is unwarranted and uninformed because they don't know you as deeply, and you can simply blow it away like a feather.

REFLECTION Do you ever think about your "bull's-eye of influence" when you're processing criticism? Perfectionists sometimes have the problem of weighting all criticism equally, so take a good look at this! Is this an area where you can grow to help yourself down the road?

GROWTH POTENTIAL

Be diligent in these matters; give yourself wholly to
them, so that everyone may see your progress.
1 TIMOTHY 4:15

If we have decided our "critic" is in a ring of the bull's-eye we
should pay attention to, now what? Well, it means we're going to
ask ourselves a crucial question: *How can I grow from this?*

I know. I've said it a hundred times before. But it's *so* important! We sometimes hit roadblocks, hard things, and stinging
criticism. It hurts, it's hard, and we don't like it. But if we can
think about how this will make us better, it can bring more
meaning to those hard times.

And remember, "better" doesn't always mean "How can I
improve my performance?" Oftentimes the way we grow isn't
about that. It's about improving our character. It's about becoming more mature, more sensitive to the needs of others. More
like Jesus. So think carefully about this from all angles when
asking yourself what positive takeaways might come from the
experience at hand.

REFLECTION Can you think back to a time when you received criticism
that ultimately made you grow? Even if it hurt at the time, what were your
positive takeaways?

Perfume and incense bring joy to the heart, and the
pleasantness of a friend springs from their heartfelt advice.

PROVERBS 27:9

There are times we've done all the processing we can. We've
looked for the positives, tried to determine how heavily to weight
the comments. We've calmed ourselves and truly listened. We
haven't responded in anger or defensiveness. But we're *still* not
sure if the criticism is valid.

It may be time to talk to a wise, trusted person for their
perspective. Ideally, this is someone in the center of your bull's-
eye—a very trusted individual who knows you well and loves
you enough to tell you the truth. Their perspective can be
invaluable in helping you determine how to move forward with
the criticism you received—whether to take it to heart or send
it away forever.

REFLECTION Think about the highest-trust people in your life. Who sits
right in the bull's-eye? Who would be a good person to help you properly
gauge criticism? Have a few people in mind so you're ready and don't have
to think through it in a moment of pain or confusion.

THE IMAGE OF GOD

I praise you because I am fearfully and wonderfully made; your works are wonderful, I know that full well.

PSALM 139:14

Perhaps you've gotten feedback that a piece of criticism was unwarranted or unnecessarily harsh. Maybe you've even been able to see that on your own. Perhaps it's even become apparent that, for whatever reason, the person criticizing you has done so maliciously. (Though be very careful not to quickly jump to that conclusion.)

It can be tempting to retaliate. It can be tempting to respond in anger—perhaps justified anger! Just remember, no matter what, the person before you is also made in God's image. They are human, just like you and me, and they may be going through their own mess right now. Every person we interact with should be treated with dignity and kindness whenever possible.

This is also true when someone gives us valid criticism, of course! But it's less tempting to dehumanize someone who is lovingly providing constructive criticism than it is someone who set out to hurt us.

REFLECTION Have you ever been on the receiving end of unfair criticism? Was it from someone you loved and trusted? How did you respond? Even when we recognize someone as God's child, it's okay to bump them into circles of lesser trust when they hurt us like this. Boundaries are good!

BE GENTLE

He tends his flock like a shepherd: He gathers the
lambs in his arms and carries them close to his
heart; he gently leads those that have young.

ISAIAH 40:11

Multistep processes are great. They can help provide a solid
framework for working through emotions or situations that
feel overwhelming and impossible to process. We've gone over
a good process for working through criticism. I pray it's something you'll be able to put into practice and that you will find it
helpful.

But, friend, please be gentle with yourself. Having a firm
framework is great, but it doesn't mean these situations don't
take a toll. It doesn't mean the process will be easy. So give yourself grace. Be gentle. Allow yourself time and space and a little
extra self-care, whatever that looks like for you. Treat yourself
to something fun. Take a leisurely walk. Throw in an extra work-
out (if that's your thing). Whatever helps you feel more peaceful,
centered, and like yourself: do it! You're a work in progress. Be
kind to yourself.

REFLECTION What are your favorite self-care activities? There's truly no
right or wrong answer here! Deep breathing, naps, playing with a pet, cre-
ating art. The options are limitless!

PERFECT SAUL

[They] dragged him [Stephen] out of the city and
began to stone him. Meanwhile, the witnesses laid
their coats at the feet of a young man named Saul.
ACTS 7:58

Remember that harsh criticism Stephen gave to the Sanhedrin?
The verse above happens just a bit later. Stephen was not at all
wrong when he criticized the Sanhedrin. But it cost him his life,
and he became the first Christian martyr.

This is a terrible moment in church history. It's also the
introduction to one of the church's most important figures:
Saul. As Stephen was killed, people laid their coats at Saul's feet.
He witnessed Stephen being stoned to death. And, as awful as
that is, Saul might have been considered . . . perfect.

At least in his social and religious structure. He was a
Pharisee, studying under one of the most notable Jewish teachers of the time. He followed what the religious leaders said was
right—that Jesus and his followers were rebels, deserving of
death. And yet he had so thoroughly missed the point! It's a
sobering reminder that doing something *well* doesn't mean it's
actually *good*. Let's hope we never get so caught up in completing
the task that we miss the bigger picture!

REFLECTION Have you ever thought about the disconnect between following all the rules and truly *getting* it? Saul gives us a perfect example of
that. But he also shows us there's a way out of that legalistic life!

PAUL AND HIS MISTAKES

Here is a trustworthy saying that deserves full
acceptance: Christ Jesus came into the world
to save sinners—of whom I am the worst.

1 TIMOTHY 1:15

Perhaps you already knew—or remembered from earlier in
this book—that Saul is the apostle Paul. Jesus met him in a
very powerful way. We can imagine someone as devoted to the
Pharisees as Saul would *have* to be met in this way to come to
saving faith!

If you know much about Paul's life, you know he's one of the
most important figures in church history. He wrote a lot of the
New Testament. He planted many churches and was instrumental in spreading the gospel message in the first century.

Yet . . . our high-achieving apostle still called himself the
worst of sinners in this letter to Timothy. Did Paul struggle with
his self-esteem? Was he a perfectionist, unable to see how much
good he'd done? Or had he simply framed his achievements in
healthy humility, fully embracing that God is the one to whom
all glory belongs? We can't say for sure. But we know one thing:
Paul was someone who understood the pursuit of excellence in
his work.

REFLECTION What do you think about what Paul said of himself here? Do
you think he was beating himself up like a perfectionist? Or simply using
hyperbole to express his understanding of how he fell short?

PAUL'S PERFECTION, NOT YET ATTAINED

Day 283

I do not consider myself yet to have taken hold of it. But one
thing I do: Forgetting what is behind and straining toward
what is ahead, I press on toward the goal to win the prize
for which God has called me heavenward in Christ Jesus.

PHILIPPIANS 3:13–14

Saul probably thought he had life figured out. He studied the
right things under the right teachers. He felt correct in his judgment and persecution of Christians. He likely thought he was
carrying out God's will—until the Son of God himself burst into
his life and changed everything.

Here, in his letter to the Philippian church, the apostle
Paul showed a different side of himself. Despite all the world-
changing work Paul had done, despite the ways God had
powerfully used him in ministry, Paul was quick to acknowledge that he had not yet won the prize. He had not yet attained
perfection or fully participated in the death and resurrection of
Jesus Christ (verses 10–12). It was a future hope, something he
continued to strive for in his life.

We perfectionists can relate to striving toward what's
ahead—in fact, we excel at it! Remember that the journey is
just as important as the end goal.

REFLECTION How do you feel about having work that is never going to be
finished in this life? Is that easy to accept, or is it uncomfortable? Do your
feelings change if you focus on the journey rather than the destination?

"LEAST OF THE APOSTLES"

For I am the least of the apostles and do not even deserve to be called an apostle, because I persecuted the church of God.
1 CORINTHIANS 15:9

This is a fascinating statement from Paul. The *least* of the apostles? From the author of so many New Testament letters? The man who told so many people about Jesus? The man who shaped so much of our understanding of what it means to serve Christ?

History would certainly disagree with Paul's assessment, but this is an interesting window into how he viewed himself. Again, we can't be sure if this is emotionally aware humility—a spiritual acknowledgment that his achievements don't earn him saving grace. Or if he was struggling to let go of his past mistakes, continuing to feel guilty about the choices he made before he knew Jesus.

And yet, of all people, Paul would recognize that *no one* could claim enough righteousness to save themselves.

REFLECTION What do you think of Paul's statement here? What do you think his reaction would be if he saw how his letters and his work continue to impact the church, two thousand years after he lived?

WORKED HARDER THAN ALL

But by the grace of God I am what I am, and his grace to me was not without effect. No, I worked harder than all of them—yet not I, but the grace of God that was with me.

1 CORINTHIANS 15:10

Whether Saul was a perfectionist or simply a high achiever with a very flawed worldview, we see a much greater depth and maturity in this Paul. He pointed out how hard he worked— harder than everyone else—and yet in talking about this accomplishment, he was quick to credit the grace of God within him, not his own power.

That would be quite a turnaround in thinking for someone who was used to the highest levels of achievement. We can guess that Paul's spiritual journey upended everything he previously knew. Paul's journey can give us hope in so many ways. First, no matter what kind of background we come from—even if like Paul we were once actively hostile toward Christianity—God can use us in great ways. Second, even if we struggle with some of our thought patterns, God can meet us in those struggles and help us grow and mature into people who reflect his heart.

REFLECTION Have you ever thought of Paul as a high achiever or perfectionist before? Most of our information about him has come through his own words, so his letters give us interesting insight into how he viewed himself!

WHAT IS SELF-DOUBT?

●●●●●●●●●●

Finally, be strong in the Lord and in his mighty power.
EPHESIANS 6:10

The phrase "self-doubt" might seem self-explanatory. It's doubting oneself. Feeling unsure. Lacking confidence. And almost every perfectionist struggles with it.

It's hard to say which comes first, self-doubt or a perfectionist mindset. It can be either. Feeling insecure and doubting yourself can lead to perfectionism as a way to cope with those unsteady feelings. Or being hardwired with some perfectionist tendencies—and operating in that mental space for years—can lead to harmful self-doubt where you don't trust yourself to take risks or put yourself out there, because not knowing what will happen is too much to deal with.

Either way, recovering from perfectionism requires looking that self-doubt in the face and banishing it! We're going to examine some strategies to do exactly that.

REFLECTION Do you struggle with a lack of confidence? If so, can you identify some ways this has affected your life in the past?

UNHEALTHY COPING: NOT TRYING

> All day long I have been afflicted, and every
> morning brings new punishments.
> **PSALM 73:14**

Perhaps you've already known for a while that self-doubt is an issue for you. Maybe you've even engaged in some unhealthy coping mechanisms to try to deal with that self-doubt.

Opting out is one of the most common ways we deal with self-doubt. If you see an opportunity that interests you—trying out for the school play or a sports team, entering a competition, starting an online business for your crafts—do you jump right in, even if you're not sure you'll succeed? Or do you ultimately decide not to even try, since you can't be sure you won't fail?

If the latter resonates with you, you might be opting out—not trying things because you don't have confidence. If that's how it's been for you in the past, don't worry! There are many truths we can rest on to help us overcome our doubt.

REFLECTION Have you ever decided not to try something new because you felt unsure about your ability to succeed? Now that you're further along in your journey, do you think you could work through those fears differently today than you did before?

UNHEALTHY COPING: OVERACHIEVING

●●●●●●●●●

There remains, then, a Sabbath-rest for the people of God.

HEBREWS 4:9

If you walk through life filled with unsureness—about who you are, whether you matter, whether you're worthy—then it's easy to get in the habit of trying very, very hard to prove yourself. To the world, to those around you, and even to yourself.

Enter: overachieving. Have you guessed that "overachieving" is really a synonym for "perfectionism"? Overachievers set unrealistic goals and then seek to not only meet but smash those goals. If they fail to do this, they might become ashamed or crushed. They might become angry. But underneath it all is a crushing self-doubt that's pushing them to try to feel like they're worthy.

Overachievers believe their achievements are their identities, so they relentlessly strive to prove themselves worthy of love. Given this, of course it's unsettling when those achievements falter or are not stellar. The Sabbath rest mentioned in this verse can seem miles away when there's so much to prove! But when we instead focus on who we *are*, not what we do, we can rest in our identities as children of God.

REFLECTION Has anyone ever called you an overachiever? Maybe, like many of us, you've even worn that label with pride in the past. Now write out at least ten other words to describe yourself—words that focus on your character, not your achievements.

. . . .

. . . .

. . . .

UNHEALTHY COPING: IMPOSTER SYNDROME

Day **289**

> Hear my cry, O God; listen to my prayer. From the ends of the earth I call to you, I call as my heart grows faint; lead me to the rock that is higher than I.
> **PSALM 61:1–2**

Imposter syndrome is a brutal beast. People who deal with imposter syndrome have deep-seated self-doubt that leads them to question all their achievements and abilities.

On the outside, those who suffer from imposter syndrome are high-performing. Anyone looking from the outside in would say, "This person is doing great!" And, objectively, they would be right. But for those trapped in the imposter bubble, all abilities and accomplishments are suspect. *Did I* really *deserve that A? Did I actually get cast as the lead because of my acting abilities, or did the director not have another option?*

Imposter syndrome tries to make all our past achievements meaningless, continuously telling us we didn't actually earn them. This can lead to anxiety, as we wonder if maybe today is the day we will be exposed to the world as a fraud. Yikes! If you can relate to this, stay tuned. Help is on the way.

REFLECTION Have you ever doubted the legitimacy of your past achievements? We certainly don't want to get our identity from our achievements, but it's okay to look back at them and say, "Wow! I did a cool thing!" If you struggle with imposter syndrome, see if you can reframe some of those accolades of the past right now—you *did* do a cool thing!

OVERCOMING: RECOGNIZING SELF-WORTH

Day 290

It is because of him that you are in Christ Jesus,
who has become for us wisdom from God—that is,
our righteousness, holiness and redemption.

1 CORINTHIANS 1:30

The first strategy for overcoming self-doubt is recognizing your unconditional self-worth.

First, we have to define *worth*. You may own a piece of jewelry that's worth $100. That number doesn't change based on anyone else's opinion of the item in question. It's worth $100, period. But if that jewelry used to belong to your great-grandmother and it's been passed down to you, the *personal value* of that jewelry might be far, far more than $100. If someone else thinks that jewelry is not particularly pretty, they might personally value it less than it's actually worth. Make sense? *Worth* is more objective, regardless of how we personally feel about it.

When I say we have unconditional self-worth, it is rooted in the fact that Jesus looked at humanity and said, "They are worth my life." *His* worth is fixed too, and I think we can all agree Jesus is worth everything. And no matter what mistakes we make, what we do or don't achieve in life, none of this changes. Our worth is fixed, and Jesus determined it long ago!

REFLECTION Have you ever considered the difference between *worth* and *value*? Here's some more good news to ponder: God both values you *and* says you are worth saving!

OVERCOMING: FOCUS ON GROWTH

Day **291**

> God is not unjust; he will not forget your work and the love you have shown him as you have helped his people and continue to help them. We want each of you to show this same diligence to the very end, so that what you hope for may be fully realized.

HEBREWS 6:10–11

Growth is such an important aspect of developing a healthy mindset, and—don't take this wrong—perfectionists tend to be pretty bad at appreciating growth. We want to think about achievement, getting all the way to the end of the rainbow and collecting the prize. We want to think about point Z. But even going from point A to point G is an achievement in itself.

So let's think about growth for a minute. Think about who you used to be three years ago or even five years ago. Have you grown? (I'm sure you have!) What things have you learned? How have you matured? How has your relationship with God deepened in that time?

REFLECTION What are the top three coolest ways you've grown over the last three years? Thank God for the opportunities we have to grow, change, and learn!

A cheerful heart is good medicine.
PROVERBS 17:22

If you're struggling with self-doubt, and I tell you to focus on the positives in your life, you might roll your eyes at me. I get it. Truly. But this is actually an important strategy for improving your mindset and overcoming doubt.

In fact, there's a whole book on the topic of cultivating a positive outlook where all the advice is supported by both Scripture and neuroscience (I worked on it, and it's called *Sunny Days Ahead*). We actually do have the power to improve our outlook, becoming more positive people, and the benefits of doing that are substantial!

Here are three simple ways to cultivate a more positive mindset:

1. When something is outside your control, look for silver linings to avoid focusing on a negative you can't change.
2. Find ways to laugh more—funny movies or books, spending time with friends who make you laugh, whatever works!
3. Practice random acts of kindness, and bask in the joy of serving others.

REFLECTION Would you say you're generally positive, or is being optimistic a struggle? No matter where you're starting, change is possible!

OVERCOMING: FACE REALITY

I consider everything a loss because of the surpassing worth of
knowing Christ. . . . Not having a righteousness of my own that
comes from the law, but that which is through faith in Christ.
PHILIPPIANS 3:8–9

Part of releasing self-doubt is recognizing you're going to make
mistakes. That might sound counterintuitive at first. Won't
thinking about the possibility of mistakes make us *more* uncer-
tain, more anxious, and less apt to take a risk and dive in?

Not if we have a healthy perspective about mistakes.
Remember, perfectionist brains want to say, *If you don't perform
well, you'll lose everyone's love and respect.* The truth is, everyone
makes mistakes—we've made them in the past, and we'll make
them in the future. But none of the truths about who God is,
what Christ has done for us, and who *you* are depend upon your
perfection. Literally none of them.

If you make a mistake, God still loves you. If you make a
mistake, Jesus still died for you. If you make a mistake, you
are still the unique, beautiful, brilliant person God created.
Mistakes will happen—try anyway!

REFLECTION Does fear of making a mistake ever hold you back? When
you consider that you are loved and valued, no matter what, does it help
relieve some of your fear?

GOD'S PURE LOVE

●●●●●●●●●●

Give thanks to the God of heaven. *His love endures forever.*
PSALM 136:26

When someone says, "God loves you!" it can be hard to really wrap our minds around what that means. Add in the fact that there are four distinct types of love mentioned in Scripture, and it can be really confusing to try to figure out exactly how God loves us.

Eros is the Greek word for sensual love, and the Bible is clear this type of love is reserved for marriage. *Storge* is the Greek word for familial love, and we see many examples of this type of love in the New Testament church—both between actual family members and between the believers/early Christians. *Philia* describes the emotional bond formed in close friendships. This type of love is the one Jesus said would be a hallmark of his followers (see John 13:35).

But then there's *agape*—sacrificial, pure, perfect, and unconditional. The kind of love Jesus displayed in his life and death. This is God's love.

REFLECTION Which concept from the four above do you usually think of when someone says the word *love*? Spend some time really thinking about *agape*. Does it change the way you hear the message "God loves you"?

LOVE IS PATIENT

●●●●●●●●○○

Love is patient.

1 CORINTHIANS 13:4

God's love is so big, so perfect, so far-reaching, it's wise to break it down into smaller truths we can hope to comprehend in order to gain a better understanding of what God's love means for us.

Have you ever heard the saying "Patience is a virtue"? It's true, but it doesn't come easily for many of us! Our modern world, especially, trains us to receive things on demand and delivered for free, thank you very much! We live in an impatient, instantaneous world.

But God's love is patient. His love waits for us. When we mess up, he's there waiting, ready to forgive us and accept us back into his arms. Even when he'd be justified in feeling annoyed, exhausted, or through bothering with us, he doesn't go there. His patient love chooses us, again and again.

REFLECTION Are you a patient person? Is it easy for you to wait for the things you want? What does it mean to you that God's love is patient?

....
....
....
....
....
....
....
....
....
....
....

LOVE IS KIND

Love is kind.

1 CORINTHIANS 13:14

We often equate the word *kind* with *nice*. But when we say, "God's love is nice," that doesn't give us a full picture of what's being said in this verse. Remember, we're talking about agape love—which is the word Paul used repeatedly while writing 1 Corinthians.

God's kindness flows from his goodness. We're meant to practice this kind of love toward others—being warm, generous, and welcoming. We not supposed to be self-seeking but instead think of others' good and what we can do to love on them. We are to be tenderhearted and compassionate.

Christians are supposed to display these characteristics. But God *is* love, and he demonstrates kindness *perfectly*. Can you imagine being perfect at generosity, warmth, and tenderheartedness? God's love is all of that and more!

REFLECTION Each day this week, try to perform a random act of kindness for someone. Give a compliment. Reach out to someone who seems lonely. Tell your family you love them. Do your chores without being asked. Those are just a few ideas to get you started!

NOT SELFISH

[Love] does not envy, it does not boast, it is not proud.
1 CORINTHIANS 13:4

Here, we're going to look at three different characteristics of God's perfect agape love, grouped together under one idea: love does not envy or boast, and it isn't proud. What do envy, boasting, and pride have in common? They are all signs of selfishness.

When someone is envious, it means they desire what another person has. They are thinking of their own gain. When someone is boastful, it means they arrogantly trumpet their own accomplishments to boost their ego. When someone is proud (in the sense it's being used here), they are magnifying themselves and refusing to acknowledge God in their lives.

All of these are the antithesis of what God's love is like. Through his Son, God laid down his very life for us. He sought what was best for us and redeemed our souls because of his selfless love.

REFLECTION What's one way you can reflect the kind of selfless love Jesus showed during his earthly ministry?

DOES NOT DEMAND

[Love] does not dishonor others, it is not self-seeking, it is not easily angered, it keeps no record of wrongs.

1 CORINTHIANS 13:5

Ah, "keeps no record of wrongs." That one might be tough for a perfectionist to fathom! Remember the high-powered microscope we use to analyze our own mistakes—and sometimes the mistakes of others? Often, whatever we discover under that microscope gets immediately transferred into a vault where it lives forevermore.

Maybe that's a little dramatic, but if you struggle with this, you know exactly what I mean. Forgetting the times someone has wronged us is *hard*. Forgiving ourselves is *hard*. And yet God's love is like this. He is slow to anger and quick to forgive. When we have faith in him and we practice honest repentance, he is quick to erase our wrongs—*poof!* Forgotten, for good. It's as if it never happened, because it's erased from memory.

REFLECTION Do you have a hard time forgiving people who have wronged you? Can you think of a time when you didn't forgive someone but now wish you had?

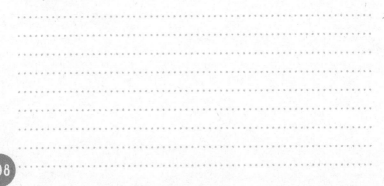

NEVER GIVES UP

●●●●●●●●●●

[Love] always protects, always trusts,
always hopes, always perseveres.

1 CORINTHIANS 13:7

That's a big word—*always*. We're used to being in relationships with other human beings, and human beings are imperfect. Even a very dear, lifelong, best friend probably doesn't *always* protect. They probably don't *perfectly* trust. They may *sometimes* give up. Because they're human, these small "failures" do not mean their love for you isn't true. They just love imperfectly.

But not God. His perfect agape love for you always protects. And he will never, ever, ever give up on you.

Did you hear that? Even if you fail. Even if you're feeling down. Even if you make tons of mistakes. God will never give up on you, and his love for you will never fade. Ever!

REFLECTION Do you feel like the love you have for others perseveres (doesn't give up)? It's easy to grow weary in relationships sometimes, but think of how you could grow in this area of agape love.

REPELS FEAR

●●●●●●●●●

For the Spirit God gave us does not make us timid,
but gives us power, love and self-discipline.
2 TIMOTHY 1:7

God's love repels fear. In him we are safe, secure, and content.
We are fully cared for, fully seen, fully known, and fully loved.
There is nothing to be afraid of—no harm that can befall us
that will ever erase our relationship with God. It's ours forever,
and fear has no home here.

If you're feeling nervous right now, like there are still a lot of
things you're afraid of, it's okay. We are not able to perfectly live
out this fearless love. We're human. We don't have perfect agape
love like God does, so rather than setting a standard we must
meet, this verse serves as an encouraging reminder.

We can rest assured that, even when we feel afraid, we can
fall back on the knowledge that God's love and our love for him
both repel fear.

REFLECTION How do you usually respond when you feel afraid? Write out
some truths about God's love to help you next time you're feeling anxious.

INSEPARABLE

●●●●●●●●●●

Who shall separate us from the love of Christ?
Shall trouble or hardship or persecution or
famine or nakedness or danger or sword?
ROMANS 8:35

Here's another wild truth about God's love: absolutely nothing can separate us from it. Remember how God's love never gives up? His love never quits on us, and external circumstances cannot separate us from him.

Do you see all those external circumstances Paul listed here? We might add political upheaval, social unrest, wars, violence, homelessness, food insecurity, and tons of other external circumstances and pressures to this list. But *nothing*—absolutely nothing—can separate us from the love of Christ.

We may—scratch that, we *will*—face adversity in our lives. Sometimes that adversity is intense. Many of the earliest followers of Jesus were actually killed for their faith. Yet even then, they were not separated from God's love. In fact, God's love for us and our faith in him are often the very things that either help us overcome adversity or give us the strength to bear it.

REFLECTION Can you think of a time when your faith gave you the strength to endure a tough situation? What about a time when you felt God's love wrapped around you during a season of hardship?

. . . .

. . . .

. . . .

. . . .

. . . .

TOO GREAT TO UNDERSTAND

And I pray that you . . . may have power . . . to grasp how
wide and long and high and deep is the love of Christ,
and to know this love that surpasses knowledge.
EPHESIANS 3:17–19

Paul prayed that the Ephesian church would have the power,
together with the church of believers at large, to understand
how big the love of Christ is. He said this might be possible
because the Ephesians (and we) are rooted and established in
love. And yet . . . he noted that this love surpasses knowledge.

That's an interesting truth about God. So much of his character and so many of his attributes are incomprehensible to us.
We can try to bring them down to human terms. We can try to
place God within our framework to attempt to understand him.
But our minds will simply never *fully* understand mysteries like
the Trinity.

But this does not free us from the responsibility of *trying* to
understand. We study and ponder and ask questions and learn
so we can gain a better grasp on the things of God, even when
they surpass knowledge!

REFLECTION How has your understanding of God and his love grown and
changed over the last year? What about over the last three or five or ten years?
Our understanding may never be complete, but it definitely gets deeper!

LIMITLESS LOVE
●●●●●●●●●

Day 303

Your love, LORD, reaches to the heavens,
your faithfulness to the skies.

PSALM 36:5

God's love and faithfulness have no bounds. If we need proof of this, think of how Jesus poured out his life for those who didn't even know God yet. Most of the Gentile world in Jesus's time had nothing whatsoever to do with the Jewish God. And of course Jesus gave his life for Jewish people too—in fact, the Jews were the ones he ministered to during his time on earth.

But his love extended beyond the bounds of God's chosen people to the entire world. That's why he called the apostle Paul and many others to share the good news beyond Galilee, Jerusalem, and Judea. And why he calls us to continue sharing the good news in our communities and beyond.

Imagine a love so big it spills out onto all of humanity. Onto every sinner, every person who knows God, every person who hasn't heard of him yet. God loves everyone. His love is limitless.

REFLECTION Is there a person you're having a hard time with right now? Maybe someone at school is bugging you, or maybe things have been tense with your parents lately. Sometimes it helps to take a deep breath and remind ourselves that God's love covers us and extends to them too. Try it!

GOD LOVES YOU, SPECIFICALLY

See what great love the Father has lavished on us, that we should be called children of God! And that is what we are! The reason the world does not know us is that it did not know him.

1 JOHN 3:1

God's love is massive, broad, far-reaching, and all-encompassing. It's also very, very precise in some ways. It stretches over everyone and funnels down to each specific person. God's love is both a big umbrella with many people standing beneath it and a one-to-one relationship, as though he's holding the hands of each individual.

God loves you, specifically. All of you. Your strengths, your talents. Even your weaknesses, when they prompt you to lean on him and ask for his help. He loves your personality (he had a hand in making it, you know). And he loves what you bring to the table.

You are wonderfully made, and your Maker delights in you. That is the love of a perfect Father. You're his child, his workmanship, and he simply adores you.

REFLECTION Several times as you've journaled through this book, I've asked you to write down some things you like about yourself. Write them out again, or write out a whole new list, if you want! Look at each item as you consider how much God loves everything on that list.

LOVED IN REBELLION

> You see, at just the right time, when we were still
> powerless, Christ died for the ungodly.
>
> **ROMANS 5:6**

We're going to take a break from focusing on perfection and look at what it means to have a real, personal relationship with God—because when that's in place, we have a perfect support in place whenever we find ourselves in doubt or anxiety over our human selves.

Remember when we talked about how limitless God's love is? We discussed how God loves those who know him and those who don't. This is something to be very thankful for, since we were once counted among those who don't know him.

Maybe you've known God (or at least *about* him) your whole life. Maybe not. But at some point, real understanding clicked. Even if you were very young when it happened, you went from not knowing or understanding God to having a personal relationship with him.

But God loved you just the same before that moment. He didn't look at you and think, *Ugh, not* him *again*. He loved you from the day you were born, and he loves you now.

REFLECTION Do you remember when your relationship with God crossed over? For some people, it wasn't one definitive experience but a series of steps that led to a deepened relationship. Write out your story!

YOU CAN'T EARN IT

••••••••••

But because of his great love for us, God, who is rich in
mercy, made us alive with Christ even when we were dead
in transgressions—it is by grace you have been saved.

EPHESIANS 2:4–5

God's love is a pretty amazing thing. Big, specific, and unfathomable.
If anyone understands even a little bit about God's love—*truly*
understands—they will want it. They will want perfect agape love
that never leaves, never fails, and never grows cold. How could we
possibly not want it?

But we can't earn it. For some people, this is a point of frustration. Earning rewards makes sense to our human brains.
We do well, then we get rewarded. Simple! But this isn't how
God's love works. He gives his love freely to those who don't
deserve it. Remember, no matter how much God loves us and
our wonderful traits, we are still sinful, and we can't fix that on
our own.

We are made alive, connected in the deepest way possible to
God's love, through Christ—and only him. God's love extends
to everyone. Saving grace and the fullest expression of God's
love only come through faith in Jesus.

REFLECTION How do you feel about not being able to earn God's love?
If this is something that puzzles or frustrates you, consider that you don't
have to earn it. You already have it. What a gift!

WE ARE FILLED

And hope does not put us to shame, because God's
love has been poured out into our hearts through
the Holy Spirit, who has been given to us.
ROMANS 5:5

Want to know something really cool? This big, deep, unfathomable, perfect love we've been talking about? Not only does it rest upon us, not only is it most fully expressed through our saving faith in Jesus, but we are actually *filled* with this love via the Holy Spirit.

When Jesus was resurrected, then ascended to heaven, he sent the Holy Spirit at Pentecost to fill his followers. This is how God operates in and through us as we live for him and grow in Christlikeness. We have his actual Spirit in us.

This is why, in the passage from 1 Corinthians 13 we read earlier, Paul was directing his comments about what agape love should look like to fellow humans. He was saying, "This is how your love should be." The love he described is *perfect*, and while we aren't capable of that, the reason we can demonstrate selfless, agape love at all is because we have the Holy Spirit within us.

REFLECTION Have you ever had a moment when you've shown love at a time that didn't make sense? For example, when someone hurt you and you were able to show immense grace and forgiveness. Have you ever considered that these moments are because the Holy Spirit is moving through you?

LOVE THAT DISCIPLINES

My son, do not despise the LORD's discipline, and do
not resent his rebuke, because the LORD disciplines
those he loves, as a father the son he delights in.
PROVERBS 3:11–12

Love that disciplines can be a hard thing for children to understand. Young minds often think, *If Mom loved me, she would give
me all the things I ask for,* or perhaps, *If she loved me, she would
never punish me.* As we get older, we understand that's not how
parental love works. If they're parenting well, caregivers lovingly
discipline us to provide boundaries, teach us important lessons,
and show us the right path to take. One day, they hope, we will
take those paths all on our own.

God's love is like this too. He loves us too much to let us
continue to make choices that ultimately hurt us. He disciplines
us to lovingly nudge us onto a better path. We're his children
and always will be, no matter old we are. But we cannot be open
to the fullness of his loving correction—and the growth that
comes with it—if we don't reject our perfectionism. Admitting
we've made mistakes is a vital part of that process!

REFLECTION Can you think of the last time your parents or caregivers
disciplined you for something? Keeping the idea of "love that disciplines" in
mind, do you see their point of view differently now?

LOVE THAT SPILLS

But the fruit of the Spirit is love, joy, peace, forbearance,
kindness, goodness, faithfulness, gentleness and
self-control. Against such things there is no law.
GALATIANS 5:22–23

It can be hard to visualize concepts like God's love or wrap our
minds around the Holy Spirit. But there are some things in the
natural world that can help us draw parallels and make our
understanding more complete.

You probably learned about states of matter in school. The
three most basic are solid, liquid, and gas. Liquids take on the
shape of whatever container they're in (like how water in a glass
is "shaped" like a cylinder). But gases will generally take up all
the available space and fill the container they're in, like when
you put helium in a balloon. If you open that container, the gas
will spill out into the air.

God's love is a bit like a gas (bear with me). If you are the
container, God's love—through the Holy Spirit—fills you up. It
becomes you-shaped as you move through life, trying to emulate
Christ. But it also spills out of you, onto others, when you open
your mouth to express love to them or to share about Jesus.

REFLECTION Have you ever thought about God's love spilling out of you
as you move through your life? Thinking about love as a liquid or a gas is a
strange analogy, but think about how his love spills from one person to the
next, filling each one as it goes. Pretty cool!

JESUS'S PERFECTION, OUR FAILURE

●●●●●●●●●

"Why do you call me good?" Jesus answered.
"No one is good—except God alone."

MARK 10:18

By now I hope we've spent enough time together that you feel seen, loved, and affirmed. You are God's beautiful creation, and he loves you so much. You don't have to be perfect—that's not what he's asked of us. He has asked us to love him and each other.

So throughout these upcoming days, keep that in mind. We're going to look at Jesus's example as the one we are to follow—*he* is the perfect one, and we're going to look at a number of ways in which he is perfect. Then we're going to compare it with how we, as humans, fail to live up to his perfection.

When we talk about our human failures, please remember these failures do not disqualify us from God's love or his calling in our lives. Never! Instead, recognizing how we fail is the first step to see where we can grow as followers of Jesus, knowing we will never reach his perfection but seeking to serve God in our lives.

REFLECTION Has it gotten easier to think about the ways we fail as you work through this book, recovering from a perfectionist mindset that tells you to be flawless? It's okay if it's still a struggle, and it's great if you feel you've made progress! Jot down some honest thoughts about where you're at today.

LIVING LIKE JESUS

"For I am the LORD your God who takes hold of your right
hand and says to you, Do not fear; I will help you."
ISAIAH 41:13

Jesus is both our Savior and example. We know this is true,
yet the idea of trying to live like him is a bit overwhelming.
Even for—perhaps especially for—a perfectionist. How can we
possibly measure up to such a high standard?

The answer is we can't. We can't achieve Jesus's level of
goodness, kindness, gentleness, or holiness. But the process of
trying is why we're here. And thankfully God doesn't command
us to follow Jesus's example, then walk away, leaving us helpless. He's *here* with us. Empowering us. The Holy Spirit dwells
within us. We have a guide, comforter, one who reminds us of
what is right, living in our hearts. The Spirit is present with us,
and he's here to help us on our journey toward living and loving
like Jesus did.

REFLECTION What's one area of your life where you'd like to grow in
Christlikeness over the next few months? Can you write out some practical
ways to encourage this growth?

PERFECT OBEDIENCE

"The one who sent me is with me; he has not left
me alone, for I always do what pleases him."
JOHN 8:29

This would be a wild statement for anyone except Jesus to make.
"I *always* do what pleases him [God the Father]." Oh, that we
could! We can't, but Jesus can and did. He stated it very plainly
right here. Of all the Gospels, John's is the one that most highlights Jesus's divinity (that is, the fact that he is God), and this
is one such example.

But this isn't the only time we see Jesus's perfect obedience
to God's will. Another example is the night before Jesus's cruci-
fixion, when he asked the Father to take "this cup" (his suffering
and death) from him, "yet not my will, but yours be done" (Luke
22:42). Jesus, in his human body, did not *want* to suffer. But,
even unto the point of death, he submitted himself to God's
perfect will.

REFLECTION Have you ever thought of how Jesus must have felt when
he was praying to the Father the night before he was killed? What kind of
emotions do you think he had in that moment?

OUR REBELLION

I do not understand what I do. For what I want
to do I do not do, but what I hate I do.
ROMANS 7:15

Ah, this is so relatable! The great apostle Paul wrote this verse, and even this man who was so instrumental in the early church, who's shaped Christianity for two thousand years with his inspired writings, said, "What am I even doing? I *want* to obey God. I *want* to serve him, but then I go off and do something else instead." Can you relate at all?

We can't know exactly what Paul was referring to here—whether it was a sticky sin he couldn't seem to fully break free from, or a bad habit, or maybe something as simple as a bad attitude he wanted to overcome. But it's probably better that we don't know the specifics. It makes it all the more relatable to know he struggled with obedience, just like the rest of us.

REFLECTION Have you ever struggled to break free from a bad habit, negative mindset, or harmful behavior? Like Paul, we should continuously seek to submit ourselves to God's will, but know that if you keep struggling, it doesn't mean your faith is false! Always feel free to reach out to a trusted person for help or accountability.

PERFECT TEACHER

●●●●●●○○○○

The people were amazed at his teaching, because he taught them as one who had authority, not as the teachers of the law.

MARK 1:22

Imagine being able to communicate everything you mean to say, just as it should be said. Being able to perfectly convey the concepts you want others to understand. Or having the ability to know exactly what your audience most wants—and needs—to learn about. I would very much like to have these skills!

Jesus's audiences didn't always understand him, but that was because of their lack, not his. Even the disciples didn't always grasp what he was trying to convey because they didn't yet understand the full context of who Jesus was and what the kingdom of heaven was like.

But Jesus's lessons were perfect. Each parable perfectly conveyed some element of the spiritual truth he was trying to illustrate. And Jesus's ultimate audience was not just the people standing before him in the moment. He knew his words and his lessons would echo through time by way of the Scriptures. He knew you and I would be learning from them two thousand years after they were spoken!

REFLECTION Have you ever had a special teacher? Maybe this teacher ignited your love for learning. Or maybe you discovered a passion for a particular subject because of this teacher's class. Think back on all your notable teachers and what you learned from them.

OUR LACK OF KNOWLEDGE

"Are you still so dull?" Jesus asked them.

MATTHEW 15:16

Oh man! Imagine Jesus asking you, point-blank, if you're still so dull. Jesus was speaking to his disciples here—his closest friends and followers—so it's all the more cringeworthy. You would think they would know exactly who Jesus is and what he's trying to teach!

But that wasn't the case then, and it's not the case now. Even as followers of Jesus, we struggle to understand him. We struggle to wrap our minds around the lessons Jesus taught because they often speak of heavenly things we haven't yet experienced. And even when we understand them intellectually, we struggle to put them into practice.

Jesus might say to us, at times, "Are you still so dull?" The answer is . . . yes, unfortunately! Which is why we're so grateful for grace. How wonderful that God doesn't ask us to grasp everything right away. He doesn't ask us to perfectly understand. He only asks us to keep seeking him, trusting him, and learning about him.

REFLECTION How do you feel when you struggle to understand something? Let's try to reframe it: instead of giving in to the frustration, thank God for his grace and patience in dealing with his children who sometimes lack understanding.

PERFECT HEALER

This was to fulfill what was spoken through the prophet
Isaiah: "He took up our infirmities and bore our diseases."

MATTHEW 8:17

This is a tricky concept. It can be tempting to think Jesus being
the perfect healer means anyone who believes in God will be
healed of all disease. But of course, many wonderful people of
faith have suffered or died from illness. Being a follower of Jesus
doesn't automatically cure you from a chronic illness or cancer.
Instead, the way Jesus is our perfect healer is *spiritual*. He bore
our spiritual illnesses and our spiritual deaths due to sin and
overcame them. In the future, his people will be resurrected and
given new physical bodies that will be physically healed.

Until then, it's absolutely appropriate to pray for healing
miracles! Jesus did many during his earthly ministry, and God
still heals people today. Just keep in mind that perfect healing
does not guarantee physical healing in this life. And that's true
no matter how closely you follow Jesus.

REFLECTION Take a few minutes to pray for those with chronic illnesses.
Maybe you or someone in your family has this kind of struggle. Maybe you
don't know anyone personally who deals with this, but it's likely you walk
past someone battling illness every day.

THE REALITY OF OUR DEATH

The dust returns to the ground it came from,
and the spirit returns to God who gave it.
ECCLESIASTES 12:7

Jesus has conquered death. This is true in the spiritual realm for us right this second. It's true physically for him now and for us in the future.

But the present reality is that our bodies will die someday, unless Jesus returns before that happens. Death comes for each of us, and we can't escape that fact, just as we can't escape our imperfection. Sin has done its destructive work in the world, and we're all beholden to that.

Except it won't last forever. Because Jesus, our perfect healer, has conquered death, our present obligation to death isn't permanent. As Jesus was before us, so we, too, will be resurrected. Christ's followers will receive remade, perfect bodies that are not vulnerable to disease or death. Hallelujah!

REFLECTION What do you think the best part of having a perfect resurrection body will be? We don't know exactly what these bodies will be like, but Jesus's body after his resurrection gives us some clues.

PERFECT COMPASSION

Jesus said, "Father, forgive them, for they do not know what they are doing." And they divided up his clothes by casting lots.

LUKE 23:34

This verse is hard to understand—incomprehensible, even. Imagine the pain Jesus was in as he hung on the cross. He was suffering in every way imaginable—physically, emotionally, and spiritually. He would have been in anguish. His human body was just like ours, capable of feeling pain. His human heart was like ours, capable of despair.

And he was an innocent man. He would have been fully justified in feeling angry at the men crucifying him. But he didn't pray for lightning to come down from heaven to smite them. Instead he prayed to the Father, asking forgiveness for the people who were hurting him. They weren't even repentant. They were actively hurting him, and still, this is what he prayed for.

His compassion was perfect. His mercy was flawless. Especially in this moment, as he died for the sins of humanity, he did not take the vengeance he was entitled to. He died so that everyone, including these men, would have a chance to repent. Wow!

REFLECTION Is there a grudge you've been holding against anyone for a while? After reading about Jesus's example, what's one way you can begin to let go of that today?

OUR VINDICTIVENESS

Do not take revenge, my dear friends, but leave room for God's wrath, for it is written: "It is mine to avenge; I will repay," says the Lord.

ROMANS 12:19

It's important to be very clear when we talk about forgiveness, compassion, and vengeance. You can forgive others and treat them with compassion *without* submitting yourself to abuse. You are *never* required to remain in an abusive situation to be a good Christian. It's always okay to draw boundaries, call out sin, and protect yourself and others.

But this does not ever give us license to seek vengeance on others. Ultimate judgment—and the dispensing of mercy, as he sees fit—belongs to the Lord. It's not for us to take revenge or seek to punish people outside the legal system. And yet seeking revenge is a very human impulse when someone causes us harm. Instinctually, we want to hurt those who hurt us.

Jesus's example shows us that this is our sinful nature at work, and we must tamp down that response, instead leaving justice to God, who judges all things perfectly.

REFLECTION How difficult do you find it to leave justice to God? Is that something you've had to wrestle with in the past? Has there been a time when you *could* have taken revenge but chose not to?

PERFECT KINDNESS

Day **320**

> "But love your enemies, do good to them, and lend to them without expecting to get anything back. Then your reward will be great, and you will be children of the Most High, because he is kind to the ungrateful and wicked. Be merciful, just as your Father is merciful."
>
> **LUKE 6:35-36**

Kind to the ungrateful and wicked? Oof! That's quite a high bar to reach. But this is true of God. Especially in the way he dispenses common grace—that is, the blessings that flow to all of humanity, regardless of whether those people know Jesus or not (this is different from *saving grace*, which comes through faith in Jesus). Sometimes we complain about this, thinking things like, *Why does this mean person have so many blessings when we're trying hard to be good?*

But if we really think about it, we should be very grateful that God shows kindness to the ungrateful and wicked . . . because sometimes, that's us! Even though we are God's children, at times we are not grateful. At times we mess up and sin. And still, the Lord is kind to us. His kindness is perfect—just as Jesus displayed during his time on earth, reaching out to the vulnerable, overlooked, and downtrodden.

REFLECTION Take some time today to think about how grateful you are that God's kindness does not depend upon our behavior—or our perfection! If you like to write out prayers, write out a prayer of thanksgiving.

OUR CALLOUSNESS

●●●●●●●●●

But because of your stubbornness and your unrepentant heart, you are storing up wrath against yourself for the day of God's wrath, when his righteous judgment will be revealed.
ROMANS 2:5

Whew boy. No one would read this verse and hope it applies to them! And if you're reading this book, actively trying to grow in your faith and walk with Jesus, I'm going to guess this *doesn't* apply to you.

Still, the verse is relatable for everyone, to some degree. Our hearts can harden, both to God and to those around us. And while Jesus displayed perfect kindness (which sometimes included a solid rebuke to those who needed it), we can become really focused on our own problems. In those times, perhaps we don't even see the suffering of those around us, let alone care about it.

It's not easy to adjust our focus, turning it outward instead of letting it stay fixed inward. But when we do, we emulate our Savior and his perfect kindness.

REFLECTION Is there someone in your life who needs a little extra kindness today? What can you do to show them you care?

PERFECT TRUTH

Jesus answered, "I am the way and the truth and the life. No one comes to the Father except through me."
JOHN 14:6

Jesus himself is truth. Because he is fully God and fully human, he is unique in that every word from his mouth is completely true. Sometimes those truths were concealed within stories, parables, and analogies. But the truth contained within them was always perfect for the message Jesus was trying to convey to his listeners—and later, us.

Because Jesus is truth, it also means he is the perfect judge. He is not biased. His perspective is never skewed. There are no gaps in his information. If Jesus judges something to be true, it is. Full stop.

Jesus stated to Pontius Pilate, as he was being questioned following his arrest, that the whole reason he was born and came into the world was "to testify to the truth. Everyone on the side of truth listens to me" (John 18:37). We, as his followers, listen to him because we are on the side of truth.

REFLECTION When you read Jesus's words in the Bible, how do they make you feel? What kinds of thoughts do they spark in you?

....
....
....
....
....
....
....

OUR LIES

Keep your tongue from evil and your lips from telling lies.
PSALM 34:13

Jesus is perfect truth, but we land somewhere sideways of perfect on this matter, to say the least. All you have to do is scroll the internet for ten minutes to see gossip, slander, misleading information, and, yes, outright lies. It's *everywhere*.

Because we get so much of our information from modern technology, it might be easy to assume this is a modern problem—people are gathered together in online spaces, swapping ideas, opinions, and falsehoods with far more people than our ancestors might have ever interacted with in their entire lives.

Yet, in Scriptures written thousands of years ago, there are dozens upon dozens of verses about lying. In both the Old and New Testaments. There are verses about slander and gossip too. So it seems this isn't so much a modern problem as it is a human problem! The good news is, that means all the advice in Scripture to deal with the issue is still relevant today as well.

REFLECTION Do you have a hard time being truthful? Sometimes it's really hard not to lie, like when we're trying to dodge getting in trouble. When do you find it's most difficult for you to tell the truth?

PERFECT WHOLENESS

For you know that it was not with perishable things such as silver or gold that you were redeemed from the empty way of life handed down to you from your ancestors, but with the precious blood of Christ, a lamb without blemish or defect.

1 PETER 1:18–19

The Law of Moses in the Old Testament had very clear instructions for many feasts and festivals that God's people were supposed to celebrate. One of those was Passover, to commemorate the time the Lord passed over the Israelites' homes when the plague of the firstborn was sent upon Egypt. They were supposed to take a one-year-old male lamb, kill it the night before the feast, then eat it the next day.

The Law demanded these lambs be without flaws. They needed to be whole—in good shape, not sick—in order for that sacrifice to be acceptable to God.

Jesus, the Lamb of God, is the ultimate fulfillment of this perfect, spotless lamb. It's probably not too hard to find a perfect lamb without obvious defect. A perfect human? Much harder—there's only ever been one! Jesus is completely whole, spiritually, without a spot of sin to mar him.

REFLECTION It's hard for us to imagine being perfectly whole in any sense, but one day we will be, when Jesus returns and sin is wiped from the world! What do you think that will be like? What are you most looking forward to?

OUR BROKENNESS

"You will not certainly die," the serpent said to the woman.
"For God knows that when you eat from it your eyes will be
opened, and you will be like God, knowing good and evil."
GENESIS 3:4–5

These are truly some of the saddest verses in the Bible. This is
where our brokenness began, the moment the serpent deceived
Eve in the garden. He was so crafty, using techniques that still
deceive people to this day. First, he undermined the truth God
spoke to Eve—he told her, "You will not certainly die." Then, he
struck at God's motivations, trying to convince Eve that God is
selfishly withholding something good from her. He appealed to
her desire to be *like* God, rather than a child of God.

And we've been making the same blunder ever since. Our
pride causes us to misunderstand and question God. Our fallen
nature leads us to sin, even when we're trying not to. Humanity
is broken and has been since the garden. In short, we desperately need a Savior.

Reminding ourselves of these truths can be difficult and
sad, but it leads us to a different kind of brokenness—a broken
spirit. One that is humbled before God, aware of its own sin—
and that's a good thing.

REFLECTION What do you think Jesus meant when he said, "Blessed
are the poor in spirit, for theirs is the kingdom of heaven" (Matthew 5:3)?

. . . .
. . . .
. . . .
. . . .
. . . .

PERFECT LAMB

The next day John saw Jesus coming toward him and said,
"Look, the Lamb of God, who takes away the sin of the world!"
JOHN 1:29

If you felt bummed after our last reading, I'm here to remind you of some good news—*the* Good News, actually! That perfect, whole, spotless Lamb with no defect and no blemish has spilled his blood for you and me. Because he's the perfect Lamb of God, we're not merely escaping the plague of the firstborn, being passed over as the angel of destruction comes through.

No, the blood of this Lamb is more powerful than that. It takes us from death to life. It seals us as children of God. It makes us coheirs in Christ, so the rights of true children belong to us too.

There has never been better news than this. It was Jesus's purpose on earth. It's the reason we're here, studying God's Word and trying to grow in our faith. It is because of the blood of the perfect Lamb that we, too, can say we are no longer slaves to sin. Hallelujah!

REFLECTION If you haven't read much about Passover before, read the story in Exodus 12. As you read, think of Jesus as the perfect Lamb. How does that change your understanding of this story?

WHAT IS IDENTITY IN CHRIST?

Consequently, you are no longer foreigners and
strangers, but fellow citizens with God's people
and also members of his household.
EPHESIANS 2:19

You may have heard that phrase before: "identity in Christ." In
fact, you may even read it several more times in this book. It's
one of those church phrases we say a lot, but have you ever really
considered what it means?

Perfectionists mistakenly get their sense of identity from
their accomplishments or their ability to perform. That's why
they begin to feel unlovable and unworthy if they fail to achieve.
As Christians, we know we should be getting our sense of self-
worth elsewhere—our identity in Christ. So we're going to look
closely at what, exactly, that means.

Our identity in Christ is a reference to how God sees us.
It's not based on who we are (though God loves who we are too)
or our accomplishments (he cares much less about them than
we do). Instead, our identity in Christ is based on Jesus and *his*
work on the cross.

REFLECTION Before we dive deeper, what are some things you think
might be tied to your identity in Christ?

. . . .
. . . .
. . . .
. . . .
. . . .
. . . .

CREATED IN HIS IMAGE

So God created mankind in his own image, in the image of
God he created them; male and female he created them.

GENESIS 1:27

Before we get to the specifics about our identity in Christ, let's
start with something that's true of all humanity: we are created
in God's image. Every human—no matter where they're from,
what they look like, what their personality is like, what culture
they come from, when in history they were born—is created in
the image of God.

That doesn't mean we're perfect as we are. Far from it. The
fall into sin distorted God's image in us. We no longer represent him as perfectly as Adam and Eve did before they sinned.
But for Christians, we can work to set aside that old version
and instead live as our "new self" thanks to Jesus's sacrifice in
our place (Colossians 3:10)—a self that is being renewed and
refreshed to be more like that image of God we once were.

Even so, every human being—even those who don't know
Jesus—is an image bearer of God and is worthy of being treated
with dignity.

REFLECTION Can you think of some things that are unique about human
beings among all creation? How do you think those things reflect God?

YOU ARE SAVED

"Very truly I tell you, whoever hears my word and
believes him who sent me has eternal life and will not
be judged but has crossed over from death to life."
JOHN 5:24

As human beings, we are created in the image of God, but something unique about our identity in Christ is that we are saved. That's another church word we hear all the time—*saved*. But what does it mean?

Just as Jesus said in the verse above, if we hear his words and believe he "who sent [him]" (God the Father), then we have eternal life and have crossed from death to life. We know, then, that if we don't hear Jesus's words and believe, we remain in death. Obviously, this is not referring to physical death. Jesus was talking about spiritual death and the judgment to come. When we're saved, we no longer need to worry about judgment for our sins!

REFLECTION Have you ever thought about what it means to be saved? How do you feel when you think about it?

YOU ARE FORGIVEN

Be kind and compassionate to one another, forgiving
each other, just as in Christ God forgave you.

EPHESIANS 4:32

An essential part of our identity in Christ—and directly connected to being saved from judgment—is the fact that we are forgiven. Because Christ paid the debt for all our sins, they are no longer counted against us. When God looks at followers of Jesus, he doesn't see a bunch of hopeless, wayward sinners. Instead, he sees his beloved children who have been ransomed by Jesus's sacrifice. We are forgiven—amen!

Now for the tougher part of this truth. Because *we* have been so graciously forgiven of our sins and God counts Jesus's righteousness as our own, because his grace has been absolutely lavished upon us when we didn't earn it, we must forgive others. I know. It's not always easy. It's hard to work on a relationship with another imperfect human. But, especially when both people involved are followers of Jesus who love God and want to serve him, forgiveness and restoration are beautiful!

REFLECTION Have you ever been in a situation where you did something wrong or even made an honest mistake, but the person who was hurt by it refused to forgive you? How did that feel? Were you ever able to restore the relationship?

YOU WILL HAVE TROUBLE

●●●●●●●●●

"I have told you these things, so that in me you
may have peace. In this world you will have trouble.
But take heart! I have overcome the world."

JOHN 16:33

Wait one minute! Isn't our identity in Christ supposed to be a
good thing? What does Jesus mean part of that identity is that
we'll have trouble? Can't we go back to salvation and forgiveness?

Sorry, friend. This is part of the package deal. Everyone on
earth has troubles and hardships and heartaches in their life,
but followers of Jesus have a little extra rolled into the mix.
Jesus said some families would split because of him. We know
many members of the early church were martyred. Not everyone
understands our faith, and that can bring misinterpretation and
hurt—or even persecution and violence.

But even as Jesus promised this trouble, in the next breath
he offered encouragement. He has overcome the world! The
things that get us down in this life—even the deaths of those
who have been killed for their faith—are not permanent. We
have a much greater future on the horizon, and our suffering
here is only temporary.

REFLECTION Have you ever thought of suffering and trouble as part of
your identity in Christ? It can feel like a bummer at first, but it doesn't have
to! What are some good things that have come from the hard times you've
had to endure?

. . . .

. . . .

. . . .

. . . .

YOU ARE SEEN AND LOVED

●●●●●●●●●

She [Hagar] gave this name to the LORD who spoke
to her: "You are the God who sees me," for she
said, "I have now seen the One who sees me."
GENESIS 16:13

If you don't know Hagar, she was the maidservant of Sarai,
Abram's wife (who would later become Sarah and Abraham).
Sarai mistreated Hagar, so Hagar ran away and hid in the
desert. In this passage, the Lord meets her and instructs her to
return to Sarai because he has plans to fulfill for each of them.
Hagar became a mother of nations, just like Sarai. And Hagar's
response was to give the Lord the name El Roi—the God who
sees me.

Friend, you are seen by the same God. And I mean *seen*. He
knows all about you. Everything you faced today? He saw it.
Everything you'll face tomorrow? Yep, he'll be there for that too.

But here's the best part: not only are you seen, you are loved.
And God has a plan for your life as well.

REFLECTION When you're in the midst of a hard moment, do you ever
think of God being there with you? Do you ever think about God watching
you as you move throughout your day? When we think of him like this,
sometimes it makes it easier and more natural to talk to him often.

YOU ARE BLESSED

And God is able to bless you abundantly, so that in all things at all times, having all that you need, you will abound in every good work.

2 CORINTHIANS 9:8

Sometimes our materialistic culture leaks into how we think about God. We begin to equate God's blessings in our lives with how much money we have, how many luxuries we experience, what kind of vacation we get to take. It's true that God sometimes lavishes these types of blessings on us. And there is nothing wrong with enjoying those things and thanking God for giving so generously.

But pay close attention to Paul's words. He said God will give us *all that we need*. Not every single thing we want. Not every passing fancy or outlandish desire we might have. But everything we *need*.

Paul even told us why God blesses us with everything we need. So "you will abound in every good work." There probably aren't many good works that require a fancy car. There's not much kingdom work that requires expensive clothes, the latest smartphone, or living in a big, new house. As followers of Jesus, we are already blessed with what we need in order to do God's work.

REFLECTION Take a moment to sort through the list of things you want versus things you actually need. Which list is longer? It's actually surprising how little we need, when you think about it!

YOU ARE HEARD

And if we know that he hears us—whatever we ask—
we know that we have what we asked of him.

1 JOHN 5:15

Remember those wants we talked about yesterday? Wanting things isn't wrong, especially when those "things" aren't material items at all. Sometimes what we want is the fulfillment of a big dream or goal. Sometimes we have a big vision, whether for something in our personal lives, our careers, or our ministries. It's not wrong to want those things.

And, as part of our identity in Christ, we can rest assured that God always hears us when we ask him. We don't always *get* everything we ask for. But because we know he hears us when we ask, if he says no to something, it's not because he ignored us or didn't understand the request. It simply means it wasn't in his plan and he has something better in mind. His plans for us are always good, even when they don't line up with what we thought we wanted.

REFLECTION How does it feel to know God hears every request you make? Does this influence what you will or won't ask of him?

YOU HAVE GIFTS

●●●●●●●●●

Our people must learn to devote themselves to
doing what is good, in order to provide for urgent
needs and not live unproductive lives.

TITUS 3:14

You already know this is true—everyone has gifts, both the practical variety and the spiritual variety—since we've gone over this in detail before. But did you realize this is part of your identity in Christ?

Anybody can be born with a practical gift—whether they're gifted in the arts, excellent with money management, good at building things, or thousands of other options. But followers of Jesus, filled with the Holy Spirit, are given something extra. These are gifts specifically used for the kingdom of God. And there's often a lot of overlap between our natural gifts and our supernatural gifts!

Everyone has something to contribute by lending their talents. It's part of our identity in Christ. We are equipped to do specific works God has prepared in advance for each of us.

REFLECTION What are some of your natural or practical giftings? Have you identified any of your spiritual gifts yet? Do you see any areas where your practical and spiritual gifts overlap? How would you like to use these gifts as you get older?

YOU ARE MADE NEW

Praise be to the God and Father of our Lord Jesus Christ! In his great mercy he has given us new birth into a living hope through the resurrection of Jesus Christ from the dead.

1 PETER 1:3

We are remade. Renewed. Born again.

We will never completely shake off our sinful nature in this life. It's just part of being human in this fallen world, and we will have to wait until Jesus returns to receive the complete fulfillment of being born again. But as we grow in our faith, as we walk in Jesus's footsteps and try to transform into his likeness more and more, we are changed. We're not the same people we were before we knew him. We're not even the same as we were a year ago!

We are spiritually born anew, and we are continuously transformed to be more like our Savior. This is a crucial part of our identity in Christ—something only believers get to experience!

REFLECTION Can you think of some evidence in your life that you have been made new? If you've been a Christian for a long time, it might be easy to think of examples of that transforming work—or it might be hard to even remember what you were like before Jesus!

YOU ARE LOVED

> In all these things we are more than conquerors through him who loved us. For I am convinced that neither death nor life, neither angels nor demons, neither the present nor the future, nor any powers, neither height nor depth, nor anything else in all creation, will be able to separate us from the love of God that is in Christ Jesus our Lord.
>
> **ROMANS 8:37–39**

Nothing can separate you from the love of God. *Nothing*. Not life or death. Not angels or demons. Nothing that's happened in the past or will happen in the future. *Nothing* in all creation can separate you from the love of God that is in Jesus.

Notice that last caveat Paul added—this ironclad love of God is specific to those found in Christ Jesus our Lord. God loves all people. He desires all people to be saved, brought into relationship with him. But there is something special about his love for those who are already engaged in that amazing relationship through Jesus. That's you, friend. You have that unbreakable love of God.

REFLECTION Picture the strongest thing you can think of. Maybe the steel supports of a high-rise building. Or diamonds. Or Kevlar. Think of all of that and more supporting the love of God for you. And give him praise!

YOU ARE VICTORIOUS

"Where, O death, is your victory? Where, O death, is your sting?" The sting of death is sin, and the power of sin is the law. But thanks be to God! He gives us the victory through our Lord Jesus Christ.

1 CORINTHIANS 15:55–57

Victory. Winning. Triumph! We are (recovering) perfectionists, so we tend to appreciate these words. Even if the person we are most often competing with is ourselves, we usually love to win—to smash the goal, grab the prize, beat the top score. To level up.

But being victorious in Christ is not about winning a prize—at least not in the competitive, worldly sense. Paul told us in today's verse where our victory lies, and it's got nothing to do with achievements or accolades or goals.

Through Christ, we are victorious over death. While our physical bodies will die, that death is not permanent. We will be raised again, just as Christ was raised before us. Though our spirits were dead before we knew Jesus, now they are alive. Death holds no dominion over us, in this life or the next, because Jesus has conquered the grave. This is a glorious part of our identity in Christ, and it's something only Jesus's followers can claim.

REFLECTION How does knowing death holds no victory over you change the way you live now—in this life, or in the future?

. . . .
. . . .
. . . .
. . . .
. . . .

IDENTITY CRISIS: MOSES

When the child grew older, she took him to Pharaoh's daughter and he became her son. She named him Moses, saying, "I drew him out of the water."
EXODUS 2:10

If you've ever struggled with your identity, you're in good company. Even some of our biblical heroes had a hard time understanding who they were, how they fit into the world, and how they fit into God's big-picture plan.

Moses is one of these heroes. We get more information about his life than almost anyone else in the Bible. We see his highs and lows, get to witness his special relationship with God, and watch him lead the tribes of Israel through one of the most critical moments of their history. He was certainly someone who was special to God.

And yet Moses didn't always understand how he fit in. He was stuck between two worlds, and they could not have been more different. He was Hebrew, born at a time when his people were enslaved in Egypt and all the baby boys were meant to be drowned in the Nile. Instead, Moses was placed in a basket in the river, only to be discovered by Pharaoh's daughter and adopted into the royal household. That's quite a reversal!

REFLECTION Have you ever struggled to understand your place in God's plans? That feeling is nearly universal! Reflect on some ways God has used you in the past.

MOSES: UNSURE

●●●●●●●●●●

But Moses said to God, "Who am I that I should go to
Pharaoh and bring the Israelites out of Egypt?"
EXODUS 3:11

At this point, Moses's life had taken several more dramatic
turns. Then, at eighty years old, God came to him and told him
to go to Pharaoh. The time had come for the Israelites to be
rescued from their captivity and brought into the land God had
promised them.

But even though God was speaking directly to him, we see
that Moses was not at all sure about this idea. "Who am I?" he
asked. How could he possibly go to Pharaoh and ask this of him?
We have the benefit of time and perspective, so we can look back
at Moses's life and shout, "Don't worry! God's with you in this!"
But at the time, Moses felt very unsure of the role God called
him to.

Does that seem relatable? Have you ever wondered who you
are and how you'll ever be so bold as to step into the things God
has called you to? If so, you're in very good company! Moses and
many of God's powerful prophets felt the same.

REFLECTION We've just looked at several details of your identity in Christ,
and those truths never change! When you feel unsure, you can always look
back at those to remind yourself of who you are in him and find assurance
that you *are* equipped for the work he calls you to do.

MOSES: CALLING

●●●●●●●●●●

Moses said to the LORD, "Pardon your servant, Lord.
I have never been eloquent. . . . I am slow of speech
and tongue." The LORD said to him, "Who gave human
beings their mouths? . . . Is it not I, the LORD? Now go; I
will help you speak and will teach you what to say."
EXODUS 4:10–12

We looked at Moses's calling earlier in this book, but let's examine it from a slightly different angle. Even though Moses felt
unsure of who he was and what authority he could possibly
carry, God reassured him. His calling didn't depend on how
secure he felt or even how gifted he was. In fact, God asked him
to do something he was *not* gifted in. His calling depended on
who God was and the work he prepared for his servant.

Full stop. No more qualifiers needed. God said, "Do this for
me," and everything was set in place for Moses to do it and succeed. Moses's doubt made things go down slightly differently,
of course. In Exodus 4:13, he begged God to send someone else,
and God was not thrilled with that request. And still, he honored
it, making Aaron the mouthpiece, even if Moses was the leader.

As with Moses, God will never ask us to do something without making a way for us to follow through on it.

REFLECTION Have you ever felt God calling you to do something you usually
consider one of your weaknesses? If so, how did you grow from that experience?

AUTHENTICITY

Day 342

"Peace I leave with you; my peace I give you. I do not give to you as the world gives. Do not let your hearts be troubled and do not be afraid."

JOHN 14:27

Authenticity is a big buzzword these days. Marketing experts who study such things say generations like yours really care about authenticity.[5] These people want brands—and individuals—to be their authentic selves, not hiding behind masks or facades. They want sincerity, truth, and realness. This is why even big-name brands are moving away from airbrushed models and selecting representatives of all body types, ethnicities, and abilities. We now want people who feel real.

But being real—authentic and transparent—is hard for perfectionists. When we're well aware of our flaws, it can hinder us from showing our true, messy selves to others. Social media especially makes it easy to hide our flaws, when face-altering filters and slick edits are commonplace. In real life, it's even harder to open up, to show everyone the truth, when we're afraid they will judge us as unworthy. But we're going to take a deep look at authenticity—why it matters and how we can pursue it as we recover from a perfectionist mindset.

REFLECTION Do you notice when companies use unedited images in their advertising? How do you feel about that versus heavily altered or "perfected" images?

TRUE VULNERABILITY

That is why, for Christ's sake, I delight in weaknesses, in insults, in hardships, in persecutions, in difficulties.

2 CORINTHIANS 12:10

Authenticity starts in our relationship with God. Sometimes we fall back into Adam and Eve mode, covering our faces and hiding from the Father as he strolls through the garden looking for us. But we know better than that. We know we *can't* hide from God. He's everywhere. He sees everything. Until we're able to be real with him, who we know can see through our mask, it's going to be really hard to be real with others.

True vulnerability is letting our perfect, sinless God see the real us. Not pretending we have it all together, and not ignoring him when we feel guilty, ashamed, or less than perfect. Authenticity with God is acknowledging our weaknesses and strengths, crying out to him in moments of need, and above all else remembering we are loved at all times.

REFLECTION How real do you feel you're able to be with God? Do you feel like you're able to share your emotions with him? Your fears? What about the times you're angry or confused? God is there to listen, always, and he cares about every part of you.

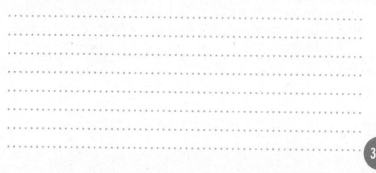

The righteous choose their friends carefully, but
the way of the wicked leads them astray.

PROVERBS 12:26

Once we feel like we're able to be open with God, honestly showing him all parts of ourselves, even when they're not pretty, we can begin to be open with others. This can be harder because oftentimes we fear losing the love of other people more than we do losing the love of God. The love of God may matter more to us, but we feel more secure in it because his love is perfect.

Here's something to keep in mind as you open up to others and show them your true, authentic self: not everyone gets invited into the deepest parts of who you are. Remember the bull's-eye we talked about before? It's wise to be selective about who you let into the inner circle of your life. It's a high-trust position.

But those whom you've chosen to let in deserve to see the real you. They *want* to see the real you, and you probably want to show it to them. You wouldn't have let them into your inner circle if not!

REFLECTION Think about the people in your inner circle. Do you think you let them see the real, authentic you? Is there someone you're pretty close to whom you've kept in an outer ring because you're afraid to let them in?

BIBLICAL SELF-ESTEEM

When you believed, you were marked in him with a seal, the promised Holy Spirit, who is a deposit guaranteeing our inheritance until the redemption of those who are God's possession.
EPHESIANS 1:13–14

God's possession. That's you. You belong to him. It's personal and it's deep. You're a beloved, treasured possession, someone he values and adores. He says you are worth . . . everything. And that's never going to change.

If you're ever feeling bad about yourself, I want you to reread that paragraph. Because our self-esteem is based on *that*. All that truth up above—it's how much God values us. We know it's not based on our achievements. We know it doesn't rise or fall on our successes and failures. But it also doesn't hinge on what other people think of us. It doesn't even hinge on what you think of yourself.

This truth is grounding. Foundational. It's a solid rock on which we can build our authenticity with others. We are free to be ourselves, to openly serve and honor God, because God says we're loved.

REFLECTION Do you worry a lot about what people think of you? It's hard not to. If your sense of self-worth is built upon others' opinions of you, then imagine swapping out that platform for one that says "God's unconditional love" on it.

GOD'S HELP

> But thanks be to God, who always leads us as captives
> in Christ's triumphal procession and uses us to spread
> the aroma of the knowledge of him everywhere.
>
> **2 CORINTHIANS 2:14**

Are you ready for some truths that will help you open up to others and be more authentic with them—and yourself? The first is that we need God's help not to sin. In other words, you are not perfect.

I know. This is not shocking or fresh news, this deep into our journey together! But sometimes the biggest roadblock to true authenticity is feeling like we must present a perfect, tidy package to everyone else, like we need to be the most airbrushed versions of ourselves. It would be nice if we could say this is true everywhere *except* church, but in reality, sometimes church is the place where we airbrush the most.

We gloss over the fact we're struggling. We don't mention we're in a rough place with God right now. We're afraid of judgment, so we put a filter on the photo of our faith. But we don't have to. If we can be honest with God about needing his help not to sin—and we can—we can be honest with others!

REFLECTION You don't have to write them down if you don't want to, but think about the top things you're struggling with in life right now. Have you been open with anyone about them? Have you talked to God about them? Remember, he wants to help us avoid sin, and he's there for you.

NOT IN CONTROL

"For my thoughts are not your thoughts, neither are your ways my ways," declares the LORD. "As the heavens are higher than the earth, so are my ways higher than your ways and my thoughts than your thoughts.

ISAIAH 55:8–9

Argh! Why does this truth sting so much? Can't our ways be as good as God's ways? Can't we be in control of everything so we can make it go according to plan?

Frankly, no. And that's hard to accept sometimes! But releasing the need to feel like we're in control of everything is a beautiful step on the path to being authentic with others. Recognizing that we're not in control allows us to be more vulnerable. It gives us the freedom to admit we're not perfect, we don't have it all together, and life throws major curveballs sometimes.

And it's really okay. Everyone is walking that path. When we're open, honest, and accepting of that, we are able to support and rely on each other.

REFLECTION Is it hard to admit when you're not in control of something? Or do you find that idea freeing?

THE PUZZLE

"Are not five sparrows sold for two pennies? Yet not one of them is forgotten by God. Indeed, the very hairs of your head are all numbered. Don't be afraid; you are worth more than many sparrows."

LUKE 12:6–7

Here's another truth to help you open up to others and show them your true self. Each of us is only one small piece of the big, global puzzle. Even the most influential, "important" people are just itty-bitty cogs in the grand machine of humanity. Very few people have changed the course of civilization or even left a mark on history. And yet we all have value. Every single person has inherent worth.

Rather than discouraging us or making us feel unimportant, this can release us from pressure. How? It's a reminder not to take yourself too seriously. It's okay to take a risk. It's okay to wear your heart on your sleeve if that's your style. Find your people and take the leap—be real with them, and let them be real with you. We're all each just one small piece in a very big puzzle.

REFLECTION Imagine zooming out on all of history. Think of all the many billions of people who have lived across time. How does it make you feel when you think about being one of them? Now consider that God loves each of us specifically!

OUR STRENGTH

As the mountains surround Jerusalem, so the LORD surrounds his people both now and forevermore.
PSALM 125:2

If you think about your truest self, all the way down to your very core, where does your sense of strength come from? There's probably several areas where you feel strong. But what's the *source* of your strength?

If you answered, "God," you're exactly right! It's okay to show our true selves because God is the core of our strength. We rely on him in everything we do. Even when we're operating in our gifts and the talents he's blessed us with, we are still leaning on God's strength.

Like all of these truths, this is both bolstering and freeing. Some people won't get you. That's okay. You won't be great at everything in life. That's okay too. The Lord is your strength, your center, your reason for living as you live, loving as you love. It's a beautiful thing to show that to the world.

REFLECTION When do you most connect with the truth that God is your strength? Is it when you're operating in your gifts, knocking it out of the park? Or is it in the moments where you feel weak or helpless? Something in between? God is there in all those moments!

RELYING ON HIM

●●●●●○○○○○

I can do all this through him who gives me strength.

PHILIPPIANS 4:13

Because God is our strength and our source, we must rely on him. He is the one who shines through our weak spaces. He is the glue that holds us together in the places we're fractured. When being real with others, we don't need to shy away from this. We don't need to be ashamed to say, "This area is a struggle for me." Or, "I'm not good at this, but I'm willing to learn." Or how about, "This is what I think, but I could be wrong."

The truth is that our weaknesses make us lean harder into God. They make us humble. They show the rest of the world we're just like them—vulnerable and imperfect, but allowing God's glory to shine through and his Spirit to work in our lives. And what could be more real than that?

REFLECTION Do you have a hard time admitting your weaknesses to others? Think about the ways God has displayed his strength through one of your weaknesses in the past.

. . . .

. . . .

. . . .

. . . .

. . . .

. . . .

. . . .

. . . .

. . . .

. . . .

. . . .

EXPOSING OUR BROKENNESS

Put off your old self, which is being corrupted by its
deceitful desires . . . put on the new self, created to
be like God in true righteousness and holiness.
EPHESIANS 4:22–24

Sometimes we're afraid of showing our true selves because, let's face it, it's not always pretty in there. We're broken and sometimes confused or ashamed. There are pieces of us we'd rather not confront, let alone share.

But the truth for followers of Jesus is all that brokenness we're afraid to show others is part of our old selves. This doesn't mean we no longer sin. But it does mean we have a new self. That broken person has been rewrapped in God's grace. You are in the process of being renewed. Transformed. Turned into something even more beautiful than what you were before.

Don't be afraid to tell your whole story. Don't be afraid to show what God has done—and continues to do—in your life. We're all works in progress, being renewed by the Master.

REFLECTION As with your inner circle, it's wise to be selective about who gets to know your whole story. Is there anyone in your life who knows your full testimony? Is that something you're comfortable sharing with others?

AN AUTHENTIC LIFE

Then he said to them all: "Whoever wants to
be my disciple must deny themselves and take
up their cross daily and follow me."
LUKE 9:23

What is the best, truest way we can live an authentic life? Jesus
said it right here: we must take up our cross daily and follow him.
That's the way a follower of Jesus lives their most authentic life.

What does that mean? When we take up our cross daily,
we deny what our human nature wants to do and follow him
and his example. We think about what God wants for our lives,
rather than what we want for ourselves. We think about serving his kingdom above serving our desires. If something was
important to Jesus, we make it important to us. Examples of
this include looking out for the marginalized, spending time in
prayer with God, and spreading the message of truth.

We are to practice these habits daily. They should become
second nature—or rather, our primary nature! The more we follow him, the more we are transformed.

REFLECTION Have you heard the phrase "take up your cross" before?
How have you understood it in the past? What are some ways you can level
up in applying it to your life now?

ENCOURAGEMENT

●●●●●●●●●

Day 353

But to each one of us grace has been
given as Christ apportioned it.
EPHESIANS 4:7

I hope by this point, you have released yourself from perfectionist prison and are well on your way to becoming a recovered perfectionist, secure in who you are, just as God made you. I'd like to wrap up our time together with words of encouragement, and I hope you'll use them to propel you toward even greater recovery!

Mistakes happen; that's why pencils have erasers. Cheesy? Yes. Cliché? Probably. But oh so true? Also yes. In life, we're all writing our stories in pencil. It doesn't mean we get to undo—erase, rewind, delete—when we mess up. We'd need a time machine for that. But it does mean we can change moving forward. It does mean our past mistakes do not have the power to ink our futures. God redeemed us—he can redeem our mistakes too!

REFLECTION When you think back on your life so far, how set in stone has it felt to you? The past is not changeable, but do you feel a greater sense of freedom moving into your future?

YOUR BEST EFFORT

●●●●●●●●●●

"For my yoke is easy and my burden is light."
MATTHEW 11:30

Are you ready for one of the greatest truths I hope you take away from this book? Your best effort is good enough. Whether we're talking about school, your future job, your life at home, your relationships, and everything you set your hand to, now and in the future—hear it again. Your best effort *is* good enough. Full stop.

There's no qualifier there. It's not good enough only if you win. It's not good enough only if you get an A+. It's not good enough only if you smash your goal and grab the prize. If it's your best effort—if you tried your hardest and did everything to the glory of God—then it's enough.

This is all God asks of us. He never asked us to be first, best, prettiest, most talented, or most successful. He asked us to trust him, to work diligently, and to do everything for his glory. Your work is good enough, and *you* are good enough.

REFLECTION Write down on a sticky note or index card, "My best effort is good enough." Put it someplace you'll often see it. When you're feeling overwhelmed with demands or like you've failed somehow, repeat the words to yourself.

ONLY GOD

●●●●●○○○○○

As for God, his way is perfect: The LORD's word is
flawless; he shields all who take refuge in him.
PSALM 18:30

Only God is perfect. I know—you already know this. You knew
this before you even opened this book! But consider again, in
light of all we know now, what this means for you and me.

God never asks us to be him. In fact, it's a bit offensive when
we try to do that. It's not our job, and we're comically bad at trying to do God's job. We were not built to carry the weight of our
own world on our shoulders, let alone the weight of *the* world.

No, instead God only asks us to trust him. Simple. Not
always easy, but simple. And even this simple task, we don't do
perfectly. It's okay. God knows who he's dealing with. He knows
that our best effort will fall short. He says, "Try anyway, and
trust me."

REFLECTION How does it make you feel when you consider that God doesn't
expect you to be flawless? Is it a freeing thought? Puzzling? Wonderful?

GROWTH

When I was a child, I talked like a child, I thought
like a child, I reasoned like a child. When I became
a man, I put the ways of childhood behind me.

1 CORINTHIANS 13:11

If God doesn't expect us to be perfect, if that's not even the
point, then what is the point of working diligently to his glory?
What is God expecting of us as we go through our process of
sanctification and renewal?

Growth. Growth is the point. He wants to see us get closer
and closer to the next point on our journey, becoming more and
more "us" at every stop. And you want to know something that
would poke any perfectionist right in the soft spot? *Mistakes
help us grow*.

Argh! Why mistakes and not winning? It's just the way it
works, my friend. It's great when we knock it out of the park.
God will grant us those successes too. But the times when we
fail? When things don't go to plan? When we have to lean on
God and not rely on our wits? Those are the times that will have
us sprinting to the next point on our path of growth.

REFLECTION What "mistakes" have you made over the last year that, looking back, were beneficial and changed you for the better? How different do
you think you'd be today if those things hadn't happened?

EFFORT IS PRAISEWORTHY

Those who work their land will have abundant food,
but those who chase fantasies have no sense.
PROVERBS 12:11

This is an important piece of reframing you must do when you're recovering from perfectionism: your effort is praiseworthy. We must learn to measure success based on the effort we put in, not the end result. We can hope the end result is fantastic too (more on that in a minute). But just the fact that we tried needs to become our focus.

As I reach the end of writing this book, my recovering perfectionist mind is already throwing self-doubting questions at me. *Is it worse than my other books? What if everyone hates it? What if I'm the only one who needs this message, and everyone else reading this book thinks I'm crazy?*

Time to reframe! Instead of allowing myself to worry about these questions, I'm focusing on the months of research and prayer that went into this book. I'm remembering days spent at the keyboard thinking of you, who would eventually read these words. Some of those days were grueling. Others felt easier. But a ton of energy was expended and effort was poured into it. And no matter what, that means I succeeded.

REFLECTION Are you reaching the end of any big projects? The next time you do, think back on your effort and give yourself a big pat on the back, no matter the end result.

TRYING

⬤⬤⬤⬤◍◍◍◍◍

"Have I not commanded you? Be strong and courageous.
Do not be afraid; do not be discouraged, for the LORD
your God will be with you wherever you go."

JOSHUA 1:9

The thought of making mistakes is scary. We don't like to think
of messing up, failing, falling flat. That's not just a perfectionist
thing, by the way. No one sets out to fail!

But for perfectionists, sometimes the fear of failing holds
us back from doing things we want to do. Sometimes it holds
us back from doing things we *should* do. Right now, let's make a
commitment to no longer give in to that fear.

Because you know what? Trying, even when you're afraid,
even when you know you might make a mistake, is very, very
brave. I mean it. Taking risks is hard. Putting yourself out there
is hard. Some people live their whole lives afraid, and they make
themselves smaller than they should be—smaller than God created them to be. Don't let that be you!

REFLECTION What's the big leap you've been hesitant to take? Is it something you think you're being called to? Is it a deep desire of your heart? Is it
time to go for it? Be brave!

EMBRACE EXCELLENCE

In everything set them an example by doing what is
good. In your teaching show integrity, seriousness
and soundness of speech that cannot be condemned,
so that those who oppose you may be ashamed
because they have nothing bad to say about us.
TITUS 2:7–8

I've spent a lot of time telling you not to focus on the end result.
Growth is the point. Effort is what is to be noticed and praised.
I assure you I mean every word of that!

But striving for excellence is probably part of your DNA. I
get it. It's likely built into your personality to care about doing
excellent work. And that's really okay. You can embrace that part
of yourself while simultaneously applying every piece of advice
you've read over the last year. It's all about where you get your
sense of identity and self-worth. As long as you're striving for
excellence and setting goals not because you feel you have to,
but because it gives you joy and fulfillment, you're channeling
this part of your personality in a positive way.

God made you with and on purpose. Be you. Delight in you.
God sure does.

REFLECTION Write out the things you most like about yourself. Either
look back at the lists you've already journaled throughout this book or
create one totally from scratch. Focus on the character traits God built you
with, your gifts, your heart. Thank God for making such a specific you!

REJECT PERFECTION

In peace I will lie down and sleep, for you
alone, Lᴏʀᴅ, make me dwell in safety.

PSALM 4:8

Yep, that's right. Embrace excellence, but reject perfection. Excellence and perfection are not synonymous. Perfection is not an attainable standard, and it's not one we've been asked to reach. So why in the world would we waste one more breath, one more heartbeat caught up in it?

Nothing is perfect except God. No one is perfect except God. But there are many things in this world that are very, very good. There are many things that are excellent and praiseworthy and lovely and kind. These are the things we are to focus on. These are the things we are to allow our minds to dwell upon, not the unattainable standard we were never asked to meet.

So go ahead. Right now, picture banishing the idea of perfection in yourself or your work. Perfection belongs to God alone, so let's leave it with him and focus on doing our best and serving our Lord.

REFLECTION Write out your top five excellent, praiseworthy, lovely things from this week. If you're having a hard time coming up with some, take a walk in nature. There's no shortage of beauty in this world God made.

YOU'RE ALLOWED TO REST

In vain you rise early and stay up late, toiling for food
to eat—for he grants sleep to those he loves.
PSALM 127:2

Ah, perfectionist workaholics. Noses always to the grindstone,
every minute of the day sucked up by schoolwork, activities,
extracurriculars, maybe even a job. Chores, ministry work, community service, sports. If your days look like this—all day, every
day—you may need to hear this truth: you are allowed to rest.

Didn't hear me? I'll try again: you are *commanded* to rest.
Right alongside "Don't steal" and "Honor your parents" and
"Don't murder," God said, "Take a break." Rest. Later, Jesus clar-
ified that the Sabbath day of rest was made for man. In other
words, it was commanded to be a benefit to God's people. He
gave us rest as a gift!

We all have responsibilities we can't skip out on. But if you
find you have no time to rest, you probably need to commit
to fewer activities. Or you need to assess how you're spending
your downtime. Sometimes we *feel* like we have no rest, but it's
because we're spending our downtime doing something that's
stressing our brains, like scrolling social media. So rest! Be
intentional about allowing yourself true downtime.

REFLECTION Sketch out an overview of your typical week. Do you have
pockets of time for rest? If not, can you create some?

TAKE A MOMENT

Rejoice in the Lord always. I will say it again: Rejoice!
PHILIPPIANS 4:4

I'm about to give you a wild piece of advice. Are you ready? Take a moment to have fun. I know. Insane. But you're allowed, I promise. And it's healthy!

God did not create us to be perpetually somber. He didn't create us to be constantly working, constantly striving. In addition to needing rest, people need to have fun as well. God gave us the gift of laughter. He gave us the gift of friendship and soul-lifting hobbies and pets and art and all kinds of wonderful things that are there for our enjoyment. They're here to bless us.

Embrace that. Embrace the idea that you're allowed to have fun and be carefree, and thank God for that!

REFLECTION What are some things that bring you joy? Write out a list of activities you find the most fun and people you love to spend time with. Over the next month, make sure you have time to devote to these activities and relationships.

YOU ARE ACCEPTED

"All those the Father gives me will come to me, and whoever comes to me I will never drive away."

JOHN 6:37

Do you have faith in Jesus? Do you believe in him as your Savior? If so, then you've come to him in the sense he described in this verse. And do you see what Jesus said about those who the Father gives to him? He will *never* drive us away.

You're his. He is yours, and that will never change as long as you live. You are accepted. You're in! The love, faithfulness, and gratitude this sparks in our hearts spurs us on to being better people, better representations of Christ to the world who needs him.

But you are not striving for that place beside Jesus. You're already there. You're not desperately working to gain that approval. You already have it, because it's based on Christ's work, not your own. You are accepted, my friend!

REFLECTION Write out a prayer of thanksgiving today. What are you most thankful for? That you're able to stand beside Jesus and he'll never drive you away? That this acceptance is based on his work alone?

INHALE, EXHALE

Day **364**

When I am afraid, I put my trust in you. In God,
whose word I praise—in God I trust and am not
afraid. What can mere mortals do to me?

PSALM 56:3–4

You've read many of God's promises to us in this book. We've
talked about lots of different freeing, soul-warming truths.
We've dived deeper into who God is and why we should trust
him. We've looked closely at Jesus's character and his work on
the cross. I want you to imagine inhaling all of those deep, profound truths as you breathe in.

Then exhale slowly, imagining all your fear, self-doubt, negative thought patterns, and anxiety leaving your body through
that breath. You can repeat this process as many times as you
want, whenever you want.

Whenever you need to be reminded of your identity in
Christ, breathe it in, then exhale that imposter syndrome.
Breathe in God's promises; exhale insecurity. Breathe in God's
acceptance; exhale perfectionism. Inhale. Exhale. Repeat.

REFLECTION Write out a list of things you would like to inhale. Focus on
things that are true and good, like what God says about you and how much
he loves you. Then write out a list of things you'd like to exhale—negative
thought patterns, insecurities, harmful lies you've believed about yourself.
Practice inhaling and exhaling these things during prayer time, before bed,
or whenever makes the most sense to you.

YOU ARE BELOVED

For those who are led by the Spirit of
God are the children of God.

ROMANS 8:14

If you know Jesus, you have received the Holy Spirit. If you have the Spirit and are led by him, you are a child of God. And you are beloved.

God looked at you and said, "Yes. She is worth dying for." God looked at you and said, "Yes. He belongs to me. I love him to the ends of the earth." You are treasured. Adored. Worth absolutely *everything*. God's love is about you. But it's also about him. Loving you brings him glory.

That's because his love changes us. We see him clearer, understand him better, worship him more and in greater truth because of his love. And this relationship with him will last forever. God and his beloved children will spend eternity in this loving relationship, with him being forever glorified through our worship and praise. And do you know what that will be like? Simply, perfection.

REFLECTION If you fully embraced the idea that you are the treasured possession of the Most High God, what's one thing you would change about the way you live your life? Would you worry less? Love harder? Take more healthy risks? Share the love of Christ more boldly with others? Do it! Start today!

NOTES

1. Steinert, Christiane et al. "Procrastination, Perfectionism, and Other Work-Related Mental Problems: Prevalence, Types, Assessment, and Treatment-A Scoping Review." *Frontiers in Psychiatry* vol. 12 736776. 11 Oct. 2021, doi:10.3389/fpsyt.2021.736776.

2. "Cortisol: What It Is, Function, Symptoms & Levels." Cleveland Clinic, https://my.clevelandclinic.org/health/articles/22187-cortisol. "Epinephrine (Adrenaline): What It Is, Function, Deficiency & Side Effects." Cleveland Clinic, https://my.clevelandclinic.org/health/articles/22611-epinephrine-adrenaline.

3. "Cortisol: What It Is, Function, Symptoms & Levels." Cleveland Clinic, https://my.clevelandclinic.org/health/articles/22187-cortisol. "Epinephrine (Adrenaline): What It Is, Function, Deficiency & Side Effects." Cleveland Clinic, https://my.clevelandclinic.org/health/articles/22611-epinephrine-adrenaline.

4. Zaraska, Marta. "With Age Comes Happiness: Here's Why." *Scientific American*, November 2015, accessed via https://www.scientificamerican.com/article/with-age-comes-happiness-here-s-why/.

5. Willaims, Robert. "Gen Z wants brands to be 'fun,' 'authentic' and 'good,' study says." Marketing Dive, July 8, 2020, https://www.marketingdive.com/news/gen-z-wants-brands-to-be-fun-authentic-and-good-study-says/581191/.

Additional Journaling Space (if you need it!)